T0316729

Compelling Communication

Do your communication skills let you down? Do you struggle to explain and influence, persuade and inspire? Are you failing to fulfil your potential because of your inability to wield words in the ways you'd like?

This book has the solution.

Written by a University of Cambridge communication course lead, journalist and former BBC broadcaster, it covers everything from the essentials of effective communication to the most advanced skills.

Whether you want to write a razor sharp briefing, shine in an important presentation, hone your online presence, or just get yourself noticed and picked out for promotion, all you need to know is here.

From writing and public speaking, to the beautiful and stirring art of storytelling, and even using smartphone photography to help convey your message, this invaluable book will empower you to become a truly compelling communicator.

Simon Hall is a course leader in writing, public speaking and storytelling skills at the University of Cambridge. He also runs his own communication agency, Creative Warehouse. He has published twelve books on business and communication, along with eight novels, and previously was a BBC Television, Radio and Online news correspondent for twenty years.

'If you want to cut through with your communication and get on in life, this is the book for you. Whether it's writing, public speaking, storytelling, how to make a mark online, or getting yourself featured in the media, it's the perfect guide for professional success. Highly recommended.'

Jonathan Rosenberg, former Senior Vice President, Google

'This wonderful book is just what you have been looking for, even if you didn't know it. Simon Hall's talent, honed by many years of newscasting and reporting at the BBC, is that most valuable of things, a hugely valuable Bible of communication skills. In it he explains how so many of us with a great story to tell end up with our words falling on deaf ears or our ideas left underfoot on the cutting room floor. His genius lies in understanding that our deepest desire is to capture the interest and imaginations of others, yet the dark arts of how to do this successfully remain painfully just out of reach. This is the Secret Sauce, the insider's step-by-step score for the symphony of your story. No more waffling or meandering ... an end to boring people to death and anger at others who seem so effortlessly able to get their message across. This is the good stuff ... a seriously important message given by as agreeable a companion as you'd ever wish for. Buy it and be happy.'

Tim Smit, founder of The Eden Project

'As an academic who has done a fair few presentations to different audiences, I found this book enormously valuable. It provides a smarter and more systematic approach to getting your message across effectively and really engaging the audience. I would heartily recommend it, particularly for those looking to step up their media and communications work.'

Professor Anna Vignoles, CBE FBA, Director,
The Leverhulme Trust

Compelling Communication

Writing, Public Speaking and Storytelling for Professional Success

Simon Hall

University of Cambridge

Shaftesbury Road, Cambridge CB2 8EA, United Kingdom

One Liberty Plaza, 20th Floor, New York, NY 10006, USA

477 Williamstown Road, Port Melbourne, VIC 3207, Australia

314–321, 3rd Floor, Plot 3, Splendor Forum, Jasola District Centre, New Delhi – 110025, India

103 Penang Road, #05-06/07, Visioncrest Commercial, Singapore 238467

Cambridge University Press is part of Cambridge University Press & Assessment, a department of the University of Cambridge.

We share the University's mission to contribute to society through the pursuit of education, learning and research at the highest international levels of excellence.

www.cambridge.org
Information on this title: www.cambridge.org/9781009447430
DOI: 10.1017/9781009447447

First published 2024

A catalogue record for this publication is available from the British Library

A Cataloging-in-Publication data record for this book is available from the Library of Congress

ISBN 978-1-009-44743-0 Hardback
ISBN 978-1-009-44741-6 Paperback

For Jess and Niamh, for obvious reasons, and for Nigel and Jerry, for reasons which will become obvious

Contents

Introduction

Communication is nothing less than a secret superpower for success.

Now, I realise that's quite a claim to start our odyssey together. But stay with me. Because I've got plenty of evidence to back it up.

Firstly, an insight of my own. A confession, if you like:

I fear that without the world of words I would have achieved nothing much in life.

I've never counted myself particularly bright. Certainly not in comparison with the brilliant minds which surround me here at the celebrated University of Cambridge. And yes, I appreciate it may not be smart to admit that, given you've invested time and money in *Compelling Communication*. But I make my confession for a reason.

It turns out I'm fortunate to be blessed with a gift those wonderful Cambridge minds, and many others besides, need. A certain talent with writing, public speaking, storytelling and the strategic use of communication. Because if there's one lesson I've learned in life, it's this:

> Explaining your vision, inspiring a team, being noticed as an incredible employee, seeking an important promotion, spreading news of a world-changing discovery, starting your own business, strutting your stuff on the world stage, wooing the love of your life, forging lasting friendships, influencing and persuading anyone at any time, or any of a range of other noble aspirations is unlikely to make headway unless . . .
> You can communicate. And not just do so, but do so well.

In short, you may be the most remarkable person, with the most wonderful ideas, that can make our beautiful planet a far better place. But if you can't explain, enthuse and energise with any of that, then what will it all come to?

Enough said, I hope.

Happily, that's where *Compelling Communication* steps in. It offers all the insights you need to make a mark with your message in any situation whatsoever. That goes from writing an elegant and effective report, or even social media post, to telling a story which leaves an audience spellbound, to giving a barnstorming speech before a crowd of thousands.

Importantly, there's something we'd best get straight from the start. This is not – repeat NOT – a dusty academic tome. You're banned from leaving it on the coffee table in order to impress visitors.

The book is for reading and using. It's intended to be rigorously practical, easily accessible and instantly actionable. Some of the points will be accompanied by videos and interactive exercises to offer added illumination. You can find those on the companion website to the book, www.cambridge.org/compellingcommunication.

Storytelling is a star turn of the communication cabaret, as we'll see. So *Compelling Communication* is designed to tell a story. We'll start at the beginning with the foundations of powerful communication, before moving on to the various elements, as well as strategic and sometimes shamelessly cunning ways to deploy your new skills.

On a personal note, I can highly recommend becoming an effective communicator. For me, it's meant an incredible life. With the BBC, I was privileged to meet a range of remarkable people in a series of memorable places while witnessing a catalogue of extraordinary events. My novel writing has been a fascinating exploration of the world and the self. My non-fiction books have brought travel and a fulfilling lifestyle.

But at the pinnacle of all sits my work here in Cambridge. I moved to this city of learning and enterprise as a break from the BBC, seeking a new adventure. I expected to pick up work helping academics and businesses with their writing and presentation skills. But I was far from prepared for the demand for my insights and experience.

Having witnessed my work across the historic colleges and faculties, a kind professor suggested I create an online course for the University. I'm happy (and more than a little relieved!) to say that *Compelling Communication Skills* was a success. Demand came from across society and around the world, and the feedback was uplifting. People far and wide were using what they had learned to make a real difference in their lives, their careers and their countries.

That wonderful experience was the inspiration for this book.

I hope it will prove as effective as the course in helping a range of readers fulfil their potential by mastering the joyous art of compelling communication. For example, some of those I've worked with, and the difference their new skill set has made:

- A renowned Cambridge professor approached me for help with a prestigious lecture. Although he had given thousands of talks in his time, he confessed: *I never really think I truly nail it. I fear something's not quite there.* The result? In his own words: *That was what was missing. The showbiz of the talk, the tricks of the trade which you taught me. This time, I felt I truly connected with the audience and made a real impression.*
- A director of a major public service, who had an extraordinary story to share, needed support to ensure it made the impact it deserved. I helped create the presentation and media package, and the story was picked up by almost 5,000 news outlets internationally. After the talk the director gave on the experience, she was surrounded by people telling her what an amazing lecture it was and how they were entranced and inspired by her storytelling.
- An executive needed to change the way her company was working, but encountered strong resistance. She asked for my help and together we created a story imagining two different futures for the business. One led to prosperity, the other decline. She began to weave the storytelling into her communications, and, after a few months, succeeded in making the changes the company required.

- A researcher wanted to heighten her profile as she sought a new opportunity. Together, we produced a media release about her ground-breaking work in artificial intelligence. The story was picked up by newspapers, radio, television and news websites around the world, helping her to become far more prominent in her field, and to secure a prestigious new position.
- The chief executive of a medical technology business needed to raise tens of millions of pounds in funding. But he was struggling to make investors understand and support the venture. I spent a week working on the company's core messages, its website and the executive's pitch. Now the business has the investment it sought and is thriving.
- A PhD student was asked to give a high profile presentation about her work producing laboratory grown meat, but suffered a fear of public speaking. We drew out the narrative of her talk, added elements of entertainment, built her confidence, and it was a great success. She now looks forward to, rather than dreads, giving presentations, something she thought would never happen.

But anecdotes aside, and finally for this introduction – not to mention most importantly – a simple question. What single theme unites this array of very different experiences?

Yes, that's a no-brainer if ever you saw one. And surprise, surprise, given the nature of this book . . .

The answer is the power of effective communication in helping to achieve our aims, whatever they might be.

That's the motivation which lies behind *Compelling Communication*. To pass on this secret superpower, so that you too can achieve your ambitions and fulfil your aspirations.

The Foundations of Effective Communication

At a glance: Compelling communication requires a series of critical components: clarity, brevity, simplicity, authenticity and – perhaps surprisingly – humility.

Let's begin at the beginning, as the old saying wisely suggests. Which means the two fundamental foundations of compelling communication.

The first might sound screamingly obvious, but nevertheless is far too often forgotten:

- Always be ruthlessly clear on your story.

You wouldn't believe the number of people I've worked with whom I've asked: *What message do you want to come across?* And whether it's a report, presentation, strategy document or whatever, they wave their hands around and reply:

- Well, it's kind of this, with a bit of that, oh, and a slice of something else . . . I think. Probably, anyway. Sort of. I mean, maybe. Isn't it?

I won't reveal how that makes me feel, but I suspect you can guess. Suffice to say I know the upcoming assignment will be far from painless.

If you find yourself uttering anything like that bumbling ramble of waffle, consider it a red flag. For effective communication, it's essential to be

Figure 1.1 Message overload. Taken from the Compelling Communication Skills course, reprinted with kind permission of Cambridge Advance Online © University of Cambridge.

absolutely clear and concise about the single, simple message you want to send.

Why? Well, imagine I had a whole lot of messages I wanted to convey. I wrote them down on pieces of paper and threw them at you, all in one go, just like in Figure 1.1.

How many of the pieces of paper would you manage to catch? One, perhaps? And even then, it's unlikely it would contain the most important message I wanted to get across.

Now let's rerun the scenario. This time, imagine you have a single, clear and simple message you want to send. I throw it to you (Figure 1.2), and . . .

How's that for a far better result? As another old saying goes, message received and understood.

Figure 1.2 The impact of clarity. Taken from the Compelling Communication Skills course, reprinted with kind permission of Cambridge Advance Online © University of Cambridge.

We'll look at how to ensure you have a simple and clear story later in the chapter. But first, a brief aside. Why am I being so insistent about this? Making the point, then making it again. And, indeed, again once more.

The reason is that we'll learn lessons from some of history's greatest communicators as we journey through this book. First onto our imaginary stage is the British wartime Prime Minister, author and noted public speaker, Sir Winston Churchill. He has wise words for us:

> If you have an important point to make, don't try to be subtle or clever. Use a pile driver. Hit the point once. Then come back and hit again. Then hit a third time – a tremendous whack.

So, fulfilling Churchill's principle for communication that really hits home (excuse the pun), here's a question. It's about the importance of being completely clear on your message. Would you have been more or less inclined to buy *Compelling Communication* if I described it like this:

I think you'll probably pick up some tips about how to communicate in a range of different situations, or that's the hope, anyway. Plus I'll tell you a few stories about my career along the way, most of which will be relevant, particularly the one about how to deal with the imposter syndrome. That was an amazing moment in life, one I'll never forget. Anyway, sorry, where was I? Oh yes, I promise I won't go on about my love of nature, and wild swimming, or not much, anyway. But whatever, I'm reasonably sure you'll find the book interesting. And overall, you're fairly likely to come away with an ability to communicate which is pretty decent. I might even tell you the story about one of the most ridiculous things I had to do in my BBC career, too. It involved a frozen otter, would you believe?

OK, enough. I'm sure you've had your fill of that meandering outline by now. No wonder my editors didn't allow me to use it to promote the book!

But seriously, how does the above compare as a sales pitch when set against:

This book explores a range of communication skills which will enable you to impress, influence and inspire any audience in any situation.

To make our time together more interesting than just me monologuing along, I'll set some challenges as we go. We've only just begun our voyage, so as a warm up let's start with the world's easiest compare and contrast exercise.

Which of the two pitches, above, was the more effective? *Hmmm*, I think I can hear you saying. *That's a tricky one. Not.*

I don't think you've taken long to answer, have you? Remember our illustrations earlier, and the very different outcomes from a chaotic bombardment of waffle versus simplicity and brevity.

Which goes to show the importance of a clear and concise focus on your story if you want to be understood and appreciated. So next, let's look at how to achieve that.

Clarity of Story

To ensure we're clear on our story, we can borrow a trick from my former profession, journalism. If you visit any newsroom, you'll be struck by various experiences. The shouted conversations, the swearing and the running around you may have expected.

But what might come as more of a surprise is a question you hear time and again as story after story is discussed. It's only brief. Just three words, in fact. But it's critical in making a news report, and indeed any form of communication, work:

- *What's the angle?*

The angle is the narrative which runs through a story. It captures the importance of what's being written and why an audience should be interested. It also determines what the story is about, the sole theme that story is about, and only what the story is about. Just as with my two different pitches for this book, there's no room for digression, waffle, or wandering off the point.

The angle should be summed up in only a handful of words, and is usually contained in the headline or opening sentence of the story. For example, some of the most famous newspaper headlines that history has seen:

- Peace!
  The Sun, Sydney, Australia, 15 August 1945, after Japan surrendered, marking the end of the Second World War
- Mandela Goes Free Today
  City Press, South Africa, 11 February 1990, on the release from prison of Nelson Mandela
- Titanic Sinks Four Hours After Hitting Iceberg
  New York Times, United States, 16 April 1912, on the loss of the ocean liner, the *Titanic*
- Diana Dead
  News of the World, United Kingdom, 31 August 1997, on the death of Princess Diana

To experience angles in modern day action, click on a well-known media outlet where you are. Now scan through the reports which are being featured.

Each of the headlines, whether contemporary or historic, illustrates the impact of complete and concise clarity. They capture the essence of the story, the most important or interesting point. All define what you will be reading about, and nothing else. Furthermore, none is more than a few words long. Even, occasionally, as in the case of 'Peace!' and the Sydney *Sun*, just one word.

That's the art of the angle.

Importantly, the angle should be decided *before any content is written*. That goes for news stories, presentations, briefings, emails, books, or anything whatsoever. Being clear on your angle from the start can save a lot of pain.

In my BBC days, I was always amazed how many reporters went out on a story and cast around interviewing people endlessly until they chanced upon an angle. That took time and energy, caused a great deal of stress, annoyed plenty of editors and marked out these individuals as less than talented. Far better for yourself and all around to do your thinking first, then start creating your content.

Which is all very well for news, you might think. But what about the rest of life? Happily, the principle of being clear on your story applies just as much there, too. Take a website, like Cambridge Advance Online, the University's internet learning platform (Figure 1.3).

What's the angle here, the service the website is offering? Funnily enough, it's exactly as written, precise, prominent and proud:

- Improve your professional thinking and performance through flexible online learning led by University of Cambridge academics.

Everything on the site is about improving your professional skillset and nothing else. But what would you think if you browsed around and it suddenly digressed into talking about the flora and fauna of the fenlands

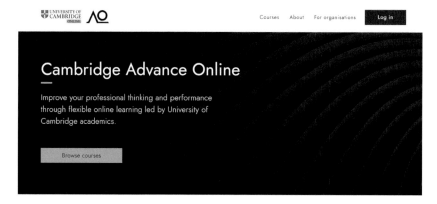

Figure 1.3 Cambridge Advance Online website. © Cambridge University Press & Assessment

of the east of England? You'd probably suspect there was an error, or that someone was having a strange day.

Whichever it may be, you certainly wouldn't be impressed with the business and so far less inclined to sign up for a course. How could you possibly trust the organisation if it's prone to irrelevant meanders like that?

Now let's put the power of the angle into action with an exercise. Here's a blurb I wrote for one of my courses. What do you think the angle was, the brief sentence which sums up the story? The one which would sit above this paragraph on a website, to attract attention and make it very obvious what was being offered.

> You're a pretty good public speaker, but how would you like to be great? That one who people remember, talk about, and who always has a waiting list of invitations. This workshop can help you make that happen.
>
> Featuring captivating your audience from your very first words, the magical power of storytelling, how to use slides economically and effectively, tricks for ensuring you hold the attention, ways to make your key messages memorable, and the art of a storming finale.

This highly interactive, high energy, and always entertaining workshop takes you through all you need to become that presenter you've always wanted to be.

Have you come up with an angle? If not, give it a few seconds more before I whisk the metaphorical curtain away for the big reveal.

If you've suggested *Learn the art of powerful public speaking*, or *Master advanced presentation skills*, or *Become a brilliant public speaker*, or something similar, then I'd say you were right.

As a contrast, here's a brief description of a talk a friend was planning to give at a conference. Are you clear what you would be hearing about from this? Would you be tempted to attend?

Most managers are short of time and often stressed. That can seriously damage the quality of their work, along with their emotional and physical wellbeing, with harmful consequences for family and professional life. Many complain of having too many meetings. A strategy to cut the number can help. Restructuring teams may be useful, along with reducing the number of people directly reporting to them. Other factors to consider include making sure a manager's office is ideally suited to their physical and psychological requirements, along with exercise and mindfulness. But the most important element is managing time, and there are ways to do this which can enhance productivity, health and wellbeing.

He sent it to me for feedback. I asked what the main thrust of his talk was, the most important point. The angle, in other words. And after a little back and forth, we agreed on:

- Learn the art of time management for a more productive, healthier, happier working life.

We began the outline with that, then added a couple of lines about the content, including cutting meetings, restructuring your team, etc. And guess what? That blurb helped to get a good crowd along.

Now try applying the principle of the angle to your work. Think about something you have to communicate, whether in a simple email, a longer report, or a presentation. Can you sum up exactly what you're trying to convey in just a handful of words?

If so, you're good to go. That precious snippet will guide you through the creation of your content. But if you're struggling, think about why. Are you trying to say too much? Are there too many elements competing for your audience's attention? Is what you're trying to get across confused?

Strip out anything which isn't the essence of the narrative you want to communicate. Be absolutely ruthless. Focus on the one, critical point you need to convey. Then try again.

Being clear on what you're trying to get across is a foundation of effective communication. It applies to any form, from a hefty book like this, to an hour-long speech, to a brief memo. People simply don't have the band-width, time or tolerance for irrelevancies.

So before you begin work on any content, set yourself a challenge. Write down precisely what you're trying to say in no more than a few words. That all-important and utterly indispensable angle will ensure the message you want to convey comes across loud and clear.

The Golden Thread

Once you're clear on your story – and only then – you can start to put it together. This is where the angle will be an invaluable aide. Because it gives rise to a lovely concept known as *the golden thread*.

You might have heard of the legendary thread. But if you haven't, it's the storyline which runs through every communication.

In the case of this book, all that you read will be about improving your communication skills. That's the golden thread, set up – of course – by the angle. Which you find in the headline, or title, *Compelling Communication.*

Once again, the golden thread works for any form of content. Think about a well-known film. *Alien*, for example. What's the golden thread? Have a muse for a moment. Then read on for the answer:

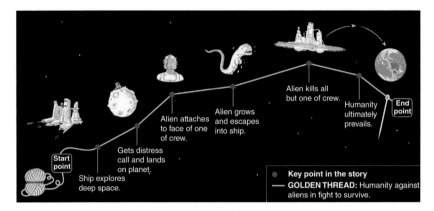

Figure 1.4 The golden thread. Taken from the Compelling Communication Skills course, reprinted with kind permission of Cambridge Advance Online © University of Cambridge.

- A battle for survival between humanity and a very ill-tempered extra-terrestrial.

Everything that happens in the film follows that golden thread, as you can see from Figure 1.4.

The concept even works for pop songs. Look up, or sing to yourself, the classic 'My Way'. What's the golden thread which runs through it?

- A person reflecting on their life, and being proud they lived it in the way they chose.

Now take a classic book, Maya Angelou's *I Know Why the Caged Bird Sings*. What's the golden thread here?

- The story of a childhood, often troubled and traumatic.

The thread helps us by determining what's relevant for our content and what isn't. It keeps us focused on the narrative, so preventing any confusion in our audience. It also has the splendid side effect of saving us work, by stopping dead any digressions before they can begin.

Let's put the golden thread into action with a challenge based on one of the most tedious chores of modern life. Imagine you've joined a new organisation. You've been given an email address and want to activate it. Below are the instructions.

First of all, what should be the golden thread of this message? Can you sum it up in one simple line, as we explored earlier? Next, spot the departures from the thread. Finally, how irritating are you finding them? I've numbered the paragraphs so you can easily jot down which you would cut.

1. Open any internet browser.
2. Which is your favourite, by the way? We know most people use Google, but have you ever tried Firefox? It's got a lovely colour palette.
3. Type in goldenthreaddigressions.com and hit return.
4. Do you like the page? We worked hard to make it simple to use. Not easy for us tech types!
5. We did wonder if the website address was a little too long, but we thought it made the point. Don't you agree?
6. Type your email address into the grey box. Hit return.
7. We'd love it if you'd notice how quick the process is. We put loads of work into that.
8. It's highly reliable, too. Only a 1 per cent failure rate. Which is impressive, if we do say so ourselves.
9. And if you see any of our bosses, please mention how easy the activation process is. We don't always feel appreciated, down here in the basement.
10. Click ok on the page you've been taken to, and that's it. Your email address is now active.

So, in terms of an angle, what do you suggest? Something as simple and clear as: *Email activation instructions*?

If so, I would agree. And as for putting a line through my wanderings of waffle, points 2, 4, 5, 7, 8 and 9 would benefit from the red pen.

Most importantly, see how much sharper and more effective the content is, as well as less annoying, when it follows the golden thread? Not to mention saving both author and reader time by removing those irrelevant asides.

The Beauty of a KISS

What am I talking about now, you may well ask. How does a kiss fit into a book on communication skills?

Don't worry. All is well. That kiss is a favourite acronym of the communication trade. It becomes relevant now as we move on to the second of our foundations of the art. As with being clear on your message, this might sound equally obvious but is often forgotten:

- Always remember your audience.

What do I mean by that? Well, take a look at the photo in Figure 1.5.

Figure 1.5 An advanced maths lecture. © Ravil Sayfullin/Shutterstock

Scary isn't it? For those of us who are less than maths-minded, anyway. That blackboard took me back to schooldays and sitting stumped, hopelessly trying to comprehend what looked like some mystical ancient language.

The point being this. What the lecturer has created is fine for a class of talented maths students. They would understand. But imagine he'd written all that to try to impress a group of visiting dignitaries from the local council, come to see what good work the college was doing. They'd be utterly baffled.

Such is the importance of adjusting your message according to your audience. Every job has its jargon, each industry its insider talk. But when we come to communicate outside of those circles, we have to translate our particular ways of speaking and writing. Otherwise, we won't be understood.

If in doubt about the language you're using, remember the acronym which inspired the title of this section:

- KISS: Keep It Simple, Silly

To explore the importance of KISS further, and for a little fun, I'll give you some of my favourite examples of jargon in action. These would be fine for people who knew this particular language, whatever it might be. But do you understand what's being communicated? See if you can work it out before I give you the answers.

We'll start with Cockney rhyming slang. If you're not familiar, it's a celebrated manner of speaking which originated in the East End of London. To give you a clue with your translation challenge, as the name suggests, the tradition is based on rhymes.

- *OK me old china plate, I've come into some bees and honey so let's have a bubble bath down the rub a dub.*

Any ideas what that means? Can I sense you scratching your head and looking puzzled? If you're not versed in Cockney rhyming slang, I imagine you're struggling. So here's the answer:

- OK mate, I've come into some money so let's have a laugh down the pub.

See how it works? China plate means mate, bees and honey is money, and so on. It's a classic quirk of Englishness, and wonderfully colourful. But it does need translating if your audience doesn't happen to be fluent in such slang.

Next we come to a particular delight of mine, management speak. I used to sit in BBC meetings and wince as various less than inspiring bosses would trot out reams of this nonsense.

- *I want a deep dive to self-source us a magic bullet which is both holistic and actionable.*

In fairness, such gibberish did at least raise a few much needed smiles in those meetings. Even if the offending manager was usually oblivious to the amusement they were causing. So, when you've had a ponder, here's the answer:

- *I'd like us to think carefully and creatively to come up with an effective, comprehensive and practical solution.*

How much fresher, easier and – perhaps most importantly – less ridiculous is that? And all from taking just a few seconds to think about what you're saying and finding a straightforward and accessible way of communicating.

Finally, let's explore a classic issue with jargon. Behold the dreaded science-speak. Some brilliant people are just too smart to remember that not everyone boasts their hyper-intelligence. That can cause problems when the rest of the world is trying to understand what they're talking about.

This is an example of a pitch a company I work with was using to promote their business:

- *Utilising Brownian motion models, non-regime switching data universes, multiple quantitative data source complex clustering and characterisation algorithms, we forecast equities' shifts.*

If you're blinking hard and frowning even harder, I know how you feel. I didn't have a clue what they were talking about either. No wonder they weren't selling much in the way of their service. But, after talking to the boss, I translated the company's offering this way:

- We use advanced maths to call the stock markets.

Isn't that far easier to understand? I'm happy to report the company are doing very nicely now, in part perhaps because customers can finally comprehend what it is they're offering.

That's the power of kissing. Or, in other words, keeping it simple, silly. Different people, from different professions and backgrounds, have different ways of writing and speaking. One of the key challenges of compelling communication is bridging the gaps between them. And simplicity can be a huge help.

But don't just take it from me. Another of our great communicators has important words for us on the subject. This time Clare Boothe Luce, one of the first female American Ambassadors, who was also a playwright and noted public speaker:

- The height of sophistication is simplicity.

Lastly for this section, a challenge. As I've mentioned, my former employer, the dear old BBC, wasn't above a sprinkling of jargon. Below is a sentence you could easily hear in a morning newsroom meeting. It would be fine for us, versed in TV talk. But if we had to explain what we were planning to someone outside of the television news industry, what do you think we should say?

- *PM's Presser @12 ex Downing Street, location POLCORR 2-way.*

Have a think, and even do some internet searching to see if you can put together a more accessible translation. Have you managed something like this?

- Prime Minister press conference at noon at Downing Street, political correspondent live report from Downing Street.

Now, isn't that much simpler for the vast majority of people to comprehend?

The same goes for elongated, protracted or prolonged lexemes. Or perhaps I just mean long words. Some people seem to think peppering your work with such examples is sagacious. Or indeed clever.

Wrong. Cut the long words. Stick to the short.

Never forget to keep it simple, silly. Remember the lesson this way. As I've said a fair few times already, and will keep right on saying, when it comes to compelling communication:

- Simple isn't stupid. Simple is smart.

Here endeth the lesson on the importance of remembering your audience and adjusting your content accordingly. When you're putting together any form of communication, look through it and check. Have you lapsed into the talk of your trade? Are there long and pompous words, or terms which are for the initiated only?

If so, remember to KISS. Get translating and make sure what you have to say is easily understood.

- Exercise: Look at a briefing, report or even email you've written. Are there any jargon terms, words or phrases which might need translating?

A Magical Miracle

I love so much of the wonderful world of words. But now it's time to introduce a favourite principle, hence the title of this section. OK, I may be exaggerating a little. Yet this is a true beacon of the foundations of effective communication.

I find it delightful because it's so simple, but so effective. It also means you can make much greater impact for less work, and what's not to like about that?

With all due fanfare, drum roll, and even twenty-one-gun salute, I proudly present the magical miracle of . . .

- Less is more.

It's interesting that, when I teach this, the audience often takes some persuading. After all, it goes against pretty much everything we were taught, not to mention what our instincts are yelling.

Want to make it clear you've worked hard on an assignment, whether from schooldays or a recent work project? Then make it weighty! Present loads of pages. Ensure it hits the target intray with a booming thud.

Got an important presentation to deliver? Then make it good and long! Talk, talk, and talk some more. Right?

Wrong. Very wrong. In fact, to hammer home another important point, Winston Churchill-style, super-wrong squared.

People have only a finite amount of working memory. There's a limit to what they can take in and retain, just as with a computer. In order to make the maximum impact, it's critical to choose your key points, then deploy those and those alone. Everything else is likely to be lost. Communicate less information and you'll make more impact. Because what you do convey will stand out and stay with your audience.

Do I still sense a certain amount of scepticism about the concept of less is more? I wonder if you're thinking: *Surely it's too good to be true.* So let me offer you some solid, yet surprising evidence.

Firstly, courtesy of one of the most iconic speeches in human history. We're talking the Gettysburg Address and its author and orator, the much loved American President, Abraham Lincoln.

Most people have heard of the Gettysburg Address. It's famous and feted, often cited as a masterpiece of speechmaking. Because it's so celebrated, the assumption tends to be that the Address must have gone on a long time. But do you know how long the speech actually lasted?

Have a ponder before I give you the answer. Here's a hint. What's the briefest you think it could have been to make such an impact? Half an hour? Fifteen minutes? Ten, even?

Then prepare yourself for a surprise. Because ...

Wait for it ... wait for it ...

The Gettysburg Address probably lasted around two minutes.

Yes, you did read that right, and no, it's not a misprint. *Around two minutes.*

Remarkably, the speech contained only about 270 words. Half a page of A4-size paper, in other words. The reason I say *about* in the context of the word count is that there are several copies of the Address containing slightly different numbers of words.

However, the central point remains. The Gettysburg Address was surprisingly short. And if you're still doubtful of such a surprising fact, here's the Address itself quoted from a very good source, the US Library of Congress:

> Four score and seven years ago our fathers brought forth on this continent a new nation, conceived in liberty, and dedicated to the proposition that all men are created equal.
>
> Now we are engaged in a great civil war, testing whether that nation, or any nation so conceived and so dedicated, can long endure. We are met on a great battlefield of that war.
>
> We have come to dedicate a portion of that field as a final resting place for those who here gave their lives that that nation might live. It is altogether fitting and proper that we should do this.
>
> But in a larger sense we cannot dedicate, we cannot consecrate, we cannot hallow this ground. The brave men, living and dead, who struggled here have consecrated it, far above our poor power to add or detract.
>
> The world will little note, nor long remember, what we say here, but it can never forget what they did here. It is for us the living,

rather, to be dedicated here to the unfinished work which they who fought here have thus far so nobly advanced.

It is rather for us to be here dedicated to the great task remaining before us, that from these honored dead we take increased devotion to that cause for which they gave the last full measure of devotion, that we here highly resolve that these dead shall not have died in vain, that this nation, under God, shall have a new birth of freedom, and that government of the people, by the people, for the people, shall not perish from the earth.

Abraham Lincoln, Gettysburg, Pennsylvania, 19 November 1863

So, there it is, in black and white, a telling tale of less being more. Which brings us back to the critical point. Despite the Gettysburg Address containing so few words, it went down in history.

The lesson being ... that you should never forget ...

- It's not the word count, but how much the words count.

The Wisdom of Mark Twain, or Beatrix Potter, or Woodrow Wilson, or Someone

Yes, I know that's another strange title. But it has a reason. Which is that I'm a fan of the old saying, *Success has many fathers, but failure is an orphan.*

There are multiple claims to the authorship of that quotation. Just as there are for a large number of popular sayings.

But, earlier in the book, I said we'd learn lessons from some of history's finest communicators as we journeyed. So here we turn to an insight – several, in fact – about the power of less is more. The legendary American writer and wit Mark Twain is reported to have said:

- *I'm sorry I wrote you a long letter, I didn't have time to write a short one.*

But it's disputed whether he actually did. So to other variations on the theme, which are backed by evidence:

- *I have already made this paper too long, for which I must crave pardon, not having now time to make it shorter.*
  Benjamin Franklin, one of the founding fathers of the United States, in a letter to a member of the Royal Society
- *Not that the story need be long, but it will take a long while to make it short.*
  Henry David Thoreau, American writer, naturalist and philosopher, also in a letter

Another fine example comes from Beatrix Potter, the great writer, illustrator, scientist and conservationist:

- *The shorter and the plainer the better.*

But my favourite take on the popular theme comes from the former American President Woodrow Wilson. Once again, it's disputed if he used these exact words. But the sentiment holds true, nonetheless.

Wilson was asked about the amount of time it took to prepare his speeches and replied:

> *That depends on the length of the speech. If it is a ten-minute speech it takes me all of two weeks to prepare it; if it is a half-hour speech it takes me a week; if I can talk as long as I want to it requires no preparation at all. I am ready now.*

Let's put the power of less is more into action with an exercise. Below is a rough transcript of something I once heard a professor say. I noted it down as I found it so striking, if not necessarily in a positive way.

What do you make of this statement on first reading? Does the point the professor is trying to make come through loud and clear? Or is it somewhat lost in the deluge of words?

> Allow me to venture a thought, notwithstanding that others may disagree, and taking into account, of course, the range of competing viewpoints, but nonetheless, I contend it can be argued that, given

the evidence, even in the context of other great institutions around the world, that the University of Cambridge could be claimed to occupy the very pinnacle of all of the body of higher education establishments globally.

Your challenge is to translate that paragraph into one simple sentence, less is more style. What is the professor trying to say? When you've cracked it, check your thoughts against my answer:

- I think the University of Cambridge is the best in the world.

Which leads us to another of my compare and contrast challenges. Of the two versions, which is more effective in communicating what the professor thinks? Not to mention requiring less work for both creator and consumer. The paragraph or the sentence?

That's the might of less is more.

Making Yourself Popular

The joyous principle of less is more can help to make you popular in working life. Whatever your position or rank, those above, below and around you are always busy. As are you, of course.

So, how do you feel when an important report arrives, which demands your attention . . .

And it's twenty-six pages long, plus a whole load of appendices.

What's that look I can sense forming on your face? Not to mention those unkind words you've just mouthed? How rude!

But seriously, now let's rerun that scenario. The awaited report arrives, your attention immediately switches to it . . .

And this time, on this wonderful occasion, it's only four pages long. With no appendices.

I suspect you're feeling rather better about life now, aren't you?

No doubt that little game, however entertaining, has raised a question in your mind. Is it really possible to keep important documents to only a few pages long?

The answer is an emphatic yes. In my time here at the University of Cambridge, I've produced a range of briefings, strategy documents and reports for various important people. None have numbered more than a handful of pages.

On several occasions, I've been asked the obvious question: *Is that it?* In reply, I said: *Have a read and see if it tells you what you need to know.*

They have, and by and large that's been the end of the matter. There have been a couple of times when they've asked me to pop in for a chat to further discuss certain points. But far more often than not, just a few pages is all you need.

Struggling to believe me? Wondering how it's possible to include all you need to say and still practise the beauty of brevity? Then read on. Because less is more is a trick greatly valued even at the highest and most historic levels. Which leads us once again to a certain Winston Churchill.

In August 1940, with the Second World War raging, Churchill wrote a memo appealing for crisp and concise communication.

> To do our work, we all have to read a mass of papers. Nearly all of them are far too long. This wastes time, while energy has to be spent in looking for the essential points. I ask my colleagues to see to it that their Reports are shorter.

Churchill also offered important advice on putting into action the art of less is more, requesting:

- Reports which set out the main points in a series of short, crisp paragraphs.
- If a report relies on detailed analysis, or some complicated factors, these should be set out in an Appendix.

- Let us have an end of such phrases as these: 'It is also of importance to bear in mind the following considerations ...' or, 'Consideration should be given to the possibility of carrying into effect ...' Most of these woolly phrases are mere padding.
- Let us not shrink from using the short, expressive phrase, even if it is conversational.

Winston Churchill, from the National Archives, UK

I must contend that attention should be given unto the considerations outlined in the excerpts above, which are arguably an important contribution to ensuring communication is effective, whilst still allowing that some may find such an approach somewhat contrary to the norms adopted by they themselves.

Sorry, sorry. Perhaps I meant that the Churchill memo has cracking advice for us on nailing the art of less is more. Now, isn't that more pithy, punchy, conversational and compelling?

Churchill was also ahead of his time. A commonly used abbreviation online is TLDR. If you're not familiar with it, the initials stand for Too Long, Didn't Read. Which helps to make the point that brevity is even more important in the internet age.

That brings us to a quick challenge. Try using Churchill's wisdom to polish this paragraph:

> I am saddened to inform you of a serious issue with financial flow. Without labouring the point, and wishing to cause alarm, this could be nothing less than an existential matter. Should we not be able to succeed in bringing in more revenue by the end of the month, consideration will have to be given to the reduction of the current employee head count.

So, what have you come up with? If you've produced something similar to the below, I'd say it's reading a lot better. The words are now far more likely to cut through and be acted upon.

> We've got a serious cashflow issue. It's so bad, it could threaten the future of the business. If we don't bring in more money by the end of the month, we may have to sack staff.

Oh, and one final point. Because no doubt you're asking. How long was Churchill's memo on brevity?

Well, surprise, surprise. I suspect you may have guessed. But here's the answer, if only to confirm your expectations.

The memo was one page long. Just one page, and one page only. Of course it was.

- Exercise: Look at a briefing, report, or any document you've written. Could it be improved by adopting the principle of less is more?

The Business of Less Is More

The wonder of less is more doesn't just work with words. It encompasses all areas of good communication. In fact, there's a brilliant business case I'd like to share.

This is a world beating service. It's cornered more than 90 per cent of the market in its field and is worth billions upon billions of pounds. You'll probably use it many times a day without ever noticing the power of less is more being put into the most excellent effect.

It's so dominant and prevalent in modern life that the name of the service has become a verb. If you're still struggling to guess what I'm talking about, don't worry. I'll stop teasing and reveal all in a minute.

What is this world conquering business, much of whose success is built on the principle of less is more? The answer is . . .

- Google

Just look at that screen in Figure 1.6 for a moment. And remember, this is an app which searches the vast landscape of the World Wide Web for the information you need. Now imagine how complicated it might be.

But no. Complexity doesn't get a look in. Google is built on the basis of less is more. It could scarcely be more simple. Type your query into the box and hit return. And that's it. Job done.

Figure 1.6 The Google homepage. © Beata Zawrzel/NurPhoto/Getty Images

To push the point further, do you remember what search engines were like in the early days? If not, have a quick look online. It's both interesting and instructive.

To be frank, they were a pain to use. You often had to tick a range of boxes, including the period of time you were interested in. Then there was the subject area. I also remember having to add the geographical locations I might want to know about, and other information besides.

In other words, a lot of fuss. Which was annoying and wasted time.

Then, like help from the heavens, along came Google. Type your query and hit return. It was as simple as that.

OK, Google provides a great service. That's a given. No business tends to do well without mastering the basics. But aside from that, what was a large part of the reason for Google's remarkable success?

You got it. We're talking the magical miracle of less is more.

Finding Yourself

We're not going all deep, philosophical and existential, don't worry. It would be venturing far too far from the sacred golden thread of this book, and we know by now that's not allowed.

No, what we're talking here is discovering your unique style as a communicator.

Often known as the writer's *voice*, this is where your character emerges. Which sounds simple, but is much harder to achieve, not to mention scary. Because here, you start to reveal something of your true self. And that's always more daunting than just presenting a list of facts and figures. Yet finding your voice, and using the power of your character, is critical for truly compelling communication.

Here's a simple example. We're not far into the book, but have you already got a sense of my character? If so, how would you describe it in just a handful of words? Jot down some thoughts. But be kind, please!

I'm hoping you might use words such as playful, warm and humorous, but also knowledgeable, authoritative and passionate about the art of communication.

And here comes the key point. When you bought *Compelling Communication*, was that what you expected in terms of style? Or, given the 800-year history and high academic tradition of the University of Cambridge, were you perchance anticipating something rather more upright and formal? A stiffer array of sentences, similar to this, and the instance preceding it, for example.

I'm wondering if you thought this book would provide the information you needed. But that reading it would be far from an enjoyable experience. Instead, however, are you finding the journey more entertaining than you expected?

That's the impact which allowing your character to emerge can have.

But don't just take the example of this book. Let me quote a few lines from a far better known and much loved author. I suspect you'll immediately recognise the stories, and the words will bring a smile to your face.

- *If you live to be a hundred, I want to live to be a hundred minus one day so I never have to live without you.*
- *Sometimes the smallest things take up the most room in your heart.*
- *Piglet: How do you spell 'love'?*
  Pooh: You don't spell it . . . you feel it.

OK, I've given it away with the last quotation. But it was so lovely, I couldn't resist. And I imagine it brought a warm and fuzzy feeling, didn't it? Yes, those are words from the Winnie-the-Pooh stories, by A. A. Milne.

The tales were written way back in the 1920s. Yet the books are still bought and read today. Films and TV programmes continue to be made about the beloved bear, the stories still lift our hearts, and much of the reason for that?

You guessed it. Because of the character of the writing.

It transports us back to the sunshine land of childhood. Where everything was love, kindness and adventure, those long ago times before we had to pay the mortgage, and get the kids to school, and the car fixed, and then there's this awful, persistent backache, and that job to do for the boss, and so on and so on.

Would the books have become so celebrated if they'd been written in a more straightforward style? In an adult manner, for instance:

- *Piglet: How do you spell 'love'?*
  Pooh: L-O-V-E, idiot. Duh.

Somehow, I don't think they would have made quite the same mark on the world.

Away from the blessed realm of children's fiction, letting your character emerge works in the real world too. Here are some famous quotations from a noted wit. Do you recognise them? I suspect you will know most, if not all. So who uttered these famous lines?

- *I can resist everything except temptation.*
- *There is only one thing in the world worse than being talked about, and that is not being talked about.*

- *I have nothing to declare except my genius.*

(at the New York Custom House)

And the answer is . . .

The legendary Oscar Wilde.

Those words date from the nineteenth century. Yet they're still admired, often cited, and much loved today. And why? Of course, because of the character of the creator. Which comes through to great effect in the quotations.

In a more modern context, what about these famous words? Do you recognise them? And can you identify the author?

- *It is in your hands, to make a better world for all who live in it.*
- *Education is the most powerful weapon which you can use to change the world.*
- *Do not judge me by my successes, judge me by how many times I fell down and got back up again.*
- *A winner is a dreamer who never gives up.*

Once again, I expect you recognised some of the quotations. They come from the former freedom fighter and political prisoner, risen to become President of South Africa, great leader and statesman, Nelson Mandela. And why have the words become so celebrated? Is a telling factor, perhaps, that you get a strong sense of Mandela's character from them?

All this talk of character calls for another of our quotations from the great men and women of words. This time, we reach back to the actress and writer Mae West, and beautiful imagery from a bygone age:

Personality is the glitter that sends your little gleam across the footlights and the orchestra pit into that big black space where the audience is.

Strutting Your Style

So, how to make sure your style emerges in your communication, whether written or spoken? The answer is, first of all, to be clear on what your character is.

Remember that earlier I challenged you to sum up my personality in a handful of words? Now it's time for revenge. Turn the spotlight around and do the same with yourself. Don't just think about it, write the words down.

When you've done that, etch those words into your memory and begin to lace examples into your work. I appreciate this can be quite a step, so start small. When I'm coaching executives, I often suggest email as a useful test ground. For instance, in her weekly message, one director of a charity used to write:

- I'm pleased to be able to report the securing of a large new legacy, which has enabled the allocation of funds to three more deserving causes. A great deal of work has gone into the completion of this bequest, for which I would like to thank the fundraising team.

That was OK. It passed on the information, albeit rather starkly and stiffly. But! She's such a passionate person, and believes so strongly in the charity's work, we agreed there was scope for far more character. So, now she writes:

- Some terrific work by the fundraising team has secured a big new legacy. They've been finalising this for months, so here's a huge well done from me and all on the management team. Even better, their success means we've been able to fund three more excellent causes. What a wonderful week, I'm so proud of everyone involved, thank you all.

Which of the two versions do you think made a much stronger connection with her staff?

Gradual is good when it comes to liberating your character. So build on the emails with a little more of you in any reports you have to write. Then do likewise in presentations. Expressing character is easier there. You've got the warmth of your voice, the expressions on your face, and your body language to help.

However, always judge the situation carefully. If you're speaking or writing to people you don't know, or they're more old school and formal, a neutral tone may be preferable. If in doubt, test out your words on friends and colleagues.

Growing comfortable and confident with using your character takes practice and time. But I can promise you, it's well worth the investment. Because, to reiterate the reiteration, and hammer home the point once more:

Why do we want to live in certain houses? Or eat at particular restaurants, or get together at favourite pubs? Because, as we often say . . .

They've got character.

And why do we talk fondly of some friends and colleagues?

Because they're characters.

People engage far more with character than the bland and boring. It's as simple as that.

- Exercise: Look at a briefing, report, or any document you've written. Does it contain a sense of your character? If not, could it be improved if you added a little of your unique voice?

Surprise!

Twists are a delightful component of compelling communication. We'll talk more about that later, when we get to the chapters on storytelling.

But first, a surprise, or twist, to end our tour of the foundations of effective communication. Do you remember the *At a glance* paragraph, right at the start of this chapter? And its rather cryptic mention of humility?

All is about to be revealed.

This book is about getting your message across. We'll cover writing, presenting, public speaking, telling stories, social media, the conventional media, the whole lot.

There is, however, another element which I'm going to mention now, because it's one of the great essentials of truly compelling communication. This is where humility comes in. If almost everything else in the book concerns transmitting, here we're talking about receiving.

Yes, it's the indispensable art of listening.

You can't communicate powerfully unless you listen to others. You'll never be heard properly unless you listen to others. You won't make your way in the world effectively unless you listen to others.

Here's a famous example of the power of true listening. Without it, this iconic relationship would never have got going. I've abridged and rearranged the scene, and generally made a scandalous mess of its beauty. But nonetheless, you'll appreciate the intensity and effect of the couple listening to each other.

ROMEO: But, soft! what light through yonder window breaks?
                    It is the east, and Juliet is the sun.
JULIET: Ay me! How camest thou hither, tell me, and wherefore?
ROMEO: With love's light wings did I o'er-perch these walls;
                    For stony limits cannot hold love out.
JULIET: If that thy bent of love be honourable,
                    Thy purpose marriage, send me word to-morrow.
ROMEO: O blessed, blessed night! I am afeard.
                    Being in night, all this is but a dream.
JULIET: Good night, good night! Parting is such
                    sweet sorrow.

Do you think the balcony scene would have become so celebrated if there wasn't such focused listening between the lovers? If it had unfolded in this, sadly more modern way:

ROMEO: But, soft! what light through yonder window breaks?
                    It is the east, and Juliet is the sun.
JULIET: What? Sorry, I'm just finishing an email.
ROMEO: With love's light wings did I o'er-perch these walls;
                    For stony limits cannot hold love out.
JULIET: Darn phone's almost out of power.
ROMEO: O blessed, blessed night! I am afeard.
                    Being in night, all this is but a dream.
JULIET: The blooming wi-fi's dodgy tonight as well.

That's just my fun, even if I might now expect a vengeful visit from Shakespeare's ghost. But you get the point about the importance of listening to people.

By which, critically, I mean really listening. Focus on what they're saying, don't let your mind wander to what emails are arriving. Understand what they're expressing, rather than wondering what to have for tea tonight. Engage with their words, nodding, smiling, frowning, prompting, questioning, agreeing, dissenting, supporting, challenging. Not prejudging and interrupting, but respecting, thinking, considering, focusing and connecting.

In other words, many of the constituents which make for true – or active – listening.

After all, how do you feel when you're trying to speak to someone and their eyes keep slipping to their phone? Or they frequently talk over you? Or they continually ask you to repeat a point, because they've drifted off elsewhere?

Or, as in the case of my reimagined Romeo, he's trying to declare undying love and Juliet is more concerned about the message she's typing.

Enough said?

Here's another example of the power of listening. I was asked to talk to researchers at the Alzheimer's Society about how to present the importance of their work. Like far too many people, I have personal experience of the horrors of Alzheimer's. So I was honoured to help those working to defeat the disease.

I had a call with the conference organiser, during which I raised a lot of questions. For example, how experienced were the researchers at giving presentations? That would help me pitch the level of my talk, from beginner, to intermediate, to advanced.

Who would their audience be? If scientific, it would be OK for them to use the language of their trade. But if they were speaking to a more general group, we would have to cover the importance of the KISS.

How playful were they? That was an odd question, I appreciate. But it's one I usually ask. Because that way, I get a sense of how best to present the session. Would the group respond better to simply being given information? Or would they benefit from some of my games and interactions?

There were many other questions. And for everything the organiser said, I listened carefully and noted down her answers. The result was – I'm told – a highly effective talk. I was delighted to receive many kind compliments afterwards.

Of course, it would never have gone so well if I hadn't listened carefully and so understood the best way to run the session.

Here are just a few more brief examples of the importance of listening. In a job interview, would you be fully focused on the panel's questions? Or only half-interested in what you're being asked? Which is the more likely to ensure you come across well?

If you were chairing an important committee, and had to feed back the group's thoughts to the boss, would you be idly scrolling through social media during the discussions? Or listening hard, taking notes, summing up the points the committee were making, so you could pass them on accurately?

After a big presentation to the board, perhaps a pitch to have an idea adopted, would you disengage and not concentrate on the directors' questions? Or would you be listening keenly and doing your best to address the points they raise?

And finally, a less work-related but perhaps more important example. If an old friend was suffering and needed to confide their troubles,

I imagine you'd listen carefully. To try to understand, comfort and help such a precious person in your life.

I could go on and on about the importance of listening. But better perhaps to leave it to another of our masters of communication, and one of my favourite quotations.

You've probably heard of the iconic book *How to Win Friends and Influence People*. Although published back in 1936, much of its advice still holds true today. And on the subject of listening, its author, Dale Carnegie, has a gem to offer:

> *You can make more friends in two months by being interested in them, than in two years by making them interested in you.*

It might be a surprise to find listening featured here, so prominently, under the foundations of effective communication. But never underestimate its importance.

- Exercise: In your next conversation with a colleague, member of staff, or manager, challenge yourself to focus hard and really listen. Then, afterwards, reflect on the difference it made to how well you communicated.

Finally, the companion website to the book has a quiz and video exercise for you on what we've covered in this chapter. You can find it at www.cambridge.org/compellingcommunication.

Writing to Woo and Wow

At a glance: Effective writing requires focus on the start, ending, content, style, character, structure and even title of your work.

Many a great idea sank on the rocks of a badly produced report, briefing, or even email. Here we'll ensure that doesn't happen by exploring the art of writing to woo and wow.

We'll begin our quest with an important question:

- What is the typical attention span in this busy modern world?

Have a ponder before I give you the answer. Or an answer, to be more accurate. Are you thinking minutes? Maybe less? Perhaps only seconds?

There's a lot of disagreement about this, so I wouldn't want to offer a definitive figure. Some sources claim eight seconds, others say it's more like forty. Another body of opinion tells us it depends on the task.

So now try an experiment. After all, if in doubt, why not think for ourselves? So, the next time you're in a meeting, or at a presentation, have a look around. Note how quickly people drift away if there's not enough happening to keep them interested.

You might get a surprise. An unpleasant one, I suspect. Because here are the results of my own study.

The precious window of time before the audience started looking at their phones . . . checking their messages . . . reading their emails . . . browsing social media is . . .

- Ten seconds.

Yes, just ten seconds. Which might sound alarming. But remembering that figure has always served me well.

No matter precisely how long the modern attention span may be, we can say for sure it's short. And that's a critical principle which needs to be remembered in all the content we create. We can't just take an audience's attention for granted. We have to work for it.

Which means that, of all and everything we do, there's one part of any report, talk, presentation, story, email, or even social media post which is paramount.

You might have the most brilliant idea to convey, the most wonderful product to sell, or the most compelling pitch for support. But what's the point if you don't get to show it off because the audience has already tuned out?

That's the importance of a striking start. So here's how to create beginnings which command attention.

Striking Starts

I could just tell you the magic ingredients for a brilliant beginning. But that's not my style, and we know how important character is in communication. So instead, let's do this as a challenge.

I'll give you the opening lines of a couple of famous books and also a pop song. You tell me what they are. Then we'll learn the lessons which have helped to make these starts celebrated. Strangely enough, despite the examples being very different, the same principles emerge each time.

So, your first quiz question. Which book boasts this iconic opening line?

- It is a truth universally acknowledged, that a single man in possession of a good fortune must be in want of a wife.

If you're struggling, think dashing heroes and fascinating heroines, the early nineteenth century, and one of England's finest authors. Which means the answer is:

- *Pride and Prejudice*, Jane Austen

The opening line of *Pride and Prejudice* is one of the most famous and feted in English literature. But the issue, for our purposes, is why it's so celebrated. Interestingly, from just those twenty-three words, three key points emerge.

Firstly, when you read that start, you know immediately what the story is about. Will it be science fiction, crime or horror? Of course not. We understand from the outset we're going to be reading a tale of love.

Which is lesson number one in the art of striking starts. Set out your story from the very beginning. Remember how short modern attention spans are. You don't have time to waffle on and risk losing the audience. Dive right in. Cut straight to the chase.

Next comes an insight I often think of as the dinner party test. What?! Well, imagine the scene.

You're invited to an evening out, you don't know the other guests, and the group shuffles through to the table. You sit down, exchange a few words with the people on your left and right . . .

And quickly come to realise whether it's going to be a good night, or a very, very long one.

So, how does Jane Austen fare when subjected to the dinner party test? With her shrewd observer's eye, her wit and her ability to sum up a truth of human existence in just a few words, all as demonstrated in that opening line. Is she someone you're going to enjoy spending time with, or not?

That's point number two of striking starts. Give us a sense of you. Whether it's your passion, humour, charm, intellect, authority, wisdom or whatever. Make it clear you're worth investing our precious time in.

Finally, to our third insight. This is the simplest, but probably most important. When you read an opening line, such as that in *Pride and Prejudice*, does it make you want to put the book aside? Or carry on to find out what happens next? Into the second line, and then the second paragraph, the second page and so on. And before you know it, you're hooked up and hunkered down in the story.

So, finally, make sure your opening is an irresistible lure to draw in an audience.

Now see how those three principles are repeated as we move on with our quiz. Next, to the striking start of a well-known pop song:

- Load up on guns, bring your friends.

Any thoughts? There's a trap in the question, as it often gives away those who enjoyed a misspent youth! If you need a clue, think early 1990s grunge. And the answer is:

- Smells Like Teen Spirit, Nirvana

That's a very different genre and style from Jane Austen's, I think you'll agree. But here's the thing. Are the three principles of a striking start fulfilled courtesy of Kurt Cobain and company? Is the story of youthful rebellion set out from the start? Do you get a sense of the character of the authors? And finally, does that opening line make you want to find out more?

Point made?

For the final part of our quiz, it's back to a book. Here's another captivating, if disturbing, opening line:

- You better not never tell nobody but God. It'd kill your mammy.

How did you do with that one? Edgy, isn't it? The book is a powerful chronicle of an African American woman's battle for empowerment, which won a prestigious Pulitzer Prize. The answer:

- *The Color Purple*, Alice Walker

Once again, our three principles are fulfilled. The beginning cuts right to the heart of the story, an agonising struggle against a dreadful fate. It offers a clear sense of the character and talent of the author, and it draws us in to read on and find out more.

Incidentally, two more points about striking starts. These recall important lessons we explored in the previous chapter. Are any of those openings long, rambling, multiclause paragraphs, which encompass a range of ideas and information, switch back and forth between concepts, lace in a series of protracted and arcane words, waffle on windily for what seems like weeks, and strain hard to demonstrate the undoubted cleverness of the author?

No. All are short, sharp and simple. Like this paragraph. But very unlike the one above.

Yep, you got it. Our good friends less is more and the KISS are helping us along once again.

Finally for striking starts, and just to check I practise what I preach, do you recall how this book began? To save you flicking back, here's the opening line:

- Communication is nothing less than a secret superpower for success.

Does that fulfil the three principles of how to craft an effective and appealing opening? Having blown a loud blast on my own trumpet, I shall hope you agree.

- Exercise: Think about a report, briefing, document, or even email you may have to write. What will the opening line be, applying the lessons of this section about striking starts?

Enduring Endings

If the beginning is the most critical part of any communication, then the end is the second most important.

Why? Well, firstly there's simple logic. As the words you leave an audience with, they're likely to be remembered.

The theory also helps us. I won't go into the details, because this is a practical book. But if you're interested, look up the peak-end rule. It suggests people tend to recall the most intense part of an experience, and its conclusion, above all else.

So, given its importance, how to ensure an enduring ending?

This time, for variety, we'll take two famous speeches as our case studies. Although we're talking about writing in this chapter, one of the happy blessings of communication is that the great majority of principles apply just as well from one form to another.

Again, to save you from the book being just a Simon waffleathon, I'll set you a challenge. Can you identify the speeches from their opening lines?

And yes, I know we're discussing endings here. But bear with me. We'll begin with beginnings, as it were, to examine whether they fulfil the three principles of striking starts we investigated earlier. But also because the beginnings help inform the way to create enduring endings. In fact, to dip into another insight from our roll call of our renowned communicators, it's true to say:

- In my beginning is my end.
  Four Quartets (East Coker), T. S. Eliot

So then, onto the speeches. And which celebrated marvel of rhetoric begins this way? I should warn you here that this is also a way of me checking you've been paying attention to the book!

- Four score and seven years ago our fathers brought forth on this continent a new nation, conceived in liberty, and dedicated to the proposition that all men are created equal.

If the words look familiar, they should. We've already met this opening line, back in the previous chapter, when we were talking less is more. It's an American speech, from the Civil War era, if you need a hint. To save you flicking back to Chapter 1, the answer is:

Figure 2.1 *Lincoln's Address at the Dedication of the Gettysburg National Cemetery.* Pennsylvania Gettysburg, c. 1905. Chicago: Sherwood Lithograph Co. Photograph. www.loc.gov/item/2003674448.

- The Gettysburg Address, Abraham Lincoln (Figure 2.1).

So, firstly, does the opening follow our guidelines for how to create a striking start? Does it plunge straight into Lincoln's story, give us a strong sense of his character, and make us want to find out more?

That's a big tick in all three boxes for me.

But critically, for the purposes of this section, how does the Gettysburg Address end? Again, to save you checking back on the previous chapter:

- This nation, under God, shall have a new birth of freedom, and that government of the people, by the people, for the people shall not perish from the earth.

Study that conclusion for a moment before we break down the key elements. Once more, there are three to look for.

Firstly, Lincoln sums up his story, one of freedom and equality, as originally outlined in his opening. Secondly, he does so memorably with that echoing rhythm of three: *government of the people, by the people, for the people.* We'll look at how to make your messages memorable later in this chapter.

Finally, Abe ends emphatically. There's no tailing off with wasted words, such as *Thank you for listening, I hope you found this useful*, or *Please bear in mind these are only my thoughts and others may have different views*, or any one of an apparently infinite number of such equivocations and vacillations so common in the modern world.

Nope, no such nonsense. Lincoln's conclusion makes for a cymbal crash of a resoundingly resonant, utterly unqualified ending.

So onto our second speech. Can you identify it from the opening line?

- I am happy to join with you today in what will go down in history as the greatest demonstration for freedom in the history of our nation.

For a clue, you're looking at the beginning of one of the most iconic speeches in human history. Perhaps even *the* most iconic. Think America in the 1960s, and the Civil Rights movement. Which means the answer is:

- I Have a Dream, Martin Luther King

Once more, check the opening fulfils the three criteria for a striking start. I'd certainly say so. And then, on to the ending. Does King conclude by summing up his story, and in a memorable and emphatic manner? You bet!

- When we allow freedom ring, when we let it ring from every village and every hamlet, from every state and every city, we will be able to speed up that day when all of God's children, black men and white men, Jews and Gentiles, Protestants and Catholics, will be able to join hands and sing in the words of the old ***** spiritual, 'Free at last, free at last. Thank God Almighty, we are free at last.'

(A word has been removed as it may cause offence.)

That's the art of the enduring ending. Sum up your story, do so memorably and emphatically. And one further thought here.

Given the importance of beginnings and conclusions, always devote plenty of time to them. It's worth the investment to help ensure you make a lasting impression. Usefully, I also find that if you can create a striking start and an enduring ending, the rest of your content comes much easier.

- Exercise: Think again about that report, briefing, document or even email you may have to write. What will the ending be, applying the learning of this section?

Clever Content

Now we've sorted the start and end of our content, we'd better think about how to write what goes in between.

Once again, the art of less is more comes into play. It's best by far to say only what you need and then stop. But how to make sure you include all the relevant details, whilst still practising brevity and simplicity?

For the answer, we can turn to another of our great communicators, Rudyard Kipling. An author and journalist, in 1907 he became the first English-language writer to be awarded the Nobel Prize for Literature.

Yet, despite such a pedigree, Kipling embraced simplicity. And seldom more so than with the insight he offers for how to fashion clever content. In fact, the wisdom is contained in just four lines of a lovely rhyme:

> I keep six honest serving-men
> (They taught me all I knew);
> Their names are What and Why and When
> And How and Where and Who.
>
> Rudyard Kipling, *The Elephant's Child*

How splendidly smart is that? Simple, yet profound. Deal with those six questions and you should have covered everything you need to tell a complete story. That's clever content, courtesy of Kipling.

By the way, this isn't just a point of professional pride for a true compelling communicator. If you miss out one of Kipling's super six, then readers tend to notice, however instinctively. Take a brief news story, created from my imagination:

Thousands of Pounds Found in Shop Doorway

A bag containing almost £10,000 in used notes has been found in a shop doorway. It was discovered by the front entrance of the Cambridge Hypermarket on the city's High Street yesterday at 5.30 am.

Police were called and took custody of the bag. A Cambridge Police spokesperson said they had no idea how the money had come to be there, or who had left it, but that inquiries were continuing.

Have a quick read through again. Which of the answers to the six Kipling questions is missing? And does the story feel a little unsatisfying because of the lack of that small, yet fascinating detail?

What's absent is the who, in this case who found the money. Not only is that an important point, it helps us to visualise the scene. Imagine the look on the manager's or cleaner's face, to come in to work for a routine day, dreamily on autopilot, and then find . . . ooh!

Use the Kipling rhyme as a mental checklist any time you put together a piece of content and the great writer of old will help ensure you tell a complete story.

Before we move on, there's one more important point to raise. And here, I have a confession. I've tried to make this book entertaining, as well as informative. But now I'm about to say something boring, for which I apologise in advance. However, it's important, so I'm going to say it anyway.

Remember those dreaded school days, when we were given an essay to write? And the teacher always told us to plan it in advance. But we never did. We just went ahead, wrote the essay, then scribbled down a fake plan afterwards.

Sadly, I've got news for you. It's so uncool and dull it hurts to say, but teacher was right. If you've got an important piece of content to put together, plan it out first. It really helps. And wouldn't you just know? All we've covered so far feeds into that inglorious yet essential planning moment.

Start by being completely clear on your story. Remember your audience and KISS: keep it simple, silly. Decide how you're going to begin and end, because you know now how important those elements are. Fill in the facts, courtesy of Kipling. Stick to the golden thread, say only what you need to say and stop, and that should be that. Job done, and done well. Splendid!

- Exercise: Think about some content you may have to write. Sketch out a plan for how you'll do so using the learning we've worked through, particularly in this chapter, but also from the previous one.

The 'Rules' of Writing

Communication is an art, not a science, and there are no rules. Hence that heading. What works, works. But if not rules, there are handy guidelines which can help us to write with real impact.

It's time, once again, to learn from the wisdom of another of our great communicators. And in this case, courtesy of thoughts far more profound than just a single quotation.

My favourite author is George Orwell. He's a truly magnificent word-smith, with much to teach us about how to write with style and substance.

Just about everyone knows *1984*, Orwell's dissection of totalitarian regimes, a book prompted by the horrors of Hitler's Germany and Stalin's Soviet Union. But I find *Down and Out in Paris and London* his most compelling work. It's a story of poverty in the two cities in the late 1920s and early 1930s, and both fascinating and moving. For me, Orwell's brilliance is using clear and simple language to explore complex issues and stir deep emotions.

Anyway, eulogy aside, Orwell kindly left six rules of writing to help we scribblers who follow in his noble wake. They were published in 1946, in his essay 'Politics and the English Language', and remain as true today as back then:

1. Never use a metaphor, simile or other figure of speech which you are used to seeing in print.
2. Never use a long word where a short one will do.
3. If it is possible to cut a word out, always cut it out.
4. Never use the passive where you can use the active.
5. Never use a foreign phrase, a scientific word or a jargon word if you can think of an everyday English equivalent.
6. Break any of these rules sooner than say anything outright barbarous.

These six rules are splendid aides to help us write in ways which woo and wow. You only need break them to feel the jarring impact on your attempts at effective communication. For example, what credibility would I have, and how much notice would you take of the rules, if I put them like this:

1. Basically, with all due respect, you shouldn't be caught dead using clichés, know what I mean?
2. Banish a protracted word in favour of a breviloquent version.
3. Should you perchance be availed of the opportunity of excising a word from a sentence, or paragraph, a page, or indeed any element, piece or form of writing whatsoever, invariably and always opt immediately and forthwith in favour of doing so, without hesitation or delay.
4. The passive voice should be replaced by the active.
5. It is strictly verboten to adopt a modus operandi based on an a priori principle regarding patois if you can think of an ordinarius English equivalent.
6. Break any of these rules, no matter what they might be, rather than create something ugly and offensive, brutal and primitive, despite the evident fact that the rules are the rules are the rules, even in a creative art like communication.

Yes, that rewriting of the six rules is my side-splitting style in action again. But naff Hall humour aside, I hope the point is made. Orwell's 'rules' can help us on the beautiful path to excellence in writing.

Figure 2.2 Statue of George Orwell. Chris J. Ratcliffe/Bloomberg via Getty Images

By the way, it's not just me who looks up to George Orwell. And I mean that literally as well as metaphorically, as you can see in Figure 2.2.

Orwell's statue stands guard outside the BBC's headquarters in London. That's quite an honour, and an illustration of the great regard in which he's held in the world of communication.

- Exercise: Return to the piece of content you may have to write. Now edit it, applying Orwell's rules. How much has it changed? Does it read better now?

Making Your Messages Memorable

Once again, we're going to explore a concept of compelling communication which can be applied across the various forms. That goes from writing, to storytelling, to speechmaking, to formal presentations and even appearing in the media.

We're talking soundbites as a way to make your key messages memorable.

When I mention soundbites, there's often an interesting reaction. People tend to roll their eyes and zone out. *Soundbites*, they groan. *That means modern politics. Boring!*

So first, to try to ensure you don't switch off, let me deal with the notion that soundbites are all about politics and in any way modern. To do so, it's time for another of my quizzes (come on, you know you love them!) Which writer coined this fine set of soundbites?

- To thine own self be true
- The milk of human kindness
- All the world's a stage
- If music be the food of love, play on
- The course of true love never did run smooth

I doubt it's taken you long to come up with the answer. Which is, of course, a certain William Shakespeare, probably the most famous playwright in the history of the English language.

Those snippets of the Bard's work are not political, and certainly not modern. They were created around the year 1600. But they sure encapsulate the art of the soundbite. Rather than write something in a bland and boring way, Shakespeare took a little time, applied his remarkable talent, and found a far more memorable manner in which to express himself.

He could have written: *They had a few rows, but they got it together in the end.* Instead, Shakespeare made a much greater impact by creating a lovely soundbite: *The course of true love never did run smooth.* The result was words which lived down the years – down the centuries, in fact – and which are still commonly quoted today. Not a bad result on the effective writing front.

But soundbites go back even further than the seventeenth century. Much further. I wonder if you can identify this example of a soundbite in action:

- Veni, vidi, vici

Recognise the phrase? It was attributed to Julius Caesar, pronouncing *I came, I saw, I conquered* in response to a rapid victory for the Roman Empire. The words were probably uttered way back in 46 BC. It's another soundbite, and in this case it's lived on for thousands of years, not just hundreds.

Our historical guides, Shakespeare and Caesar, have both kindly illustrated the art of soundbites. They tend to be short, pithy phrases, which use tricks of catchy language to lodge in the memory.

So, assuming I've convinced you that soundbites are worth incorporating into your work, how do we create them? Let's take a look at probably the four most common methods.

The Threes

The first of our four journeys into the land of soundbites is the rule of threes. There's something about trios which the mind finds pleasantly memorable.

In my experience, using threes has the added advantage of being the easiest way to create a soundbite. It's certainly my go-to strategy if I'm writing an important document, or speech, and I'm struggling to find a catchy way to phrase a key message.

Here are some fine examples of the threes in action. Again, rather than me just telling you who the authors are, see if you can get them before all is revealed. We'll start with a very well-known soundbite:

- Never in the field of human conflict was so much owed by so many to so few.

That dates from August 1940, and is a tribute to the pilots of the British Royal Air Force, fighting the German Luftwaffe. The words were spoken by Winston Churchill in one of his most famous speeches. Say it out loud and feel the rhythm of *so much ... so many ... so few* settling into your mind.

Next, consider this another sneaky test of mine to check you've been paying due attention!

- Government of the people, by the people, for the people.

I suspect you recognised Abraham Lincoln, drawing the Gettysburg Address to a close. The year was 1863.

Finally for our fun with threes, a change of direction and a pop music challenge. Did I mention that once, long ago, I was a disc jockey? If you're wondering, that's where my love of lyrics comes from. Anyway, back to the point and your pop soundbite threes challenge:

- Gimme, gimme, gimme a man after midnight.

Can I sense you singing along? Isn't the enduring appeal of ABBA wonderful? That song dates back to 1979, yet it's still played aplenty today. And there it is, the rhythm of three, proud and prominent.

Incidentally, now I've highlighted the use of threes in soundbites you'll probably start seeing them everywhere. For example:

- Friends, Romans, Countrymen – Faith, Hope and Charity – The Good, the Bad and the Ugly – Lies, Damned Lies and Statistics – Faster, Higher, Stronger – Bacon, Lettuce, Tomato

Counterpoint

There are other ways to construct soundbites, aside from the trick of trios. Another commonly used technique is counterpoint. This involves setting out one concept and then switching to its opposite. For example:

- I know I have the body but of a weak and feeble woman; but I have the heart and stomach of a king.

That fine example of counterpoint dates from 1588. The words were spoken by Queen Elizabeth I of England, rallying her troops in preparation for an expected invasion by the Spanish Armada.

Here's a much more modern example, but every syllable is just as powerful:

- We realise the importance of light when we see darkness. We realise the importance of our voice when we are silenced . . .
  We realised the importance of pens and books when we saw the guns.

Stirring, isn't it? And, of course, memorable. The counterpoint of light and darkness, voice and silenced, pens and books versus guns works magnificently.

That was Malala Yousafzai, who was shot in the head by the Taliban in Pakistan for having the gross cheek to campaign for the rights of girls and women to an education. The words were part of her speech to the United Nations Youth Assembly in 2013.

Finally for our exploration of counterpoint, a literary example:

- It was the best of times, it was the worst of times, it was the age of wisdom, it was the age of foolishness, it was the epoch of belief, it was the epoch of incredulity, it was the season of Light, it was the season of Darkness, it was the spring of hope, it was the winter of despair . . .

That's the beginning of the novel *A Tale of Two Cities*, by Charles Dickens. It's another celebrated opening line, and why? Much because of the use of counterpoint.

Alliteration

Another standard trick for creating soundbites is alliteration, the repetition of the same letter or sound. Although most often associated with speech-making, it works for writing too. So here we go with the last leg of our quiz, and it's back to my DJ decks as we begin with a couple of pop songs:

- Whisper words of wisdom . . .

Once again, I suspect I can hear you singing along. Yes, that's the Beatles and the enchanting 'Let It Be'. Isn't the alliteration beautiful?

On then to another example:

- They paved paradise
  And put up a parking lot

If you need a clue here, we're back in 1970 with one of the iconic songwriters of the period. And the answer is Joni Mitchell, with 'Big Yellow Taxi'.

Lastly, to end this section with a bang, we'll get serious. It's time to stand back and admire alliteration in speechmaking with one of the most celebrated examples:

- I have a dream that my four little children will one day live in a nation where they will not be judged by the color of their skin but by the content of their character.

There are no bonus points here for identifying Martin Luther King and 'I Have a Dream'. Not since I gave the answer away in the first line of the quotation. But isn't the alliteration powerful? And notice particularly how it helps to drive home his message.

Analogy

There's a final common method for constructing soundbites to examine, and that's analogy. Comparing one thing to another is particularly useful in the field of science and innovation. There, it can help an audience understand something they may never have heard of through reference to a concept they know.

All too often, the origin of great quotations is disputed. That's the case with these words, commonly attributed to Albert Einstein, even if he may never have used them. But they're worth mentioning as they make the point about analogies explaining new technology. In this case, radio.

- Wire telegraph is a kind of a very, very long cat. You pull his tail in New York and his head is meowing in Los Angeles. Radio operates exactly the same way: you send signals here, they receive them there. The only difference is that there is no cat.

That's a longer analogy, almost a story. They can be much shorter, but still effective:

- The immune system is like the police force of the body.
- Finding the right room in this building is like finding a needle in a haystack.
- The meeting was as enjoyable as going to the dentist.

When they work well, analogies can become part of everyday language. For example, to dismiss a less than inspired suggestion:

- That's as much use as rearranging the deckchairs on the *Titanic*.

Far more profoundly, one of the most famous analogies was coined by Winston Churchill. In 1946, he used it to describe the division of Europe between the democratic west and the totalitarian east.

- An iron curtain has descended across the continent.

You'll often hear journalists use analogies to help the public appreciate sizes. It's almost a media rule that any large volume of water will be compared to a certain number of Olympic swimming pools. Likewise, a sizeable area will be the equivalent of so many football pitches. Well used though such analogies may be, they can still be helpful in aiding an audience's understanding.

Finally, before we leave them behind, say bye-bye, and bid them farewell (see what I did there?!), one word of caution:

- Use soundbites sparingly.

If you splash soundbites around, here, there and everywhere, an audience will grow jaded, tune out and turn off. They'll sense a triumph of style over substance, no matter how smart the soundbites. Which is never a winner.

In just about any piece of content, be it a report, briefing, speech, talk, presentation or whatever, I will use only one soundbite. One only and only one. And I'll bring it to bear on the most important message I'm trying to convey. Wielded that way a soundbite should stand out, stick in the mind, and so have the effect which you intend.

- Exercise: Return to the content you have to write. Can you create a soundbite to include, to help make your key message memorable?

The Voice

We talked about finding your unique writer's voice, or character, in the previous chapter. But I want to mention it again here to illustrate how important it is, and the impact it can have when put to use in your writing.

We'll take the words of three famous writers and see how their use of voice helps their work stand out. Our starter is another famous opening line of a book. And see here how the character makes the words rise from the page and feel alive.

- If you really want to hear about it, the first thing you'll probably want to know is where I was born and what my lousy childhood was like, and how my parents were occupied and all before they had me, and all that David Copperfield kind of crap, but I don't feel like going into it, if you want to know the truth.

Any ideas what book that is? Published in 1951, the answer is . . .

The Catcher in the Rye, by J. D. Salinger.

It's become a classic, and much of that is down to the voice of the narrator, Holden Caulfield. If you don't know the book, see how you get an immediate sense of Holden's character from that beginning alone. The story carries on in just the same vein.

You've probably understood in only a few words that Holden is a young man going through the classic teenage trials. There's anger, disenchantment, confusion, uncertainty and much more.

So, think about this question. Would the book have made such an impact if Salinger hadn't written it with that striking character?

On then to another voice, also famous and celebrated, but very different from young Mr Caulfield. The point being, it doesn't much matter what the character of the narrative is, so long as it's there. Can you recognise these quotations from the author's renowned series of books?

- Far away there in the sunshine are my highest aspirations. I may not reach them, but I can look up and see their beauty, believe in them, and try to follow where they lead.
- Preserve your memories, keep them well, what you forget you can never retell.
- Life and love are very precious when both are in full bloom.

Isn't the voice of hope and happiness wonderfully uplifting? That's Louisa May Alcott, the American writer and poet. She's probably best known for her novel *Little Women*, which was published in two parts in 1868 and 1869. Her words have lived down the years, and much of that is because of the beautiful character of the writing.

Finally, another abrupt change of direction, and a very different voice again.

- I could see that, if not actually disgruntled, he was far from being gruntled.
- She fitted into my biggest arm-chair as if it had been built round her by someone who knew they were wearing arm-chairs tight about the hips that season.
- The lunches of fifty-seven years had caused his chest to slip down into the mezzanine floor.

That could hardly be more different from the previous example. What kind of a world does this feel like to you? Classic English aristocracy, perhaps? If so, good. Because that's exactly what it represents.

The writing is from the Jeeves novels and short stories by P. G. Wodehouse, which became popular in the 1920s. If you're not familiar,

Jeeves is the long-suffering valet for Bertie Wooster, a rich but lazy gentleman of the English upper classes. As you can tell from the excerpts, Jeeves is very much the smart one, with a wonderful dry wit of a voice.

The stories are still widely enjoyed today, more than 100 years on. And yet again the reason for that is much to do with the voice of the writing.

Now, I suspect I know what you're thinking here. That this is all well and good, an interesting tour of various forms of literature, thank you Simon. But I bought *Compelling Communication* to help me in working life, not to write a novel.

No problem. I'm not necessarily expecting dry wit, or teenage angst, or sunshine optimism to infuse your work. But just some form of voice can really help you to write in ways which woo and wow.

For example, returning to a point I raised back in Chapter 1. This book is a highly professional, beautifully produced tome from the University of Cambridge, a hallmark of quality. And I trust the content has proved useful. But I also hope the incorporation of my character, however strange, has made the learning more interesting than a dull and dry plod.

Here's another illustration of the impact of voice from working life. Imagine I sent a brief email with a headline review of the year to the team at Creative Warehouse, my company. How engaged do you think they would be if I wrote it this way:

> Dear team, I'm pleased to report we have had a very successful year. For this, I would like to convey my gratitude and indeed pride at your efforts.
>
> Key to note is that profits were up a remarkable 45 per cent. The two new members of staff we took on at the beginning of the year, Eric and Ellie, have bedded in well and become established members of the team.

The local charities we support will enjoy the benefits of your efforts. We have been able to increase our donations to them by 10 per cent.

I would also like to show my appreciation for all your hard and excellent work in the form of the annual bonus. This year, I'm happy to say, it will be equal to a third of your salary.

As a summary, that's OK. It's informative. It tells the team what they need to know. But I wonder whether they would get a real sense of my pleasure and pride, and come away buzzing from reading the message.

Now contrast that rather characterless effort with how the Simon you've come to know would actually write the message. Then think about the difference in terms of effect:

Team, you've absolutely smashed it this year. I couldn't be more impressed and proud.

Profits are up a massive 45 per cent. And before you ask, no, that's not a typo, and yes, I did say 45 per cent. That's an extraordinary achievement.

Our new colleagues, Eric and Ellie, have blended in so well it's as though they've always been here. Some lovely local charities are going to benefit from your work. I'm delighted to say we've upped donations to them by 10 per cent.

Finally, the news you've all been waiting for. Because of your hard, and – let's be frank – excellent work, it's bonus time. Which will be . . . wait for it . . . wait for it . . .

No less than a third of your salary – and very well deserved, too. Thank you.

Notice the word counts of the two messages are very similar. Less is more, after all. You don't have to go on and on to make good use of your character. But most importantly, I hope that compare and contrast exercise illustrates the point about the importance of voice and the impact it can have.

- Exercise: Look back on the piece of content you may have to write. Can you introduce your voice into it?

Clichés

George Orwell warned us not to use clichés in his six rules of writing. But I want to briefly expand on why they're worth avoiding.

The simple reason is that few lapses have the power to tarnish your writing so quickly and effectively. Clichés reek of sloppiness, laziness, a lack of thought and imagination. There is always a better way to express yourself, if only you take a few seconds to think. And doing so can make your content feel much fresher. To borrow a quotation from one of our great communicators, Khaled Hosseini, here's a little wry humour from his novel *The Kite Runner*:

- About clichés. Avoid them like the plague.

Here are some of my most detested clichés. Once again, I've got a challenge for you. I'll outline five grating banalities which always make me wince, you can help me think up alternatives. My ideas follow the clichés in question:

- From the cradle to the grave
- At a crossroads
- Locked horns
- Big cheeses
- All ears

Now you've stopped grinding your teeth – hopefully – what have you come up with in terms of replacements for those clichés? Here are my thoughts:

- From birth to death
- Facing an important decision
- Disputed/debated
- Senior managers
- Listening carefully

Don't worry if your words don't match mine. This is very subjective. Just so long as you're in roughly the same place with your suggestions.

I hope you found that it didn't take much effort to replace those hackneyed old phrases with far better substitutes. That's the pleasure of being a cliché hunter. It doesn't require a lot of work, but the benefits can be significant in terms of improving your writing.

- Exercise: Check back over the content you've been putting together for the exercises in this chapter. Now get hunting. Have you included any clichés? If so, start excising!

Triumphant Titles

I've left titles as this chapter's final stop for a reason. It's because they tend to be thought about last when creating content. But prepare yourself for a surprise here.

- Titles should actually be the first thing you think about.

Why? Well, the reason goes back to a point I've made time and again, and then time and again, again. I harp on about this because it's so important in effective communication. Surprise, surprise, once more it's down to the busyness of the modern world.

Carry out another of my everyday life experiments. Turn off your email for an hour. Don't recoil in shock. I know it can be hard in our super-connected, always available existence, but give it a try. When you turn email back on, how many new messages have you received?

If you're like me, it'll be plenty enough to prompt a growl.

Now scan through the subject headings, or titles. Which emails are you tempted to read first? Aside from those sent by the boss, or your partner, I'm betting it's the messages with the most interesting titles. Which goes to show how a good title can offer you an edge in attracting attention.

I'll give you another illustration of the importance of titles. In a newsroom, which job usually falls to the most senior or talented journalists?

Figure 2.3 London, England – 30 November 2018: Pile of newspapers from the UK. © Lenscap Photography/Shutterstock

It's also one of the most coveted, by the way. Not just due to its importance, but because it can be fun.

Well, wouldn't you know it? The answer is the headline writers (Figure 2.3).

In the publishing trade, ages of agonies can go into creating the titles of books, and for good reason. Take the very book you're reading. Did it help to attract your interest, make you want to find out more, and then actually buy *Compelling Communication*?

Once again, that's the importance of titles, headlines, subject boxes or whatever.

So, how do we go about creating appealing and effective titles? To answer that, let's have a look at some, along with a sprinkling of news headlines too. The lessons are the same for both.

To make this more interesting, we'll play another of my jolly games. I'll list ten titles, you work out whether they're from blogs, academic research papers or books, or are newspaper headlines. Then we'll examine what they can teach us.

- Dancing with Cats
- The Three Worst Starts to a Presentation
- Over £100m! Is This the Rail Price? Is This Just Fantasy? Caught up in Land Buys. No Escape from Bureaucracy!
- The Nature of Navel Fluff
- Tips to Keep Your New Year's Resolution
- The Man Who Mistook His Wife for a Hat
- Effects of Cocaine on Honey Bee Dance Behaviour
- Headless Body in Topless Bar
- Three Powerful Words Every Top-Performing Leader Should Use Daily
- Everything I Want to Do Is Illegal

Now let's see how you got on. It's time to mark your homework:

- Dancing with Cats – book
- The Three Worst Starts to a Presentation – blog
- Over £100m! Is This the Rail Price? Is This Just Fantasy? Caught up in Land Buys. No Escape from Bureaucracy! – news headline
- The Nature of Navel Fluff – research paper
- Tips to Keep Your New Year's Resolution – blog
- The Man Who Mistook His Wife for a Hat – book
- Effects of Cocaine on Honey Bee Dance Behaviour – research paper
- Headless Body in Topless Bar – news headline
- Three Powerful Words Every Top-Performing Leader Should Use Daily – blog
- Everything I Want to Do Is Illegal – book

Just before we move on, a couple of notes. For full disclosure, 'The Three Worst Starts to a Presentation' is one of my blogs. I've included it because it attracted a lot of interest. 'Is This the Rail Price? Is This Just Fantasy? . . .' is a legendary newspaper headline, courtesy of the genius of the *Ulster Gazette* in Northern Ireland. If you're struggling to see its smartness, hum to yourself the opening lines of Queen's pop classic 'Bohemian Rhapsody'.

So, back to the point. What can we learn from that exercise? Yet again, as with starts and endings, there are three insights to note. And that goes whether we're talking news headlines, blog titles or whatever.

First, notice how each title captures the most interesting or important aspect of the content. Just like way back in Chapter 1, when we discussed angles. And all are written to catch the eye.

It might be in an unusual way, such as with 'The Nature of Navel Fluff', or 'Headless Body in Topless Bar'. It could simply be usefully informative, as with 'Tips to Keep Your New Year's Resolution'. But in any case, it's critical a title attracts your interest or it's not doing its job.

Imagine a reader in a bookshop, browsing the racks, a scroller scanning through internet pages, or a customer in a newsagent's. Competition for attention is intense in all those scenarios. You've got to stand out to have a chance of your work being read.

But! As ever in life, there's a but, which leads us onto point two. You can't just make up an interesting title at random. It has to at least give a hint of what the content is about. And all ten we've featured do just that.

Finally, a title should intrigue. Having attracted a reader's interest, and informed them about the story, you have to encourage them to find out more. Whether, as before, that's by picking up a book in a store and leafing through it, clicking on a blog, or choosing a certain newspaper from a stand.

Follow the principles of those three letter Is – interest, inform, intrigue – and you won't go wrong in creating an effective title.

Given which, here's a question. Remember the compare and contrast exercise from the section on voice, a little earlier? The one about the success of Creative Warehouse. Which of these two titles do you think works best for the email I'm going to send?

- Review of the year
- Smash of a year, bonuses all round

And one final thought. Going back to *Compelling Communication*, how would you say the title does in meeting the measure of the three Is?

- Exercise: Can you come up with a title which interests, informs and intrigues for the piece of content you have to write?

3

The Tricks of the Writing Trade

At a glance: Writers use a range of techniques to give their work impact. These include effective structures, layouts, styles, textures and editing, along with ensuring their words engage the reader and appeal to all.

We've now covered all you should need to write cracking content. But there remain some tricks worth knowing to help ensure your work gets read, digested, and, to be frank . . .

Admired.

Yes, that's right. It's time to elevate you from the level of good writer to wordsmith. Someone about whom colleagues and contacts might even say the magic words, those which every content creator wants to hear:

I wish I could write like them.

Don't believe me? Then read on.

Smart Structures

Have I mentioned that people are busy and modern attention spans are short? What's that, I hear you groan? Endlessly!

Given which, it helps not just to give your audience the information they need, but to do so in a way which means they read and keep right on

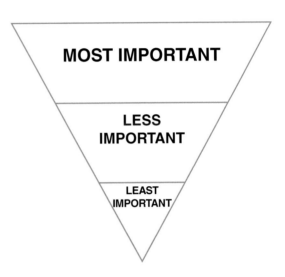

Figure 3.1 The inverted pyramid structure of communication

reading. All the way to the very end of your work. To achieve that, once again we'll borrow a trick from journalism. Allow me to introduce the inverted pyramid structure (Figure 3.1).

The principle is simple. In whatever content you're creating, you should put the most important information first. It's a technique also sometimes known as *news ordering*. You start with what a reader simply must know, then work downwards to details which are useful to know, and finally interesting to know.

Once again, click on a news website where you are. National, local or international, it doesn't matter. Read a couple of the stories and analyse the way they're structured. Do you see how they start with the most important information, then work their way to the less critical in the manner of the inverted pyramid?

You might also notice that the six Kipling facts – the who, what, where, why, when and how – are high up in the story. That's because they're essential to know in order to understand the content. Whereas less important information, such as background and context, comes further down.

A word of warning here. The inverted pyramid isn't a rule. It's a guideline. Although, in general, news ordering is a useful aid to how we structure content, there may be occasions when the most important information comes last. That's often the case in storytelling, for example, as we'll find out later in the book. After all, a murder mystery where the killer is revealed at the start of the book wouldn't be much of a mystery.

Another point to bear in mind is this. Although it is a simple concept, don't worry too much if the inverted pyramid is initially difficult to master. When I'm teaching writing skills, I often find a group will struggle with it.

The reason is that it goes against the way most people have been taught to write, and have been doing so for years. As may be the case with you, they tend to set out the background first, then discuss a subject, their thoughts or research on it, before coming to a conclusion.

News ordering usually starts with the conclusion, as that tends to be the most important piece of information. It then works in reverse, to the research and background.

Let's put the inverted pyramid structure to work with an exercise. Remember the illustration of the use of my voice, from the previous chapter? When I wrote a note to the Creative Warehouse team about how well they had done last year. To save you flicking back, here it is:

> Team, you've absolutely smashed it this year. I couldn't be more impressed and proud.
>
> Profits are up a massive 45 per cent. And before you ask, no, that's not a typo, and yes, I did say 45 per cent. That's an extraordinary achievement.
>
> Our new colleagues, Eric and Ellie, have blended in so well it's as though they've always been here. Some lovely local charities are going to benefit from your work. I'm delighted to say we've upped donations to them by 10 per cent.
>
> Finally, the news you've all been waiting for. Because of your hard, and – let's be frank – excellent work, it's bonus time. Which will be . . . wait for it . . . wait for it . . .

No less than a third of your salary – and very well deserved, too. Thank you.

Try putting that into news order, or inverted pyramid style. You'll probably have to rewrite some of it to ensure the message makes sense. Don't forget the importance of remembering your audience. What do you think will be the most important information for my team?

When you've finished, have a look at my version, below, and see if we agree:

Team, we've had a great year, so I'm delighted to be able to give you all a bonus. And the magic figure will be ... no less than a third of your salary.

How can we afford that? Because profits are up a massive 45 per cent. And before you ask, no, that's not a typo, and yes, I did say 45 per cent. That's an extraordinary achievement.

Other highlights from the year: Some lovely local charities are going to benefit from your work. I'm delighted to say we've upped donations to them by 10 per cent.

Our new colleagues, Eric and Ellie, have blended in so well it's as though they've always been here.

Team, you've absolutely darn well smashed it this year. I couldn't be more impressed and proud.

I decided the bonus news would be the most interesting and important for the team, so began with it. Who wouldn't want to read about that? Next came the rise in our profits, which is also a very strong element. Additionally, it helps to set the bonus award in context. Then came the extra funding for charities, a powerful detail, and finally our colleagues settling in well. That was probably the least important information, even if still well worth sharing.

Now compare and contrast. Do you think the second version would be more likely to draw the team into my message and keep them reading until the end? And even if they were super busy, and could only scan the first three or four lines, would they still know what they needed?

That's the power of the inverted pyramid.

Once more, don't worry if your version doesn't tally exactly with mine. There are bound to be differences in the way we've written the story, communication being an art. Plus the inverted pyramid is subjective. Just so long as you understand the principle, and can see its benefits for your writing, then all is well.

- Exercise: Go back to the piece of content you might have to write from the exercises in the previous chapter. Is it set out in the inverted pyramid structure? If not, what happens if you try ordering the information that way? Is it more effective now?

Modern Writing Styles

Compelling Communication has been written in a certain style. I'm not talking voice here. You've already got a clear sense of my character, however unfortunate that may be for you. No, in this section, I want to mention something more subtle, but which still has an important role in ensuring your writing woos and wows.

What is it? Well, imagine I continued on the theme of said concept by suddenly writing in this kind of manner, one with elongated sentences, which they themselves contain multiple clauses, occasionally perchance trespassing into a form of language which might be of a long winded and even verbose nature, the sum tending to create an effect of working through a word maze, and losing your avid attention at some juncture within the remarkably convoluted structure, which, in fact, comes to resemble more of a short story than the mere sentence which was its lofty ambition at the outset.

At this point, you might be wondering what's going on. And I wouldn't blame you. But fear not, there's no need to worry for my health. With all the usual subtlety, I'm just making a point. Which is that some writing styles work well for the modern world, whereas others very much don't. Compare this paragraph, for example, with the one above. Which is by far the easier to understand?

Let's explore the point further by checking in on two celebrated writers of bygone days. I hope you'll find the concept easy to remember this way. Beware and be warned. I'm working towards a soundbite to sum up modern writing styles.

First, let's travel back to 1871. Take this example of the style of Thomas Hardy, the great British Victorian novelist, from his novel *Desperate Remedies*:

- It is commonly said that no man was ever converted by argument, but there is a single one which will make any Laodicean in England, let him be once love-sick, wear prayer-books and become a zealous Episcopalian – the argument that his sweetheart can be seen from his pew.

That's quite a sentence, I think you'll agree. It runs to almost fifty words, and boasts clauses aplenty. The couple of longer words also had me scurrying for a dictionary, which, to be frank, wasted my time and was annoying. Incidentally, that's another illustration of the importance of the KISS, keeping it simple, silly.

But the main point here is the extended and convoluted nature of the paragraph. There were so many clauses that I had to read, and then re-read, before re-reading once again to work out what it meant. Do you know? And if so, how long has it taken you to understand?

Personally, I think Hardy is saying that someone might not like the church. But if the person they fancy is there, they'll be along in double quick time.

Now contrast that crossword clue type writing with the trademark style of another famous author:

- I'm clear enough in the head, he thought. Too clear. I am as clear as the stars that are my brothers.

That's Ernest Hemingway, taken from his novella *The Old Man and the Sea*, published in 1952. What a different approach from Thomas Hardy.

How long did Hemingway's paragraph take you to understand? I imagine you got what he was saying instantly, if not sooner.

I hope that's point made about which style works best for the modern world. And if ever you're in doubt, remember that a great deal of content will be viewed on a mobile phone. Which means a small screen. And that, in turn, lends itself to equally small and simple sentences. In summary, with that soundbite I've been working towards:

- For happy modern writing, be a Hemingway not a Hardy.

One word of advice, before we move on. Beware of making every single one of your sentences terse.

The impact can feel abrupt. Staccato. Sometimes dizzying. Or disjointed. Often very macho. Perhaps disorientating. Machinegun-like, even. And certainly aggressive. Not what you want. Unless you're trying to intimidate. Which I doubt you are. Right?

It's far better to use a mixture of sentence lengths. That way your meaning is easily understood, but you don't come across as combative. Your work also feels more interesting and elegant. Longer sentences will often follow one or two shorter versions, as you might have noticed from this paragraph. Then it can be back to shorter sentences again. Look through some of the rest of the book and you should find plenty of evidence of the technique.

- Exercise: Check back on the piece of content you might have to write from the exercises in the previous chapter. Look at the sentences. Are any too long, given what we've just discussed? Can you edit them to make your content clearer and easier to navigate, whilst still ensuring your work doesn't feel staccato and abrupt?

Lovely Layouts

If you're generous, you might already have concluded my communication voice is populist. I won't go into what you might be thinking if you're particularly forthright!

If you're not feeling benevolent about my style, prepare yourself for a shock. We're about to head downhill rapidly. Because I'm going to get unashamedly superficial. Next we move to a simple trick, which nonetheless can be a great help in ensuring your writing actually gets read.

We're talking the layout of your work.

Why are layouts important? Well, scan back over this section. Each paragraph has been relatively brief. None has contained more than five sentences. The benevolent insulation of white space has helped to make sure they're well separated.

Which, I hope, has made the layout of the page kind and simple to navigate. And that, in turn, encourages you to read it. After all, we can hardly write with impact if no one bothers working their way through our content.

Now contrast that considerate approach with the layout of the paragraph below:

If you're generous, you might already have concluded my writing voice is populist. I won't go into what you might be thinking if you're particularly forthright! If you're not feeling benevolent about my style, prepare yourself for a shock. We're about to head downhill rapidly. Because I'm going to get unashamedly superficial. Next we move to a simple trick, which nonetheless can be a great help in ensuring your writing actually gets read. We're talking the layout of your work. Why are layouts important? Well, scan back over this section. Each paragraph has been relatively brief. None has contained more than five sentences. The benevolent insulation of white space has helped to make sure they're well separated. Which, I hope, has made the layout of the page kind and simple to navigate. And that, in turn, encourages you to read it. After all, we can hardly write with impact if no one bothers working their way through our content.

Did you read that paragraph? If so, you'll have noticed it's made up of exactly the same words as before. But I'm wondering if you're now going back to check, because initially you *didn't* read it. Or if you did, you were more than a little inclined to skip over it. Which, hopefully, demonstrates how the same information, presented in two different ways, can have two very different outcomes in terms of engagement.

That's the importance of a lovely layout. We're always tempted to gloss over dense blocks of brooding text. Whereas, when faced with an appealing appearance, we're far more likely to read.

So, how do we create pleasing layouts? Keep in mind the impenetrable thicket of a paragraph, above. Now contrast it with the layout of a couple of pages of the Cambridge Dictionary online (Figure 3.2).

How easy on the eye did you find those pages? Were they appealing to explore, with all the information set out in a way which made them a pleasure to navigate?

If so, take them as a case study to list the tools you can use to create an elegant and appealing layout. Then compare them with mine:

- Table of contents
- Headings and subheadings
- Bullets and lists
- White space
- Photographs and videos
- Graphs and charts
- Font types and sizes
- Quotes
- Highlighting
- Indenting
- Italics
- Bold
- Different colours
- Short paragraphs

All of those tricks are useful, but in particular I'd like to highlight indenting. You might have noticed it's a favourite device of mine. Bear in mind that it requires brevity to work, but given that I think it makes important points stand out. In fact, you might say:

- Indent to illustrate importance

New words – 6 January 2020

On **January 6, 2020** | By **Cambridge Words** | In **New words**

danielzgombic / E+ / Getty Images

spite house *noun* [C]
/ˈspaɪt.haʊs/
a house that has been built or altered in order to annoy its owner's neighbours, such as painting it a very bright colour or building an extension that blocks the neighbour's view

In the UK, the most recent spite house to make the papers was the Kensington home of … a property developer who painted candy stripes on the three-storey façade of her house in 2015. She denied that the stripes were to spite neighbours who objected to her plans to demolish the £4.75m property, which she used "for storage".

[theguardian.com, 8 September 2019]

Give yourself a pat on the back! (The language of praising)

On **January 1, 2020** | By **Kate Woodford** | In **Idioms, the English language, Vocabulary**

Comstock Images/Stockbyte/Getty Images

by Kate Woodford

I thought our **About Words** readers might enjoy a positive post this week, so today I'm focusing on the language of praise – saying nice, positive things about someone or something. We're looking at single words and phrases and, as ever, focusing on the sort of language that is in use now.

Let's start with 'compliment'. A **compliment** is a comment that praises an aspect of someone. We **pay** someone a compliment:

The host paid me a compliment on my jacket.

You might say that you believe someone's comment to you is positive by saying **I take it/that as a compliment**:

Figure 3.2 (a) and (b) The Cambridge Dictionary. © Cambridge University Press & Assessment

How's that for a soundbite? The rhythm of three and alliteration!

A preference for indenting is only an opinion, part of my writing character if you like. You may have a different technique that you favour. But the point is, so long as you think about how you present your work and ensure it's effective, then all is well.

The joy of creating a lovely layout is that it's such a simple win. How long would it take you to incorporate most of that list, above, into a report or briefing?

Probably the easiest of all is the use of white space. Even the busiest or laziest of writers will hardly shrink from hitting the return key a few times. And white space has greatly improved many a foreboding document I've been presented with here in Cambridge, believe me.

A word of guidance. Don't go crazy with your layout experiments. If you use everything on the list, and lots of it, the impact will probably be far from positive. Dizzying, more like. Choose the elements carefully and use sparingly for best effect. Remember our old friend, the beautiful principle of less is more.

Finally for this section, a challenge for you. Below is the first part of a blog I wrote on The Three Worst Endings to a Presentation. It was a follow up to The Three Worst Starts, which I mentioned when we were talking titles.

Before you recoil in horror, don't panic. The blog didn't appear in any way like this on screen. I've just removed the layout tricks we've discussed to help make the point.

Your task is to think about how you could improve this so a reader would be drawn in and encouraged to work their way through the blog. That's opposed to the current look, where the layout is more of a deterrent.

> If the start is the most important part of a presentation . . . Then the end is the second most important. As the words you leave your audience with, they're the most likely to be remembered. And drifting into the theory for a moment, research tells us that the beginnings and ends of any experience always tend to be the

most memorable. So, how do you finish a talk in a way which truly impresses an audience? The answer to that a little later. But first, based on my experience, here are the three worst ways to conclude any form of public speaking or presentation: The apology. I have no idea why people feel compelled to do this, but it is remarkably common. It might be a lack of self-confidence, or simply paranoia. But so often I see a speaker end by apologising for bothering an audience with their words, and seeking forgiveness for not putting more time and effort into their talk. In fairness, this is certainly a way to leave a lasting impression. Just not entirely a positive one! The fizzle out. I sadly enjoy this one for its comic value, as it feels like something you might find in a sitcom. It goes like this: So, that's it ... I think, anyway ... Hang on, is there anything else I need to mention? No, I think that's probably about all ... Yes, that's it, I think. For me, this is the public speaking equivalent of a visit to the dentist. It's painful, and it just goes on and on and on. The mad dash. I'm a huge fan of this for revealing who hasn't got their timings anything like right. Many presentations have a set time limit. The speaker gets the sense they're approaching the cut-off point ... Which means they have to shift gear into hyperdrive. They talk quicker and quicker and quicker, until the final few seconds are just a breathless babble. Avoid this awful fate by leaving yourself leeway when you time your talk. 10% is about right. If you're trying to speak for 5 minutes, plan for about 4 1/2. If 10, aim for 9, and so on.

To see how you did against the way I actually laid out the blog, search for The Three Worst Endings to a Presentation, Simon Hall, Creative Warehouse. Once again, don't worry if you haven't opted for exactly the same format as me. Just so long as you can see the difference an appealing layout makes to your work.

- Exercise: Look back on the piece of content you might have to write from the exercises in the previous chapter. How can you ensure it has a pleasing layout?

Texture

Texture is usually associated with furnishings, decor and homeware. But not here, not with what we're going to explore. Because it can help enhance the impact of your writing too.

The cleverness of texture is that, done well, the reader won't even notice it. We've already discussed mixing up shorter and longer sentences, when we were talking about modern writing styles. That's part of the texture of writing. But there's another element which is even more subtle.

Reflect for a moment. Can you think what I'm talking about? This brief paragraph itself offers a clue.

If you're still struggling, look back on the previous section, or any part of *Compelling Communication*. It's full of content. But here's the question.

Is it only content, content, content? Followed by more content, content, content. A bombardment of information, coming at you in quick succession, page after page. Which might be informative and useful, but does it really give you the space to understand and digest all that you're being told?

Or is there something more subtle in play? Maybe you're offered some important content, then asked to reflect on why it's worth incorporating into your work. Following that, perhaps there's more learning to take in, but next comes an exercise to put it into practice.

In short, are you served up an idea, given the opportunity to explore it, then put it into action? Which draws you into becoming a part of the narrative, rather than just passively spectating? I'm wondering if that helps the learning process, as well as making the journey more enjoyable. And if that's the subtlety of the strategy, part of the texture of the book, is it working?

I very much hope you'll say yes here, by the way. Because – believe it or not – a lot of thought has gone into how each section develops.

The upshot being that just about anyone can write a report, briefing, email or even social media post which is laden with content. But does that content really engage the reader on a deeper level, encouraging them to think about the subject and retain the information?

That's the art of texture. It might be so subtle that no one notices the trick except for you, the grand creator which you've become. But it's still highly effective in ensuring your writing has real impact.

Now let's put the technique into action with another of my challenges. I've jotted down a brief note to send out to the Creative Warehouse team. I believe this is an important issue, but I'm not sure they're going to read it, digest it, and act on it, given the way it's written.

I sense it's lacking something. And I'm wondering if it could be to do with texturing.

Can you help? Feel free to rewrite if that makes it better, just so long as the fundamentals of the request remain the same:

> Team, I'd like us to bond better as a unit.
>
> I read some research at the weekend, and it was shocking. It said members of staff at some companies can sit with people in the same office for a whole week and not talk to them once. Not once!
>
> I hope that's not us. But I wonder if it's worth us trying to talk to each other more. I imagine it could be good for teambuilding, and maybe even increase our productivity. It should surely be a positive thing, to get to know each other better.
>
> Just to be clear, I'm not talking about when we have discussions in meetings. This concerns stopping by a colleague's desk for a chat, taking a coffee break with them, or even having a natter over lunch.
>
> Maybe, by the end of the week, we can all have spoken to each other and then see if it makes us feel better personally, as well as contributing to our performance as a team.

So, what did you come up with to introduce some texture? Does the note I want to send feel more engaging now?

My thoughts about how to improve the message are below. As ever, don't worry if they don't match yours exactly. As well as being very subjective, this is also heavily influenced by the individual character of how we communicate. Just so long as you can see how texture helps you write with impact, all is well and dandy.

> Team, I'd like us to bond better as a unit.
>
> I read some research at the weekend, and it was shocking. It said members of staff at some companies can sit with people in the same office for a whole week and not talk to them once. Not once!
>
> Have a think for a moment. Do you think that could be us? Can a week go by without you speaking to everyone else in the team?
>
> Just to be clear, I'm not talking about when we have discussions in meetings. This concerns stopping by a colleague's desk for a chat, taking a coffee break with them, or even having a natter over lunch.
>
> Do you think it's worth us trying to talk to each other more? I imagine it could be good for teambuilding, and maybe even increase our productivity. It should surely be a positive thing, to get to know each other better, don't you think?
>
> Maybe by the end of the week we can all have spoken to each other and then see if it makes us feel better personally, as well as contributing to our performance as a team.

Did you spot the tricks of texturing? They tend to focus on giving the reader space to reflect, such as when I ask the team if a week goes by without them speaking to the rest of the staff. Posing direct questions, like whether it's worth us trying to talk to each other more, is another classic method.

That second version of the note feels far more engaging to me. And all because of a few seconds' thought regarding how to introduce texture to the writing.

By the way, as a last point here, you'll see more of this technique when we come to the chapters on public speaking and presentations. Texturing, or introducing interactions, is one of the most powerful tricks for making your talks come alive.

- Exercise: Look back on the piece of content you might have to write from the exercises in the previous chapter. Would it benefit from the addition of some texturing?

Inclusive Writing

Here's a real no brainer of a question. Do you want your work to be appealing to the whole of your potential audience, or would you prefer to alienate half of it?

Before you dismiss that as daft squared, hold on. My silliness has a point. We can often turn off half the population from our writing without ever realising, or meaning to do so. And just through clumsy or insensitive wording, which can be easily remedied with a little thought.

How? Well, let me tell you a fascinating story. It concerns an English utility company, Thames Water, supplier to London and the surrounds, a job vacancy and an inadvertent experiment.

Thames needed sewage works technicians. This was part of their advert:

- Are you a confident sewage champion who can see off the competition to land your dream job? You should have a background in an industrial setting to help ensure sewage is treated effectively and efficiently.

Any guesses what percentage of applicants were women, following that advert? I'll give you a clue. It's not a high number. You're looking to single figures, in fact.

And the answer is . . .

Eight per cent. Yes, just eight.

That surprised Thames Water. They expected far more women to apply. To their credit, the company investigated why so few were interested. And they discovered a problem with the language they were using.

The advert was what's known as heavily male coded. That is, subconsciously it put off many women. Words like *confident, champion* and *competition* were identified as the problems. So Thames did some rewriting and advertised again:

- This is an excellent opportunity to make a real impact on the delivery of wholesome water. Join a team with a close knit family feel. We welcome people who want to learn and be team players, and offer mentoring support to help you feel at home.

What percentage of applicants do you think were women this time? It's a very different figure from the original result.

And the answer is . . .

Forty-six per cent. Yes, 46.

Wow. That's quite a turnaround, I think you'll agree. And all from making sure the language Thames Water used wasn't a deterrent to women.

The list of words which are associated with male or female stereotypes is a long one. For an illustration, try this quick exercise. Which of these words would you say are male or female coded?

Pushy, dominant, self-reliant, emotional, risk-taking, loyal, considerate, assertive, understanding, analytical.

An interesting exercise, isn't it? And the answers, according to the research:

Male coded: Dominant, self-reliant, risk-taking, assertive, analytical
Female coded: Pushy, emotional, loyal, considerate, understanding

If you're interested in learning more about gender coded language, search online for: *Journal of Personality and Social Psychology, Evidence That Gendered Wording in Job Advertisements Exists and Sustains Gender Inequality*. It's an academic paper, which isn't our thing in this book. But on this occasion, I think you might find it intriguing. For the coded words themselves, scroll down to Appendix A.

If you struggled with the gender coded wording challenge, don't worry. I have a confession. Not ensuring your writing is inclusive is an easy mistake to make.

I once wrote a website for part of the engineering faculty, here in Cambridge. The head of the department was very keen it should be as appealing to women as men, and I tried my hardest to make it so. I was confident I could. I'm an experienced writer, after all.

So I did my work, then put the words through a checker. And would you believe it? What I'd written was still noticeably male coded. That was a telling lesson for me, which is why this section on inclusive writing features in the book, and in pretty much all my teaching.

Now let's put the learning into action with a challenge. Imagine one of my friends needs a new member of staff for his company, a London-based communication agency. He's sent the draft advert to me for feedback. And I'm starting to worry it might be rather male orientated.

What do you think? Can we improve it so the advert is equally appealing to women and men?

Incidentally, before you draw a sharp breath, and think about writing in to complain, please don't. Once again, you're witnessing my creativity and (idea of) humour in full effect, inventing an extreme example. This is not a genuine advert! Feel free to rewrite as much as you wish:

> This is a kick ass opportunity for a trailblazing writer with guts, ambition and edge to join a fast growing and highly successful, but still greedy, greedy, greedy for more company. We're a bunch of misfit weirdo creatives with strange ways but fairly decent hearts, if you can find them under the stony faced exteriors. Our clients are demanding, so you have to be 200 per cent focused, and if your social life is more important don't bother to think about applying.

How did you get on? My thoughts are below, and once again, don't worry if your work isn't an exact match. Just so long as you're spotting the macho language and making it more broadly appealing.

> This is a fulfilling opportunity for a talented writer with passion and aspiration to join a fast growing, highly successful and still expanding company. We're classic creatives who love getting lost

in the world of imagination and the writing art. But we're also a well bonded, contented and caring team. Our clients expect excellence, and we always strive to ensure they're happy.

Being a thoughtful and intellectual reader, I suspect a question will have materialised in your mind. Are you wondering whether writing which is female coded puts off men? If so then the answer, according to the research, is no, interestingly enough.

I should mention that the issue of gender coded language is controversial. But it's become sufficiently well established that many professionals screen their communications, and particularly job adverts, in an attempt to ensure inclusivity. Which brings us to a handy way to avoid falling into the non-inclusive writing trap. Like so much of modern life, it comes courtesy of the wisdom of the web.

If you search for *gender bias decoder*, you'll be presented with a range of free options to check your content. They tend to be designed for job adverts, but work equally well for any form of writing you want to assess.

I would recommend putting any content through one of the checkers before you publish, or send it out. It takes only a few seconds of cutting and pasting, and is well worthwhile to ensure your work has the broadest of appeal.

- Exercise: Look back on the piece of content you might have to write from the exercises in the previous chapter. Does it contain any gender bias? Can you rewrite it to solve the problem?

Show Not Tell, Show Not Sell

We're drawing towards the end of this chapter, so it's time to explore another advanced skill to help your writing woo and wow. Have you heard of the concept of show not tell?

If so, I wonder if it takes you back to school days and literature classes. If you're not familiar, the trick is designed to engage readers more deeply with your words. It should make them feel part of your story, giving a sense they're truly experiencing it, rather than just watching from afar.

Here's a simple example. I could tell you:

- From the way Jane walked into the office, it was obvious she was in a bad mood.

That's OK. It imparts information. But it's rather bald and bland, and hardly steeps you in the scene. So now contrast that sentence with this:

- The door crashed open and, crimson faced and glaring, Jane stalked in, threw down her bag and stomped to her desk.

Which of the two gives you a much stronger sense of the scene? And, indeed, Jane's mood.

Notice also the word count of both sentences. To save you doing the sums, the first version totals eighteen, the second twenty-two. Which I hope shows you don't need many extra words to make much more impact – if you think carefully about how to portray a scene, convey a situation, or present a point.

To further demonstrate the subtlety and effectiveness of show not tell, I've used the trick repeatedly throughout *Compelling Communication*. I wonder if you've spotted it in action?

For example, remember when we discussed layouts, just a few pages ago? And I presented you with this ogre of a paragraph:

If you're generous, you might already have concluded my writing voice is populist. I won't go into what you might be thinking if you're particularly forthright! If you're not feeling benevolent about my style, prepare yourself for a shock. We're about to head downhill rapidly. Because I'm going to get unashamedly superficial. Next we move to a simple trick, which nonetheless can be a great help in ensuring your writing actually gets read. We're talking the layout of your work. Why are layouts important? Well, scan back over this section. Each paragraph has been relatively brief. None has contained more than five sentences. The benevolent insulation of white space has helped to make sure they're well separated. Which, I hope, has made the layout of the page kind and simple to navigate. And that, in turn, encourages you to read it. After all, we can hardly write with impact if no one bothers working their way through our content.

I didn't just tell you how readers can skip over dense blocks of text. I showed you, by tempting you to do so. And I hope the point was more effective for that.

Here's yet another instance. When we talked about the danger of your writing being made up only of short sentences, I offered this warning:

> The impact can feel abrupt. Staccato. Sometimes dizzying. Or disjointed. Often very macho. Perhaps disorientating. Machinegun-like, even. And certainly aggressive. Not what you want. Unless you're trying to intimidate. Which I doubt you are. Right?

Again that's show not tell in action, amplifying the impact of the message you want to get across.

But don't just take it from me. The finest authors to have graced the earth are pretty much all masters of show not tell. Here's one notable example, from J. R. R. Tolkien's *The Two Towers*, part of the iconic *Lord of the Rings* series. This is an excerpt from how he describes the approach to Mordor, dark domain of the evil Sauron.

> Here nothing lived, not even the leprous growths that feed on rottenness. The gasping pools were choked with ash and crawling muds, sickly white and grey, as if the mountains had vomited the filth of their entrails upon the lands about. High mounds of crushed and powdered rock, great cones of earth fire-blasted and poison-stained, stood like an obscene graveyard in endless rows, slowly revealed in the reluctant light.

That passage is widely celebrated in the writing community as an example of scene setting at its finest. And why? Much because of the use of show not tell. Would it have become so feted, do you think, had Tolkien written:

It was a horrible place, full of nasty smells and ugly sights, a truly desolate scene.

I trust I need say no more. Perhaps except to quote another of our masters of communication, Anton Chekhov, the Russian playwright. These words are commonly credited as his, although they could be a more concise summary of a letter he wrote on the subject. But be that as it may, the quotation beautifully sums up the lesson of show not tell:

- Don't tell me the moon is shining; show me the glint of light on broken glass.

But, but, but! What's that I hear you say? Thank you Simon for that stroll down literature street. It's all very Cambridge, intellectual and lovely. But what's it got to do with me writing with impact in my day to day life?

It's funny you should ask that. All is about to be revealed. In show not tell style, naturally, and with a reference back to the title of this section. Which here means I'm going to start talking about show not *sell*, as it's always more effective.

Take, for example, Compelling Communication Skills, the online course from which this book blossomed. I've written a few blogs and social media posts about it. But a sum total of none, zip and zero have proclaimed *Sign up today!* Yet still I've had lots of interest in the course, with many people getting in touch to ask for more information and how to join.

What I have done, rather than straightforward selling, is talk about the benefits the course has had for our participants. Posts such as:

I'm feeling chirped like a proud father.
Today sees the last lecture of the latest run of my Compelling Communication Skills course.
What a privilege to work with such a talented group of people from across the world . . .
And to hear we've made a real difference to their lives and careers.

Many thanks to everyone who trusted us and joined the course, and the brilliant team behind it. It's a delight working with you.

Or another example of show not sell, this time from my voluntary work:

I'm proud to have reached my 15th anniversary of helping young people into careers in the media.

First at the University of Exeter, now Cambridge . . .

And still getting Christmas cards from those I've supported with messages of thanks.

Now that's what I call fulfilment.

Both those musings attracted a lot of warm comments and kind support, which meant they spread happily across the Internet. That led to a surge of interest in the course, and, on a personal level, in the charitable work I do. Which means a lot to me.

Would that have happened if I'd simply written some posts saying *Sign up for Compelling Communication Skills, it'll be a great help in your working life.* Or *I'm a former journalist turned lecturer, get in touch for insights about media careers.*

Somehow, I think not.

That's the power of show not tell. Or, in this case, show not sell.

It's also why testimonials are so important. Anyone can tell you how great they are. And, let's face it, plenty of people do. But not everyone has a file of testimonials showing that.

Do you remember an important part of how this book began? Flick back to the very start, the introduction, and have a look. There are stories from a professor, a director, a chief executive and others, about how learning effective communication skills helped them to achieve their goals.

Why were those testimonials so prominent? I'll be honest, it was pure show not sell. We know that potential purchasers often browse the first couple of pages before deciding whether to buy. And those brief stories were powerful to showcase.

- Exercise: Imagine you're filling in a job application. You go to write: *I'm a proven problem solver, who has faced many difficult challenges in their work and always found solutions.* How could you write that in a much more effective, show not tell style, but without using too many extra words? Remember, brevity is important.

Finally for this section, the power of show not tell has spread to such an extent that it might lead to the restyling of a famous figure. Do you know the story of William Tell? In legend, he was a great marksman with a crossbow, who shot an apple from his son's head to save both their lives from an evil duke.

He's heard all about show not tell, and what it can do. So now he's considering renaming himself William Show!

OK, that might be a new low for my awful humour. But, in mitigation, I thought it could prove a rather different ending to this section to help you remember the importance of show not tell.

Editing

I've left one critical, essential, indispensable and incredibly important lesson for the end of this chapter. Yes, it really is that significant in the realm of advanced writing skills. It sounds dull – hell, for many it is dull – but it remains absolutely vital. So yawn though you may, we're going to cover it.

Step on to our stage the impact of editing.

There's an old saying in the writing profession which is well worth remembering. It may only be brief, but is steeped in wisdom nonetheless:

- Writing is rewriting.

I've got a couple of questions for you, which I hope will prove telling. The first is this:

How many times is the average novel rewritten before it goes into print? I'm talking rewrites by the author themselves, then their agent, and then the publishers. Bear in mind most novels are about 80,000 words in length. What we're going to reveal is a sort of average answer, not in any way definitive, but based on my experiences and those of other writers I know.

And the answer is . . . the magic number . . .

About seven times.

Now take a news story, the kind I used to write for the BBC. An average two-minute TV report would typically contain 150 of my words. And here, in terms of edits, I'm counting my rewrites and those of my producer.

The answer is . . . and well, would you believe it . . . once again . . .

About seven times.

Which may provide a profound insight into the ideal number of rewrites. Or it might just be coincidence. But it certainly illustrates the importance of editing.

Take a renowned example from great literature. And as we haven't had one for a while, we can do this as another of my quizzes. I know how much you love them (ahem)! So, which famous book starts with this opening line?

- It was a bright cold day in April, and the clocks were striking thirteen.

And the answer is:

1984, by George Orwell.

Incidentally, to check you're paying attention, does this opening fulfil the three principles of striking starts which we discussed in the previous chapter? I'd certainly say so.

Anyway, back to the point. *1984* boasts an iconic opening line. But interestingly, it wasn't originally written that way. A copy of much of an earlier draft of the book still exists, and has a very different beginning:

- It was a cold day in early April, and a million radios were striking thirteen.

Now compare the two. The differences are only subtle, but the editing clears up clutter and makes the published opening cleaner, sharper and more effective.

That's the importance of going back over your work and editing. Even a luminary of the writing art like George Orwell can't produce masterpieces without it. To help remember the point, we can tap into the thoughts of another of our great communicators, this time Ernest Hemingway. After all, like Rudyard Kipling, he won a Nobel Prize for his writing:

- The only kind of writing is rewriting.

We'll end this chapter with an exercise. Below is a draft of how I plan to begin the next part of the book. But I just don't think I've got it right. Bearing in mind all that we've learnt in this chapter, and the previous one, do you think you can help?

- I hope you found the last chapter interesting and useful, and the ones before it too. I quite enjoyed writing them, to be honest, and I hope that came across, as well as them proving informative, of course.

  Right, so next, something special. I really love pretty much all the elements which make up the wonderful world of communication, it's no exaggeration to say. But there's one part that I love most of all, and that's storytelling.

  I've got loads of reasons for that. Loads and loads, actually. Firstly, storytelling just sounds so lovely. That's because it is lovely. Simples. The art takes us back to our childhoods, don't you think? Being read stories by our parents, discovering stories to enjoy as we browsed around, and making up stories of our own, of course.

You can see what I eventually came up with – after some hard editing, of course – very soon, when we move on to Chapter 4.

Again, don't worry if your version isn't exactly the same as mine. Just so long as you're picking up on the key points of how to make that ramble a better introduction. And, most critically of all for our purposes in this section, the indispensable importance of editing.

Finally, the book's companion website has a quiz and interactive exercise to test your knowledge of writing skills. You can find it at www.cambridge .org/compellingcommunication.

4

The Splendour of Storytelling

At a glance: Telling stories can have far more impact than merely reciting facts. But they require key elements to be effective, including structure, jeopardy, pace, morals, messages, characterisation and a fulfilling ending.

I delight in all the elements which make up the wonderful world of communication. But one I love the most, and that's storytelling.

The reasons are many and varied. Firstly, storytelling just sounds so marvellously enjoyable. Indeed, *it is* marvellously enjoyable. The noble art carries us gently back to the sunshine days of childhood, being read stories, discovering stories to enjoy, and inventing stories of our own.

Secondly, storytelling is a fundamental of the fabric of our lives. Do you happen to know what percentage of our day to day conversations are made up of stories, according to the research? The answer may surprise you.

The figure is . . . according to the eminent anthropologist, Professor Robin Dunbar, who published research on the subject in 1997 . . . no less than . . .

Sixty-five per cent.

Yes, that's right. Almost two-thirds of our daily chattering is made up of stories. But now you think about it, that makes sense. Something strange happens on the way to the office and you tell your colleagues over a coffee: *Hey, you wouldn't believe what I saw* . . . And you relate the story.

You pull off a coup at work, and you get home and let the family know: *Hey, guess what I did today?* Then you tell the story. And on it goes.

Stories stretch far back in human history. Before we had the printing press and books, and way, way before the Internet, knowledge and wisdom were handed on by elders in storytelling sessions. Our favourite novels, TV shows, films, plays, box sets, even video games, they're all based on stories and storytelling.

Thirdly comes the most important insight, the lead role which stories play when it comes to being a compelling communicator. Storytelling lights up the mind in a way which leaves mere facts floundering in its wake.

For example, have you noticed something curious when you're watching a film? The moment it comes to an action scene, you often find yourself fighting it out with the characters. Or when the story turns to sadness, you can feel the tears forming.

That's how stories infuse our minds and engage our emotions. To borrow a wisdom from another of our great communicators, this time let's hear from the English writer Philip Pullman:

- After nourishment, shelter and companionship, stories are the thing we need most in the world.

The Power of a Story

If you want a message to be noticed and remembered, turning it into a story is a wise strategy. Because, in yet another of my indented for importance mantras:

- Facts fade, but stories stick.

Don't believe me? Still need convincing? OK, let me tell you a story and we'll compare the impact it has with a bland statement.

I expect you know the imposter syndrome. That awful feeling of dark self-doubt, the fear we're not up to everything the world demands of us. Would you like to know how to beat the imposter syndrome?

I thought you might. Well, no problem at all. The solution is simple and goes like this:

> Everyone suffers with the imposter syndrome. It's a fundamental part of us all. I get it, my friends get it, the brilliant people I know from my BBC days and here in Cambridge struggle with it some-times. Even Albert Einstein complained about it, which sure tells you something.
>
> So, the next time the awful thing comes calling, remember that. Everyone suffers the imposter syndrome, not just you. It's simply a part of being human.
>
> There. I hope that helps.

Oh, hang on. What's that I sense you're thinking? Perhaps ... I was promised a remarkable story which would help me to beat the imposter syndrome. And all I've got is this Simon idiot muttering a few bland reassurances. That's rubbish! I feel cheated.

Fair enough. You've got a point. You're never going to be moved by my vaguely comforting words, let alone remember them. So, instead of a state-ment, that not to worry, everyone suffers with the imposter syndrome, how about a story instead? And one of a true life, truly remarkable experience:

> My trick for beating the dreaded imposter syndrome was born of an extraordinary moment of pure revelation.
>
> My main charitable work is visiting ordinary British schools, like my own, to talk to the students about their futures. Many don't know what they want to do with their lives, or the possibilities that are open to them.
>
> So I tell the young people about how I was once like them, unsure what I could achieve. But with hard work, and putting the talents

I had to good use, I went on to work for BBC Television, write books, run my own business, and teach at the renowned University of Cambridge.

I call my talks – modestly enough, well, you know me – *The Secrets of Success*. And one of the secrets I reveal is how to beat the imposter syndrome.

I usually cover it by talking about a couple of famous people who have suffered the horrible thing, and how they've handled it. But this time, on this day, something strange happened.

The talk was at a school not far from Cambridge. There were about 200 students in the audience, all aged 16, 17 and 18, and we were in a large, wood panelled hall. It was echoey, full of sunlight, and smelled of wood polish. I was on a stage, at the front, with the headmaster next to me, smartly dressed in his suit and tie, and there were lots of teachers in the audience. It was quite an occasion.

I came to the point about the imposter syndrome. As usual, I was going to mention the celebrities who had suffered it, when an instinct whispered from a corner of my mind. *Do something different*, it said. So I did.

I remember wondering what I was thinking. This was a big event and I could be about to make an utter fool of myself. I had a script which had worked many times before. Why take the risk and abandon it in favour of a shot in the dark? But I went with it anyway, however much a part of my mind was screaming *Nooooo!*

I paused for a second, looked around the hall, and asked: *Who here suffers from the imposter syndrome?* And there was a silence. Because, of course, these were young people and they didn't want to look uncool in front of their friends.

The silence ticked on. I think the sun even went in briefly, as if to emphasise the drama of the moment. The seconds passed and I kept waiting, waiting, waiting for a reaction.

Then, at last, near the front, one of the students, a young woman, slowly, shyly, raised her hand. And then, next to her, a young man raised his hand. Then a couple more students raised their hands. Then a teacher. Then a few more students. And then, next to me, at the front of the hall, the headmaster himself raised his hand. And I raised mine, and more and more students and teachers put their hands up, until, remarkably quickly, everyone, all 200 of us, had our hands in the air.

And it was a most incredible – most beautiful – moment of realisation.

The students were saying to each other: *You suffer like that? I always thought you were so cool and sorted. And look, look the headteacher does as well. And Simon, that guy from the BBC and Cambridge. And wow, just everyone does ...*

Revealed there in that school hall, on a sunny, springtime day, was the truth of the dreaded imposter syndrome. It's a part of us all. Maybe it's evolutionary, there to stop us being complacent, to drive us on, to keep us working and growing.

Whatever the reason, whenever the next time it bites, never forget. The imposter syndrome is just a part of being human. We all suffer it sometimes, so remember my story, remember the truth it tells us, and remember to stay strong.

And roll the credits. Relax. But remember the point. Which, of course, is this.

What will you remember? My bland statement, telling you not to worry about the imposter syndrome because it's a part of us all. Or my story?

That's the splendour of stories. So now we'll explore the secrets of storytelling, and how this simple, beautiful and uplifting art can help you become the most celebrated of compelling communicators.

The Ingredients of a Story

Just before we move on, let's briefly explore something which I think will interest you. Checklist the imposter syndrome story against all we've covered in the book so far. Specifically:

- Is the story clear? Could you sum it up in just a handful of words?

- Is the start of the story striking enough to attract your attention?
- Is there a sense of my unique communication style, or voice, coming through?
- Can you see the art of show not tell working in the story?
- Does the narrative follow the sacred golden thread?
- Is the language simple and effective?
- Is the style modern and inclusive?
- Does the story contain all the facts Kipling demands, and also follow Orwell's rules?
- Is the story relatively brief, saying only what needs to be said?
- Does the ending sum up the key message, and memorably, with the use of a soundbite?

As well as being another of my tests, there's a more significant point here.

Nearly everything we've explored so far will help to make you a splendid storyteller. That goes from a striking start, to a clear narrative, a memorable ending and all else in the checklist above.

Storytelling Structure

Although the imposter syndrome story follows the great majority of the principles of compelling communication, there is one big difference. I expect you noticed, but just in case, I'm talking about the ending.

It's in the nature of a story that the most important information is usually the conclusion. Which is the opposite of the inverted pyramid structure. That's because, in a story, you have to draw the audience in, and build up the suspense and emotion. For example:

- In the case of a thriller, it's the final showdown between hero and villain.
- With a romance, it's which character gets to walk off into the sunset, hand in hand with the hero or heroine.
- For the imposter syndrome, it's the big reveal of how to deal with the dreaded thing.

That, of course, raises a question. If stories don't unfold according to the same principles as the majority of communication, how do we structure them?

The answer is that there is no set way to tell a story, despite what some people might claim. But there is an outline which can help.

The image below demonstrates a classic narrative structure for a story. Does it look familiar? It should! You've seen a similar version when we explored the golden thread and how it worked in the film *Alien*, earlier in the book.

Once again, the line represents the thread. But this time it passes through the typical stages of a story rather than the specific events (Figure 4.1).

Stoking up the suspense, building up the drama, stepping up the tension towards the climax before the big reveal is classic storytelling. Only after

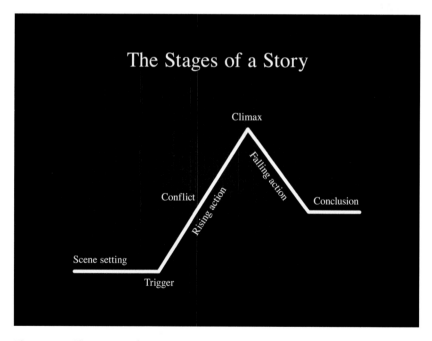

Figure 4.1 The stages of a story

the resolution can the audience breathe out again and relax. Have a look once more at my imposter syndrome tale and tick off the various stages. To explore them further:

- Setting the scene

In a thriller, for example, we might see a priceless painting put on exhibition for the first time amid high security. But we also witness background muttering from a brilliant gang of criminals about the irresistible challenge of stealing the 'unstealable' artwork. With the imposter syndrome, it's my talks at schools and describing this particular event.

- The trigger

Stories usually have a trigger moment, and it tends to come early in order to set the action in motion. For example, in our thriller it might be the theft of the painting. The rest of the story is then about the hunt to retrieve it. For me, it was the instinct whispering to *do something different*.

- Conflict

Conflict helps to raise the tension and engage the audience. For example, in *Star Wars*, it's the rebels against the Empire, a modern take on the old classic of good versus evil. In *Alien*, it's humanity versus the creature. In our thriller, it's the heroine versus the gang. In the school hall, it was my moments of internal doubt, wondering what on earth I was doing.

- Rising action

The tension increases. Perhaps our heroine, a famous art detective called out of retirement, has a series of leads, but each comes to nothing. And she's running out of time to get the painting back. For me, it was those awful seconds of silence as I waited to see if the audience would react to my question about who suffered with imposter syndrome.

- Climax

This is the moment of truth in a story, the point where the conflict is resolved. In *Star Wars*, can Luke Skywalker destroy the Death Star? Can Ripley kill the creature in *Alien*? Can our heroine retrieve the painting from the gang? Would the young people respond to my question, meaning my gamble had worked?

- Falling action

Following all that action and suspense, this is where the tension eases. In *Star Wars*, the rebels get together to celebrate their victory. In *Alien*, Ripley can finally head home to Earth. In our thriller, the heroine turns down international fame, donates the vast reward to charity, and goes back to her organic blueberry farm. Or something like that! For me, it was when the students were looking at each other and the moment of realisation.

- Conclusion

Often this is the moral of the story, the lesson we learn. It's better to be good than evil in *Star Wars*, that human resilience triumphs in *Alien*. For our heroine, perhaps it's that you don't need to seek celebrity to be happy and a success. With the imposter syndrome, it was the understanding that such darkness is part of us all.

Finally for this section, it's worth noting that the classic storytelling structure is not prescriptive. As I may have mentioned more than a couple of times already, communication is an art. Sometimes you can get impressive results from breaking the rules.

But if you're not an experienced storyteller, the architecture we've explored here will help to ensure you wield stories effectively. You can always start to experiment with your technique as your confidence grows.

- Exercise: Think about one of your favourite stories, whether a TV show, film, book, play or whatever. Does it follow the classic story structure? Then think about a story you sometimes tell. Does it do likewise?

The Long and Short of Storytelling

I'm often asked a deceptively simple question about storytelling:

- How long should a story be?

The answer is that it depends on what the story is worth. In my BBC days, the average duration of a TV news report was about one minute and forty seconds. Cue nostalgic picture of me in action in those long ago times (Figure 4.2)!

On big news days, when there was a lot to cover, the duration of a report could stretch to more than five minutes. But the stories could also be much shorter. If you were able to say all you needed in only twenty seconds, then that's how long you took.

Figure 4.2 The author during his BBC career

Once more, we return to the principles we've met before. So long as you cover the key points, say what you need and stop, you should have told an effective story.

There's much disagreement about what is the longest book, or story, ever written. *War and Peace*, by Leo Tolstoy is commonly cited as a very long book. And at 361 chapters, and almost 600,000 words, it is indeed a hefty work. But *À la recherche du temps perdu*, or *Remembrance of Things Past*, by Marcel Proust trumps it easily. The book comes in at nearly 1.3 million words, although it is split into multiple volumes. Imagine trying to read it in bed otherwise.

That, however, is a relatively quick read compared with *Marienbad My Love*, by Mark Leach. The word count here is – wait for it – 17.8 million. Yes, really, almost 18 million words, in a total of 10,700 pages. But, as the author says, it contains thirty years' worth of work both by himself and borrowed from others.

All those tomes are impressively long when set against the average length of a novel, which is generally around 80,000 to 100,000 words. But, bearing in mind our key principles of brevity and less is more, perhaps more interesting is the shortest story.

In fact, here's a question for you. What would you say is the fewest number of words which would be required to tell a story?

Once again, there is no definitive answer. But there is one which is famous and celebrated. As with many great tales, this is disputed. But legend has it that Ernest Hemingway was once challenged to write a story in only six words. And the answer he's said to have offered has become iconic.

- For sale, baby shoes, never worn.

I'm wondering what happened when you read that story. Did your imagination go flying away, exploring what could have happened, the events behind the words? Mine certainly did. Which, of course, is much of how the story works.

A hidden corner of London boasts a wonderful example of short form storytelling. Postman's Park is one of the city's best kept secrets. I often visit whenever I'm in the capital and have time.

The park is a memorial to those who have sacrificed their lives to save others. The stories are told in simple plaques, some of which you can see in Figure 4.3. And they always make my imagination spin, and often bring tears to my eyes with the results.

Try a visit to the park anytime you're in London. It's near St Paul's Cathedral, an oasis of calm and reflection, and a thoughtful way of spending half an hour.

Anyway, tour guide aside, remembering to leave space for the imagination is one of the great arts of storytelling. Writing works best when the author and the reader work together, as an old saying of the trade has it.

But, for now, the point to remember is that a story should be only as long as a story needs to be. No less, and no more. I'll leave this section with an example in action, one with just the necessary amount of words, and which also triggers the imagination to do its magical work.

There is, however, a twist. Because it's me, I'm going to share a favourite joke. Gags are often stories too, after all.

In homage to my wonderful father, who you can blame for my sense of humour, it's time for the joy of Tommy Cooper. He was Dad's favourite comedian. I fondly remember youthful days, with us sitting together on the sofa watching Cooper on the television:

> The minute I got off the plane in New York, 15,000 people started crowding around me. If you don't believe me, ask Marlon Brando. He was standing right next to me.

Did you feel your imagination fly, and your mind fill the gaps so that the joke made sense? And all that in just a handful of well-judged words, which was all the story needed.

Figure 4.3 Plaques at the Memorial to Heroic Self-Sacrifice in Postman's Park in London, UK. © Chris Dorney/Shutterstock

Figure 4.3 (*cont.*)

Pace

Some stories can last a long time. There's one I tell which goes on for about ten minutes, although much of that is due to the audience laughing. Since you ask, it dates from my BBC days, and is about what to do when you urgently need to thaw out a frozen otter.

Yes, really, you did read that right. Yes, it is all absolutely true. And yes, I will tell it later, however absurd it may be. That should keep you reading, if nothing else does!

But for now, the question is this. How can you be sure to keep an audience engaged with a longer story, when modern attention spans are so brief?

The answer is pace.

Think back on some of the films, box sets or books which have absorbed you. Why did they have you spellbound, page after page, scene after scene, or episode after episode, eagerly wanting to find out what happened next?

I'm guessing it's because there was so much going on. Take one of my favourites, the box set *Breaking Bad*. It's commonly cited as among the greatest TV shows of all time. If you don't know it, the story focuses on Walter White, an ordinary family man and chemistry teacher in New Mexico, America. He's horrified to be diagnosed with lung cancer and turns to crime to make money in order to secure his family's future.

Walt begins producing drugs, and gradually gets drawn into the sordid depths of the criminal underworld. The series is about how he, and those around him, navigate the range of mortal dangers they come to face.

There's so much to learn from *Breaking Bad* about storytelling. The characters, the settings, the plots are all outstanding. But one thing the writers always ensure is that the story develops fast. Whether it's Walt under threat of being murdered by a rival drugs gang, potential capture by the police, or his family turmoil, there's always so much going on that the viewer never loses interest.

That's the power of pace.

So when I'm thinking about telling a story, I find it useful to jot down a rough outline. Not only does that help me remember what to say, it also acts as a check to make sure enough is happening to retain an audience's interest.

As an example, take a story which is very meaningful for me. I'll tell you why a little later.

> Brothers together, Joe and Vlad played soldiers until bedtime forced a draw. Next morning, Vlad bought a new tank and won the battle. Then Joe bought a tank, then Vlad, then each bought tanks until all their pocket money was gone. Brothers together, they stopped playing and began to fight.

I'm not going into exactly what that brief tale is about yet, although I suspect you might have guessed. For now, as an exercise, just list the developments. And while you're doing so, also note the stages which the story runs through, according to the classic structure we explored earlier.

So, how many developments have you spotted?

I make it eight. We might not agree, because it's debatable whether some of these are one or two. But this is my analysis of the developments, along with the structure:

- Brothers together, Joe and Vlad played soldiers until bedtime forced a draw.
  One development, bedtime and a draw. Setting the scene.
- Next morning, Vlad bought a new tank and won the battle.
  Two developments: Vlad buying a tank, then winning the battle. Trigger.
- Then Joe bought a tank, then Vlad, then each bought tanks until all their pocket money was gone.
  Three developments: Joe buys a tank, then Vlad, then both as many as they can afford. Conflict. Action rises.

- Brothers together, they stopped playing and began to fight.
  Two developments: the brothers stop playing, then start to fight. Climax and conclusion.

Did you spot how new developments kept on unfolding, even in just one brief paragraph? That gave the story pace. It's remarkable how much can happen in so few sentences. Notice also how not a word is wasted. Or, at least, it shouldn't be. The story had to total exactly fifty words.

Why? Well, because that was the only rule of a mini-saga competition at the Littlehampton School, on the south coast of England, circa 1985. I entered the story you've just read for the simple reason that we all had to enter a story. But however much I might have complained, it led to something very strange happening. And, as I've mentioned, something even more meaningful.

I was far from a model student when I was in my teens. I was disruptive, fighting, vandalising, was suspended from school a few times and even arrested by the police on a couple of occasions. In fact, for a while, those were my sole distinctions, however unhappy.

Anything remotely to do with academic achievement had entirely passed me by. Until it was I wrote that story.

So came the day the headteacher stood up in an assembly to list the mini-saga competition winners. To be honest, I pretty much tuned out. This wasn't going to be something which would ever involve me. I remember half listening as he listed the third and second prizes, read them out, then came to talk about the winning entry.

It was brilliant, he said. An outstanding work of political and social commentary. So thoughtful, perceptive and simply darned smart. A genius of allegory, he proclaimed. And all that in just fifty words.

I began looking around the draughty, falling-down old hall, wondering which annoying creep was being praised so enthusiastically. Which meant it came as one of the greatest surprises of my life when the head called me up on stage to receive my prize.

I even remember looking around, thinking this had to be a case of mistaken identity. No one used the words genius and brilliant in relation to me. No one. No time. Never.

I should admit that I've changed the names from the original story. Vlad and Joe were Ronnie and Mike in the 1985 version. You'll appreciate why if you think back to the era of American and Soviet Presidents Reagan and Gorbachev. And OK, it might not be the most subtle of ways to invoke the fear of nuclear Armageddon, but it wasn't bad for a generally unruly and unpleasant sixteen-year-old.

I'll leave this section with one final memory. It was that story which made me think I might just have one vaguely useful talent in the world. And so, that day, perhaps began the journey which led me to working for the BBC, writing books, leading a course at the University of Cambridge, and – drumroll please – to the book you're currently reading.

Jeopardy

For a story to really make an impact, a sense of jeopardy is important. Unless there's something to win or lose, an audience is likely to wonder why they should care and switch off.

Sometimes, the stakes are as high as they can be. That's partly why extinction-of-humanity-type stories are so popular. H. G. Wells' *The War of the Worlds*, where the Martians are out to get us, is one example. Not many people who will be reading the book, watching the film (Figure 4.4), or listening to the radio adaptation won't feel a part of the fight for the survival of our species.

Likewise with the film *Armageddon*, where a giant asteroid is on a collision course with Earth. A team of astronauts, led by Bruce Willis (who else?) has to intercept the threat and blast it off course. In more modern times, stories about how climate change could mean the end of humanity have become common, for obvious reasons. *The Day After Tomorrow* is one example, with millions of people being killed by extreme weather.

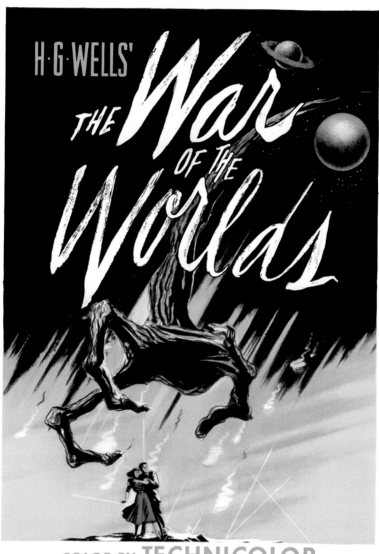

Figure 4.4 Theatrical release poster for the 1953 film *The War of the Worlds*, the first cinematic adaptation of H. G. Wells' 1897 novel of the same name. Illustrator unknown. © 1953 Paramount Pictures Corporation, via Wikimedia Commons

But the stakes don't have to be the end of life as we know it for a story to work. Which is fortunate, as for most of our real-life storytelling that's unlikely to be a realistic scenario. Hopefully, anyway!

Breaking Bad is a step down from apocalypse type plots, as the jeopardy threatens Walt, his friends and associates. Whether it concerns their lives, or their freedom, it works because we're invested in their fates. Likewise with *Alien*, when the stakes are the survival of Ripley and the crew.

But you can step down even further on the peril scale. Generally, all you need for jeopardy is an understanding that the situation matters to those involved, and preferably a great deal. That's the case with most romantic fiction, for instance. But whatever the nature of the story, you have to make sure the peril is clear soon after the outset. That way, the audience should be drawn into the plot and eager to know the outcome.

What do you think was the jeopardy in my imposter syndrome story? Look back once more and have a ponder.

I'd say it was twofold. Firstly, me risking making a fool of myself in front of a large audience. The other element was not communicating effectively how to deal with self-doubt. Which would be a loss for the young people who had come to listen.

In the otter story, the jeopardy arises from a fear of professional humiliation. If I can't thaw the creature out in the next half hour, I'll miss the deadline for the story to get on the news. By setting out at the start that not meeting a deadline is a cardinal sin of journalism, I give the audience a clear understanding of the peril in play.

OK, so it might be ridiculous, but it's clear and present nonetheless. And I can promise you, from the wonderful reactions I've enjoyed when telling the story, that the strangest jeopardy works. Just so long as it's obvious and highlighted early in the narrative.

P.S. OK, yes, I've done enough teasing. The otter story is coming in the next section. Be warned!

- Exercise: Think of a story you might tell in your professional life. What's the jeopardy? How can you make clear it matters, and also establish it early in the narrative? And while you're thinking, also check whether the story has sufficient pace to keep an audience engaged.

The Character of Your Storytelling

Storytelling, along with public speaking, is where the character of your communication style becomes most important.

I mentioned the legendary Tommy Cooper earlier as a tribute, but for another important reason too. Look him up online and watch a few minutes of one of his performances. I bet it's not long before you start laughing out loud.

But when you've got a sense of his style, next analyse some of the show. You might get a surprise. If you look at Tommy Cooper's act on paper it doesn't appear funny, let alone hilarious. Why then are most of us laughing so much?

The answer is the character that Cooper brings to the performance. With his wonderful expressions, manner of speaking and all round presence, it's hard not to start chuckling just watching him.

The lesson is to always unleash your own unique style when it comes to telling a story. And as you've got to know me reasonably well now, it's time. As promised, here comes the almost legendary tale of the frozen otter.

When you read it, imagine I'm relating this to you in person. Think about how I'd use my voice, the way I might gesture at certain points. The expressions on my face, the pauses I would leave for the audience to envisage the scene and react. Most importantly of all, on that basis, see how my character helps to make the story one which is usually a highlight of any talk I give.

> I'm going to tell you the story of the most ridiculous thing I ever had to do in my BBC career. The competition is stiff, believe me. But this is the oddest of the odd.

The story goes back to when I was an environment correspondent. I was sent down to Cornwall, in the south-west of England, to cover a sad story.

There had been a spate of otters getting run over on the roads of the county. It was springtime and the theory was that the creatures were ranging away from their territories to try to find a mate. They were crossing roads to do so, being hit by cars, and killed. My editor wanted to do the story because it tugged at the heart strings. Everyone loves otters. They're incredibly cute.

A conservation group, the Cornwall Wildlife Trust, also wanted the story on the news. They could put out a warning to drivers to take care when near rivers and hopefully save a few otters' lives.

Before I set off that morning, I popped into the newsroom to talk to the producer of the lunchtime news. He was very keen on the story and wanted it on the bulletin. So we agreed I would do a couple of hours' filming, drive back to Plymouth, where the TV station was based, and edit together a report in time for the bulletin.

There was only one concern. The story had been set up the day before, and the Wildlife Trust had warned us they couldn't guarantee we would find a dead otter while we were out filming. But, fortunately, they had a solution.

The otter corpses were not disposed of, but sent to a pathology laboratory in order that scientists could learn more about the species. So the trust arranged to have a dead otter sent back from the lab by a motorbike dispatch rider in case we needed to film one.

It wouldn't be misleading the audience, because it genuinely was an otter which had been killed on the roads of Cornwall. It was just a way of making sure we could get the story on air. TV relies on pictures, and the critical footage was a dead otter lying beside a road. We simply had to have that shot.

By the way, if you think this story sounds strange already, it gets worse. Much worse.

I had arranged to meet the cameraman, Martin, and the Rivers Officer from the Cornwall Wildlife Trust, Kate, at a service station on the main A30 road in the middle of Cornwall. I pulled in just before 10 o'clock to find them both waiting.

Kate told us there had been no otters reported killed on the roads overnight. However, that shouldn't be an issue in making the story work, because at that very moment the dispatch rider arrived. We had all we needed to do the filming.

Except! When the motorbike rider opened his pannier, I started to have my first concerns.

What he had brought was wrapped in black plastic. It was big, and it was clearly heavy, because he was struggling with it.

Oh well, I thought. Perhaps it's just a big otter.

The rider put the package down on the tarmac and rode away, leaving us to begin unwrapping it. And that was the moment when things started to go seriously wrong. Because what he had brought was an otter. Not a badger, or some other creature, as we might have feared. It was undoubtedly an otter. That was the good news.

But the bad news, the thing they hadn't told me, which would've been so useful to know was . . .

That they kept the dead otters in a deep freeze.

Which meant that what had arrived was a comedy frozen otter in a block of ice. There was no way we could put it beside the road and film it. No chance at all. It would look ridiculous.

The dearly departed and deep frozen creature would probably thaw out in a few hours, but the problem was we had very limited time. I had to drive back to Plymouth to make sure the story could feature on the lunchtime bulletin, as agreed with the producer. Missing deadlines is something you simply don't do in BBC News. It's a high crime against the corporation.

Martin, the cameraman, looked at me and cried, aghast, 'What are we going to do?' So I did some quick thinking and looked around. Was there anything here at the service station which could help?

Aha! Over there, in the corner, was a Little Chef, a branch of the roadside restaurant chain. Which prompted an idea. A ridiculous one, yes, it was true. But this was a desperate moment, and desperate moments require desperate remedies. So I wrapped the otter back up in the plastic and tried to walk nonchalantly into the restaurant with it under my arm.

I don't know if you've ever tried to walk nonchalantly with a frozen otter under your arm. It's not easy, but I just about managed, and once in the restaurant headed straight for the toilets. There I found exactly what I was hoping for. One of those hot air dryers where you run your hands underneath.

I unwrapped the otter and started playing it back-and-forth under the streams of warming air. And, however weird this may sound, however absurd, the plan was working. The otter was thawing out beautifully.

A couple of men had come in to use the toilets while I was at work, and given me strange looks. But, bless them, they didn't say anything and just left me to my task.

After a few more minutes, I had almost finished. The otter was nearly thawed out. We were going to be okay. The day had been saved. The story would make the lunchtime news. Relief flooded through my veins.

But then the door opened again, and this time I had a bad feeling. I looked around and it was the manager of the Little Chef.

I remember him standing there, stunned, in the doorway. Because clearly his training had not prepared him for what to do when you find TV reporters thawing out frozen otters in your toilets.

'What are you doing?' he eventually gibbered. And I thought, well, I'm only going to get one chance to say this in my lifetime, so I replied . . .

'I'm thawing out this frozen otter, what does it look like?'

He gawped some more, and then said, 'That's incredibly unhygienic, I'm going to have to ask you to leave.'

I replied, 'Sorry, I didn't realise it was against the rules.' After all, there was no sign on the wall saying *Please don't thaw out frozen otters in here.*

Anyway, I wrapped the otter back up in the plastic, moved as rapidly as I could out of the restaurant, we went on to do our filming and the story got on air just fine. To much relief on my part.

Finally, a confession. I do miss the BBC occasionally. But one of the pleasures of leaving the corporation is at last being able to tell that tale!

A Cautionary Tale

As well as being highly effective for getting your message across, stories are fun. A joy, in fact, as I hope I've shown (note: not told) you. I love sharing stories, as you may have noticed. Most of the people I work with come to delight in storytelling too. I hope you will, as well.

But, as a final note for this chapter, a brief word of caution is needed. The stories you tell in your professional life have to be relevant to your purpose. Otherwise, they're likely to fall flat.

What am I talking about now? It's just that I've seen presenters and hosts, bosses and staff who understand the power of stories. Which makes them desperate to include a tale in any talk they're putting together. So they choose one, a favourite, and they tell it . . .

Only for the anecdote to make no impression. Apart, perhaps, from an embarrassed silence. And why would that be, given the power of storytelling?

The answer is because the tale in question is not relevant to the setting, or event. Which leaves the audience baffled, unimpressed and sometimes even hostile. In other words, feeling disinclined to listen to whatever is being communicated, rather than highly and happily engaged.

When I tell the otter story, I make sure it's part of a clear narrative. If that's just a talk about my career and work, it's fine to introduce it as the most ridiculous experience of my BBC days. But sometimes, I also tell the anecdote when I'm teaching young journalists. In that case, I do so under the banner of always asking the right questions before you go out to cover a story. Doing so can save a lot of trouble. Or ridiculousness, as in the case of the otter.

I saw a splendid example of an irrelevant story, and the effect it can have on an audience, here in Cambridge. As I try to be kind in life, I won't name names. But it was a business event, about pitching for investment, and a sizeable one. There must have been 150 people in the lecture theatre.

The host introduced the evening, then told us a story about her son and his football boots. He had a lucky pair, apparently, which he simply had to wear or his team couldn't possibly win. But on Sunday morning, the magic boots could not be found. Despite a desperate hunt, and his protests, they set off for the game without the magic boots.

He wasn't far from distraught, she told us. He spent the whole of the twenty-minute drive lamenting that defeat was guaranteed because of the loss of the blessed boots. Even worse, how he was fated to a life of failure now that they were no longer a part of his world.

OK, it was a little melodramatic. But the set-up was effective and the story was working. The audience was swept up in it, waiting to hear what would happen. The scene was set. The drama was building. The conflict was growing. I was impressed by the classic structure of the story and the impact it was having.

So came the denouement of the tale. The suspense built a little further. The game was nil–nil. Then her son (wearing borrowed boots) broke away down the wing, beat a defender, then another, crossed the ball . . .

And it was duly headed in by the centre forward. The right team won. Cue celebrations. The curse of the magic boots was broken. Her son had his faith in the world and the chance of a happy future restored.

I remember the moment well. All of us, the whole audience, were leaning forward. We'd enjoyed the story. Now we were waiting for the punchline. Its relevance to the pitching event for which we had assembled. The moral it would impart.

But that didn't happen. Not in the slightest. Instead, she began to introduce the first business that would be presenting. Which left us in the audience looking at each other in bafflement. There were many shaking heads and puzzled frowns. Most people were just bemused, but there was some annoyance too at what felt like a random waste of our time.

To this day, I'm not sure whether the story was supposed to have some relevance and the host just forgot to mention it. Or whether it was simply a tale thrown in because it felt like the right thing to do. A way to get the session off to a good start, maybe.

But what I can say for sure is that misplaced story certainly marred the start of the event. It also eclipsed everything which followed. I can't remember anything about the pitches, or the networking session afterwards. Only that arbitrary tale of football and life. So I suppose you could say it fulfilled one of the aims of telling a story, which is to be memorable. Just not in the right way.

Contrast that with a story I sometimes tell when I'm preaching the power of simplicity. I hosted an evening with two of the executives from Google. It was at the Judge Business School, part of the University of Cambridge, and a big event. There were a couple of hundred people in the lecture hall and several hundred more joined online.

To break the ice, I started with a ridiculous question:

> *Bearing in mind the incredible achievements of Google*, I said, *I imagine everyone listening and watching has one thing they'd like to know. So I'm going to raise it right at the start. If you're ready, your opening question is this . . .*
> *What is the secret of your extraordinary success?*

The question got a good laugh, as I expected it would, which warmed the atmosphere nicely, just as I had hoped. I didn't expect the executives to answer. That wasn't the point of the exercise. But, to their credit, they did.

That Google provided a great service was a given. But in addition, there was a secret they wanted to share. And it had two critical components.

Google was firstly swift, and secondly simple.

I've never forgotten that reply and always cite it whenever I'm working with an early stage business. For the best chance of making it big, learn from the masters. Ensure your product or service is both swift and simple to use. That it works well too should go without saying.

It's only a brief story, but always powerful in emphasising the importance of simplicity and speed in modern life. And part of the reason it's effective, however obvious it might sound, is that the anecdote is 100 per cent relevant to the point I'm making.

Lastly for this chapter, be wary of relating the same stories repeatedly if there's a danger your audience may have heard them before. That can also be a turn off.

We all have favourite tales to tell. Indeed, we'll look at the value of assembling a personal library of stories in the next chapter. But remember to rotate your anecdotes. Otherwise, the experience will be like another run of repeats on the television. Eye rolling, irritating and certainly far from captivating.

5

● ● ● ● ● ● ●

Strategic Stories (Storytelling II, the Sequel)

At a glance: To use storytelling effectively, it should be deployed strategically. That requires understanding the way in which stories can influence and persuade, how to wield them to achieve your goals, and the most powerful and memorable form of the art.

Now that we've mastered the way stories work, the moment has come to look at how to use them to achieve our aims. Because they can be remarkably powerful in helping to do so.

For this, we're going on a journey. Pack your sandwiches and a flask of tea, because it's a long one. Almost a quarter of a million miles into space, in fact, and back to the start of the 1960s in terms of time.

Just for a little more drama and build up, this is one of the most iconic examples of using storytelling to help achieve a goal. And not just any goal. We're talking a true epic tale of our species.

(Stories) for All Mankind

I must be in my bracketing phase of the book. That's the second time in quick succession. Anyway, more importantly, do you recognise the words from that section heading? The unbracketed ones, I mean.

There's a splendid box set, *For All Mankind*, which is worth a watch. The storytelling is superb, a masterclass in the art. But, for our purposes, the words mark the end of one of the greatest stories in human history. It has important lessons for us in how to use storytelling to achieve our aims, so we're going to briefly explore it.

Perhaps the best place to begin is in 1962. That was the year American President John F. Kennedy made his iconic speech known as *We Choose to Go to the Moon*. In it, he tried to rally public support for his goal of landing a man on the moon by the end of the decade.

It was an important mission, not just for science and the development of humanity, but for global politics. The Cold War between the West and the Soviet Union was growing ever more icy. America was perceived as being behind the USSR in the space race after the Soviets launched the first artificial satellite, and then put the first man in space. Kennedy was determined to make up the lost ground with the challenging vision of a moon landing.

However, he faced a major problem. The American public were unconvinced. Opinion polls showed large numbers were concerned about the cost and value of landing on the moon. So Kennedy set about changing public sentiment to swing support behind the mission.

How did he do so? Yes, you guessed. In large part by using the power of storytelling. We'll look at exactly what Kennedy did in a while. But first, because it's so telling, a brief anecdote about the impact of the story he created.

You may have heard the tale. It's gone down in history, it's so touching, potent and memorable. There are variations on how it's told, but this is the essence:

Kennedy was walking around NASA headquarters late at night when he met a cleaner. The man was busily at work, and legend has it that Kennedy asked why he was still in the office at such a forsaken hour, mopping the floor.

The cleaner's answer has become renowned. Imagine how he might have responded. What would you have said, if you were in his position? Asked a question like that by the President of the USA, no less! This is what the cleaner is reputed to have replied:

- I'm not mopping the floor, I'm putting a man on the moon.

Think for a moment what that answer tells us about the vision and culture at NASA. Isn't it remarkable how the cleaner believed he was an important part of the massive operation to land on the moon, no matter how apparently humble his work?

That was what the vision of a lunar landing, told in the form of a story, had managed to achieve. Not only did the astronauts, engineers, mission controllers and all those other high profile people believe in it wholeheartedly. But those who might be considered a very long way from the actual act of the moon landing – such as cleaners – had bought into the dream as well.

The storytelling worked with the rest of the nation too. Even after John F. Kennedy was assassinated, in November 1963, the mission to the moon continued. And the rest is history, as the saying goes.

When the moon was successfully conquered, the Apollo 11 astronauts left behind a plaque to mark such a profound moment in human history. On it was engraved:

Here men from the planet Earth first set foot upon the Moon July 1969, A.D. We came in peace for all mankind.

Hence the title of this section. Given their importance in society, and our exploration of the dream of a moon landing, I thought '(Stories) for All Mankind' fitting.

It's unlikely any of us will need a story to help achieve a goal as lofty as making it to the moon. But nonetheless, we can use stories to help realise our aims in our more everyday lives. Some might be of events we've lived through, some could be the experiences of others, some may be a future we conjure up as part of a vision of a better tomorrow. As it was with Kennedy and NASA.

The Stages of a Successful Story

The story of JFK and the cleaner led to an academic study by Andrew Carton, a professor at the University of Pennsylvania. He examined how storytelling was shaped at NASA to make its work meaningful to just about everyone and anyone. That went all the way from the lowest to the highest, as we've seen.

Critically, the research found that any form of story needs to appeal to a broad range of the audience, no matter how diverse they might be. Relatability, Carton found, was indispensable.

Why? Because it makes an audience feel like individuals, rather than an anonymous mass. Each has a sense of ownership of the story and a stake in its outcome.

Remember my imposter syndrome anecdote? It was relatable because – as we came to find out – everyone in the room had a stake in it. Everyone in the human race, in fact. Likewise with my Vlad and Joe allegory. We inhabitants of the Earth all have an interest in the dangers of nuclear war destroying our beautiful planet.

Given which, now let's explore the strategies we can use to connect diverse groups of people through one common story and aim. This builds on Andrew Carton's research, and has four areas:

1. *Narrow down your story to one core and broadly appealing message.*

Remember earlier in the book, way back in the first chapter, how we talked about the importance of a simple, clear and compelling message? One which can be summed up in the angle of a story. For example, with my course on advanced presentation skills:

- Learn the art of powerful public speaking.

In the case of NASA, Kennedy focused the attention of its staff on just one aspiration that anybody could relate to:

- An iconic human achievement of science and progress.

This aim had the broadest and most understandable appeal, as it was both emotionally compelling and exciting.

> **2.** *Translate the abstract ideas into concrete objectives to which people can easily relate.*

Many people, particularly outside of NASA, might not relate to the broad appeal of advancing science. The subject is a turn off for some, after all. Which meant the core message needed to be made into a concrete objective in order to involve the wider population.

That was a classic example of adjusting a narrative according to the target audience, also as previously discussed.

Landing on the moon was the obvious firm outcome. It had the added advantage of being inspirational.

Additionally, there were associated aims of exploring the solar system, and the moon itself. But, in the noble tradition of keeping it simple, the goal of putting a man on the moon dominated the narrative.

> **3.** *Show a pathway through intermediate steps to maintain stamina and make the long term objectives more accessible.*

In the case of NASA, the objective of a moonshot took the best part of a decade. So the organisation needed intermediary steps to keep people interested and motivated in order to maintain public support. In other words, this was a way of adding pace to the story.

These steps were provided by the Mercury, Gemini, and then Apollo missions. Mercury was America's first spaceflight programme. Its goal was to put a man into orbit and return him successfully to Earth.

Gemini followed, with the aim of advancing the technology and know-how required for space travel. It succeeded in showing longer missions were possible, along with the ability to manoeuvre in space. Both were critical for a moon landing.

Apollo, the third programme, built on the work of Mercury and Gemini, allowing a spacecraft to orbit the moon before a landing was finally achieved.

That series of stages provides an important lesson for storytelling strategies. It's much easier to visualise a distant objective if the intermediary steps to reach it are obvious, simple to understand and more accessible.

4. *Bring those objectives back to an abstract and broad purpose that connects them with other aspirations.*

Abstract aspirations can be very powerful because they trigger the imagination of the audience. They also enable individuals to connect with such objectives in their own personally meaningful ways. In other words, they become part of the story, just like the cleaner in the Kennedy anecdote. And that goes to make it all the more effective.

With NASA, Kennedy looped back the concrete objectives to a broader message that made sense in the context of the Cold War:

- That knowledge and peace could be found on the moon.

In the rivalry with the Soviet Union, landing on the moon was an objective that could be achieved without conflict. Kennedy also connected the conquest of the moon to another aspiration. It spoke of patriotism, a victory for freedom and democracy against an oppressive and totalitarian system. Given the tension of the times, that message was strongly appealing to a very broad set of people.

Back to earth, as it were, and here's a more current and modest example. It's based on a scenario I worked on, but the business in question has asked to remain anonymous so I've changed some of the details. However, it's still a useful illustration of the power of storytelling.

The CEO of a company wanted to turn the car park outside her offices into a green and welcoming space. The building was in a city centre. She believed it could provide a relaxing focal point for her staff in the warmer months, and perhaps become a pleasant hub for the wider community too.

The abstract of her storytelling involved making the company a more modern and caring employer. Across the nation car use was being discouraged, care for the environment a priority. A green space outside was also far better for the mental health of employees than an expanse of tarmac.

That combination had broad appeal. First, to her core constituency, her staff. Particularly as she was careful to help those who felt they had to drive with alternative parking. The vision also appealed to the local council, which needed to give permission for a change of use of the car park.

The concrete (or grass!) objective was straightforward. Additionally, it wouldn't be fenced off but instead proudly open to the public. There would also be benches, shady and sheltered areas, and a cart supplying drinks and sandwiches.

Then it was on to the series of steps required. Plans were drawn up, the company's staff consulted and their views taken on board. The council was also spoken to, and the proposal amended to take account of their views. Approval was given, work began and was completed in only a few months.

The office garden, as it was named, opened happily in time for the arrival of spring. It was immediately popular with the company's staff and the local community.

Finally, it was back to the abstract. Thousands of people benefited from the garden. The company's staff loved it to the extent that some took on voluntary roles helping the plants and flowers to thrive. The community also appreciated the new green space, and the company's reputation was enhanced.

In summary, the initiative had broad appeal as it made for a more attractive city centre, with a happier, more welcoming business, and it pleased local residents and decision makers too.

OK, admittedly the series of steps and the outcome wasn't quite space flight and a moon landing. But the CEO's storytelling of an appealing vision worked, nonetheless. I hope you can see potential parallels in your own life, and how stories can be a useful aid in getting your ideas adopted.

Finally for this section, a brief exercise to work through. Imagine I was a brilliant scientist in the field of nuclear fusion, the process which powers the sun. That may be quite a stretch, given my intellect, but indulge me for now.

I've got a theory which might just make fusion work here on Earth. It's going to require a lot of high level backing from government types, both in terms of regulation and when it comes to financing. I'll probably need to tap into some money from the private sector as well. On top of which, I'd like to engage the public imagination, to see if I can raise support across the country. To help with that I hope to attract media interest, to spread news of my story far and wide.

In other words, I want my narrative to appeal to as wide a range of potential stakeholders as possible, in exactly the way effective good storytelling should. So, this is the story I plan to wield at every opportunity. Visualise me giving it as a brief speech, as I tour around, rallying support for my vision. Can you spot the four stages we outlined earlier in action? And do you think the story will be effective?

> For decades, humans have dreamt of finding a limitless source of cheap, clean and safe energy. The moment has now come for that dream to be realised. How? With the development of nuclear fusion.
>
> My vision is for a fusion reactor in every town and city of our nation. Conventional nuclear power works by splitting atoms. But fusion is the exact opposite. It releases enormous amounts of energy by fusing atoms together.
>
> The raw materials for the process are nothing more than seawater. Yes, ordinary, everyday seawater. There's no long-lived radioactive waste to have to dispose of afterwards. The fusion plants are relatively small, no more than an average factory in size. And from there flows endless safe and clean power.

That's power to heat your home. Power to charge up your car. Power for your smartphone, your TV, your cooker, your fridge, your game station, your toaster, your whatever. Across the country, it'll mean power for businesses and offices, power for shops and skyscrapers, power for streetlights and traffic lights, abundant power for every need, everywhere and everyone.

How will we achieve this dream? We begin in Cambridge, with the nation's first fully functional, reliable and safe fusion reactor. Built on the outskirts of the city, on the site of a derelict farmhouse, this is where we'll prove our technology works. All we need is approval from the government to start work, along with a few million pounds of funding, and we're good to go.

When the Cambridge reactor has proved a success, we'll build one in nearby Norwich. That's to show how quickly and effectively we can scale up our power production. Next we'll build a reactor in Manchester, and Edinburgh, and Cardiff, and Plymouth, and Southampton, and Brighton, and Canterbury, and soon there'll be reactors in every town and city across the United Kingdom.

We will become entirely self-sufficient in energy as a nation. No more need to worry about gas or oil supplies from unstable and unreliable countries. We will be as green a nation as the world has ever seen, generating power from humble seawater, with no waste products whatsoever. We will be the envy of the globe, before, of course, we share our technology with other nations for the good of all humanity.

And cue wild applause. My grand oration is done. OK, I know I can wax a little lyrical, and I'm prone to getting carried away. But I trust that worked in terms of being a powerful story to support my vision. Did you spot the four stages of effective storytelling in action?

Have a check through before I give you the answer. Which is . . .

The abstract was right there at the start, with my talk of a limitless source of cheap, clean and safe energy, and how nuclear fusion could provide it.

Then we moved on to the concrete objective, with power for homes, cars, phones, businesses, etc. The series of steps came next, government support, the first reactor, built in Cambridge, and then more across the nation. Finally, it was back to the abstract and a much better world. All as a result of our remarkable vision, of course.

Once again, I hope my flight of fantasy demonstrates the power of storytelling in engaging the public imagination and so generating backing for an idea.

- Exercise: Think of a project you would like to see put into action in your working life. Can you construct a story to help make it a reality? When you have, build on that by sketching out the stages the story would go through.

The Art of Persuasion

When you're wielding stories for work, you'll want to persuade your audience to buy into what you say. That could be in a job interview, influencing a panel to appoint you. It might be pitching an idea to your bosses for their backing. It could be presenting a vision for a business and asking for financial investment, potentially of millions of pounds.

Whatever the scenario may be, the power of persuasion is a great weapon to have in your compelling communication armoury. So now we'll look at how to persuade an audience of the worth of your case. And, for this, it's time for another of my quizzes. With all due oddness, I challenge you to a game of name the ancient Greek. Yes, really! Try Figure 5.1 to see how you do.

Incidentally, I like picture quizzes because they remind me of one of the greatest achievements of my life. In a pub quiz, many years ago, I scored ten out of ten in a freshwater fish picture identification round.

How about that for talent? I don't think I answered any other questions, but on the subject of fish I was the star.

Figure 5.1 Statue in a park in Stagira, Halkidiki, Greece. See the text to discover the man behind the statue.
© sneska/Shutterstock

Anyway, enough Hall quirks. Did you manage to identify our Greek friend? It was . . .

Aristotle, the famous philosopher.

The reason I mention him is that Aristotle classified the key elements required for a persuasive story. He might have done so more than 2,000 years ago, but the three pillars of persuasion remain as true today as way back then.

1. Ethos

This is probably the easiest of the three to establish when you're seeking to influence and persuade. Ethos is your moral standing in the story you have to tell, the reason the audience should listen to you.

For example, why are you reading *Compelling Communication*? That's a question I fear you may often ask yourself, given my painful humour and occasional curious aside. But the reason, from an ethos perspective, is my qualifications.

I'm a course leader in communication skills at the University of Cambridge, one of the finest higher education institutions in the world. I run a successful business communication consultancy, which has worked with well-known companies worth hundreds of millions of pounds. I'm a writer, with a series of books on communication published, along with eight novels. And I was a BBC radio, TV and online news correspondent for more than twenty years.

Hopefully that's enough of a splurge of ethos to persuade you I'm worth hearing.

By the way, establishing your ethos can sometimes be a little embarrassing. Modesty is a noble trait, after all. Many of us shy away from blowing our own trumpets, let alone playing an extended solo on them. But swallow your humility and suck it up. You have to establish your credibility to be taken seriously. It's as simple as that.

For another example of ethos in action, imagine you were talking to a board of directors. You're asking them to adopt the recommendations of a study you've worked on. In this case, your ethos might be that you've carried out 18 months of research on the subject, surveyed 800 members of the public, and consulted widely with experts in the field.

Ethos is usually the briefest part of a story, presentation or pitch. When I'm teaching, it normally takes me about thirty seconds to introduce myself as part of an hour's lecture, or even a whole day of a workshop. But it remains critical nonetheless. Otherwise your audience may be left with the lingering and entirely unhelpful question: why should I listen to this person?

2. Logos

This is the logic of your argument, and will usually take up a substantial amount of your story. That's particularly the case if you're presenting an argument driven by research and data, as will often be the case.

The logic of reading this book is that you know what a mastery of communication skills can mean for you. A promotion perhaps, because you get noticed with the way you present and argue your ideas.

You bring new customers and partners on board with the power of your persuasiveness. You attract appreciative attention for your employer with your interesting, informative and entertaining blogs and social media posts. When the time comes, you go on to absolutely smash the promotion interview, particularly the ten-minute presentation you're asked to give.

And all because of your high competence in compelling communication.

If you're presenting that study we mentioned when we were discussing ethos, much of the time would be taken up with running through your research. You'd want to be clear how it was conducted, to show the robust nature of your work. Then more time would be taken with the results and finally the conclusions, the recommendations to which your data must indisputably lead.

3. Pathos

Pathos brings us to the emotion of your argument. This is where you play to the humanity of your audience.

The pathos of reading *Compelling Communication* taps into some basic human needs. The desire to be a success, to get ahead of your competitors, to be noticed, appreciated, respected and admired. You know very well how great communicators throughout the ages are revered. Who wouldn't want to be thought of in a similar way?

But, surprising though it may be, there's also emotion involved when you're presenting the results of detailed research. I work a lot with medical technology companies here in Cambridge. They may have some amazing findings on the impact of a new device. But we always make sure to bring the story back to the humanity of their case.

The presenter might say, pointing to a lovely image of an older woman in a garden: This innovation will mean Gladys here finally having the energy and mobility to really enjoy her time with her grandchildren.

For the study we mentioned in the sections on ethos and logos, there could be a pathos element too. Adopt our ideas and our organisation thrives. We become preeminent in our field. Our staff love working here. We're widely respected for our roles in this great institution. Our founding fathers, no less, would heartily approve.

Sad to say there's no magic formula for what proportions of a story should be made up of the elements of ethos, logos and pathos. Just so long as they're all in place, you should have the foundations you need for persuading and influencing.

Here's a quick test to check you can spot the terrific trio strutting their stuff. It comes courtesy of a brief pitch I sometimes use for the course I teach on public speaking and presentations. A pitch is a form of story, after all. Despite there being very few words, only seventy-six in fact, ethos, logos and pathos are all in play. Can you spot where?

Who wants to know the much sought-after secrets of becoming a fantastic public speaker, that wonderful ability which can make you widely admired and much in demand . . .

And even better, how to use those talents to help you succeed in life, whatever it is you want to achieve, whether personal or professional?

I'm Simon Hall, course leader in communication skills at the University of Cambridge, director of communications consultancy Creative Warehouse, author and former BBC News Correspondent.

Did you tick the trio off the list? If you identified the ethos as the last paragraph, the logos as the second, and the pathos as the first, I would agree. Which also illustrates that they don't need to be in any particular order. Just so long as they're present and correct, all is well.

- Exercise: Go back to the story you might create, from the section on the stages of a successful story. Can you ensure it contains ethos, logos and pathos?

Setting the Scene for Storytelling

Here's an interesting question. Do you happen to know which of our five senses is the most strongly linked to our emotions?

The answer might surprise you. Given how much most of us rely on our eyes, many people say vision. But the actual answer, according to the research, is smell.

Once again, we won't venture too much into the theory. Suffice to say those who know believe it's because there are powerful connections between the way we process scents and the areas of the brain which deal with emotion and memory.

I asked the question because remembering that smell is such a strong emotional trigger will help you to tell stories which really make an impact.

You may not have spotted it at the time, but I was careful with how I set the scene for my imposter syndrome anecdote. To save you flicking back, this is what I wrote:

There were about 200 students in the audience, all aged 16, 17 and 18, and we were in a large, wood panelled hall. It was echoey, full of sunlight, and smelled of wood polish.

What do you notice about that brief paragraph? I describe what the scene looked like, of course. You'd expect that. Sight is the primary sense for the vast majority of the population. But I also mention how the hall sounded and smelled. Which, I hope, helped to bring the moment to life.

In the jargon of the communication trade, making use of all the senses to set a scene is called sensory language.

A classic error of scene setting is to describe only what you can see. The best writers, to really make a setting vivid, call on all the senses. It's a trick particularly well used by poets, and often to beautiful effect.

Beware, beware, culture alert. I know you don't get much of that from me, but here's some just to show I can occasionally do it. Take, for example, this excerpt from Sir John Betjeman's poem 'Greenaway':

I know the roughly blasted track
That skirts a small and smelly bay
And over squelching bladderwrack
Leads to the beach at Greenaway.

As you can probably tell, Betjeman loved that small beach in Cornwall, fair county in the far south-west of England. And how about his words for making the scene feel real? Just a few lines, but the use of touch, smell and sound are richly effective.

Betjeman was a great observer of the world, which is a useful tip for scene setting. To make it work well, imagine breathing deeply to really taste the air, feeling the ground underfoot, and listening hard to your surroundings.

This wonderful statue of Betjeman at St Pancras Station (Figure 5.2) seems to capture his delight in the world. It's a favourite of mine, which I'll sometimes enjoy when I'm in London, and worth a visit.

Figure 5.2 Statue of Sir John Betjeman by David Anstiss, CC BY-SA 2.0, https://creativecommons.org/licenses/by-sa/2.0, via Wikimedia Commons

For another example of striking scene setting, we can turn to Sylvia Plath, the American poet, and her remarkable power with words. For example, these brief excerpts, first from 'Lady Lazarus':

> *What a million filaments.*
> *The peanut-crunching crowd*
> *Shoves in to see*

Next, from 'The Moon and the Yew Tree':

> *The grasses unload their griefs on my feet as if I were God,*
> *Prickling my ankles and murmuring of their humility.*

Just a few words, yet such a vivid sense of the respective scenes. But OK, enough poetry. How does this use of the senses work with storytelling in professional life?

Well, think back to the story we were discussing earlier about a prosperous future for a company. The presenter could lace in a few words to create a happily appealing vision:

> *Imagine walking into the office and hearing that lovely low level buzz of contented conversation as the staff went about their work.*

Or, in terms of my fusion plant:

> *Local residents would walk past, hear the reassuring hum, and know all was well. Even better, with the removal of the old, polluting power plants, they'd be able to enjoy the fresh, clean air of our newly reborn city.*

The point is that hitting all the senses can help your stories to make an impact. And, even better, it only requires a few words dotted here and there. From me, about the school hall: *It was echoey, full of sunlight, and smelled of wood polish.* For the fusion plant: *the reassuring hum.* From Betjeman and Plath, respectively: *squelching bladderwrack* and *peanut-crunching crowd.*

Big wins from small amounts of thought, feeling and work. What's not to like?

I have a personal rule that whenever I set a scene, I look to tick at least two boxes of the senses other than sight. And it always seems to help immerse the listeners or readers into the world I'm trying to create.

- Exercise: Imagine a story you might tell in a work context. How can you bring the scene to life by using smells, sounds, touch and even taste?

Your Story Bank of Appealing Anecdotes

When I teach storytelling, one concern comes up time and again. I shouldn't smile when I hear it, but I do. Although only for the best of reasons, please be assured. I may be odd, but I'm not mean.

Someone in the group will generally say: *But I don't have any stories to tell.*

The reason I smile is that they do have stories to tell. And it usually only takes a couple of minutes of thought before they've come up with a list of several. Which is just the start of creating what I call your story bank of appealing anecdotes.

You've already experienced – perhaps endured might be a better word – a few of the constituents of mine. And those are just the proverbial tip of the iceberg.

It's a worthwhile, and indeed enjoyable, exercise to set aside a few minutes to think through some of the stories you can tell. Having them on standby, ready for when needed, is an essential component of your compelling communication toolkit. It's also wise to think about how a story would support a message you might want to convey.

For example, here are three more tales I could tell on any given occasion. I'll also list the relevant point I want to make, the moral, if you like. I'll keep the anecdotes brief so you don't have to read them in their entirety. But all go on much longer, if you allow for the inclusion of some scene setting and building of suspense:

- **The typo trauma**

  I once led a short writing course, Beautiful Blogs, which was specially convened for the chief executives of some sizeable Cambridge businesses. Naturally, I wanted to impress such high powered people, as that could lead to new opportunities.

  The course went well, and so, to reinforce our connection, I sent out an email afterwards. I thanked the executives for their excellent participation, said how enjoyable our time together had been, and to please call on me if I could help with anything else.

  I then sat back and basked in the glow of a good job well done. Sadly, that feeling lasted no more than a few minutes, which was when the first reply arrived.

  The CEO in question was kind, said how much she had enjoyed the workshop, and benefited from it. But she didn't realise she had taken a course which was all about . . .

  Wait for it . . . wait for it . . .

  Beautiful Bogs.

  Yes, that's BOGS, not blogs. Common slang for toilets. I had apparently led a course about lovely loos. One tiny typographical error had horribly changed the meaning of what I was trying to say. To my hideous embarrassment.

  The lesson being always to take care when typing messages, and particularly important ones.

- **Barbara and the butcherbird**

  I sometimes teach creative writing at festivals, and as part of that offer one-to-one feedback on drafts of novels. The way this works is that you're usually in a large hall, at a desk, and the aspiring authors each get about twenty minutes with you. They rotate between tutors to benefit from a range of views.

  Each changeover is an interesting moment. I'll have the person's name and manuscript in front of me, but I won't know what they look like. So, as a little game, I scan around and see if I can guess who's coming to see me.

  I was particularly looking forward to this next writer. Her name was Barbara, and the work she had submitted was excellent. I should be clear,

I mean in terms of her ability, not the topic. Content warning here. The subject in question was not pleasant at all.

Her story was about a man who planned to attack women in a forest. He had bought a hunting knife and was lying in wait, to see who his victim might be. Barbara had cleverly drawn a parallel between this horrible man and a creature known as the butcherbird, which also lived in the forest.

If you don't know this charming avian (and why would you?), it's a species of shrike which likes to impale its prey on any available spikes. Thorns, barbed wire fences, that kind of thing. I told you it was a charming creature.

Anyway, horror of subject aside, Barbara was clearly a talented writer who I was looking forward to chatting with. So came the moment of her appointment, and I began scanning the crowd, wondering who she might be among all those milling around. Perhaps in her thirties, I thought. Professional type, smartly dressed in a casual way. Determined, resolute, she would stride over, give me a cool and firm handshake, and sit down.

I couldn't see anyone who looked even vaguely like that. The crowd was thinning. Most of the writers had managed to find their tutors. But hovering uncertainly near my table was a nervous, older lady, dressed in lovely summer colours. She was grey-haired, slight and smiling shyly.

Barbara? I said, doing my best to hide the surprise in my voice.

Yes, she replied.

I made a poor attempt at trying to appear unruffled. I know it wasn't good, because Barbara kindly asked, *Are you OK? You seem flustered.*

I am, I admitted.

Oh dear, she replied, so very gently. *I feared this would happen. My writing wasn't any good, was it? You just don't know how to tell me.*

It took me several seconds to form a sentence after that. Eventually, I managed, *Barbara, your writing was great. Really good. It's just that you're not quite what I expected.*

After that stumbling introduction, we got on well and have kept in touch. I'm pleased to say Barbara went on to become a successful writer. The lesson from this story, of course, is an age-old but oh so important one. Never judge by appearances.

- **The value of values**

Remember when Covid-19 struck? No, I don't want to either, but stay with me for a moment.

Like everyone everywhere, the business community here in Cambridge was in a state of fear. I choose my words with care and try to avoid clichés, as you know. But, thinking back, panic may not be too strong a description. It was a dreadful time.

As society began to shut down, I had a chat with the boss of the Cambridge Network, the main business group in and around the city. We wanted to help our community, so I suggested putting on a webinar about crisis communication. The idea was to help businesses and organisations keep in touch with their customers, partners and indeed staff during the coming storm.

The situation being urgent, we set up the webinar for the next day, which was quite a feat. Bear in mind, none of us had ever held one before. This was one of the steepest learning curves I had faced.

But we got the technology sorted, and sent out an email advertising the event. It was free, in line with my values and those of the Network, in trying to help colleagues through difficult times.

We expected perhaps 50 people to book up, out of a capacity of 100. But guess what happened? All 100 places were taken within minutes. So we put on another webinar, and another, and eventually I ended up hosting seven.

Social media went mad with news of the events and there was lots of kind appreciation. That resulted in me being approached by a publisher to write a personal development e-book. It was a success, and I've now written no fewer than twelve e-books on business and communication.

I also made many new contacts and friends, and a great deal of work came my way as a result of those webinars. I emphasise again: that was never the reason for running them. We were simply trying to do the right thing at an awful moment in history.

So the point is this. All those books I've now had published, all those new friends and contacts, all that extra business, it all came about because . . .

Of my values. And not just having those values, but putting them into action.

The moral of the story this time, naturally enough, being the value of values.

I could go on. And on and on. And on some more. You know me and how I love storytelling.

Anyway, that's just a sample of the tales in my own story bank. I keep them in a corner of the library of my mind, ready for when needed. And they often are. It might be at a networking event, or when I'm teaching, perhaps even in my private life.

But wherever and whenever you wield them, having a story ready and being able to tell it well can be a great asset in life. Which means that creating a story bank of your very own appealing anecdotes is a wise investment of time and thought.

- Exercise: Start drawing up your own story bank of anecdotes. And because I'm being kind here, I grant you the freedom to get away from your desk and sit comfortably, with a cup of tea, or glass of wine, to do so. Aren't I lovely?!

Pat the Dog, Stroke the Cat

What am I talking about now you may well be thinking, and yet again. What could patting a dog and stroking a cat have to do with stories?

The answer is empathy.

Storytelling works best when there's a rapport between you and the audience. When there's something about you which they like, so they're drawn into the world you're creating. Which brings us to a trick of the screenwriter's trade.

Think back on a favourite film, or TV series. The writers know many viewers don't give a story long before they decide whether to keep watching or move on to the next offering. There's so much to choose from in our on-demand age.

To keep you engaged, some action or drama will often quickly develop. But the writers also know they have to make you feel for the lead character. To establish empathy, to make you care about what happens to them. Which is where stroking the cat or patting the dog comes in.

Just before the action, the character will usually do something which marks them as a person worth caring about. Showing some love for a cat or dog is a cliché, which is rarely seen nowadays. But there will be something else to hook you into wanting to know what happens to this person.

It might be giving money to a busker, making them smile as they play their guitar. It could be helping up a child after they fall over in the street. It might just be offering to take a photo for a couple trying unsuccessfully to capture themselves in a selfie. But whatever it is, the classic pat the dog, stroke the cat moment will be there. The next time you watch a TV show or film, keep an eye out for it.

So, when you tell a story, ensuring an audience is with you, feeling for you and caring about you is important. Which makes a dog-patting or cat-stroking moment worth incorporating.

Look back on the previous section about your story bank of appealing anecdotes. You know me well enough by now, so I didn't have to try too hard to engage you. Obviously, you're already charmed by my humour and wit (ahem!)

But did you spot what I did at the start of the story about bloodthirsty Barbara? By mentioning that I taught creative writing and gave one-to-one feedback to aspiring authors, I set myself up as kind and public spirited. Likewise with the value of values story, and wanting to help the business community through the pandemic.

The beautiful bogs story offers another way of connecting with an audience. Many people feel you have to be all powerful, completely confident and utterly in command when giving a presentation.

Wrong, I'd say. Showing humility is a powerful technique for making a connection. As with my embarrassing typo. By confessing fallibility you show your humanity, and that seldom fails to be well received. I'll reveal my own most moving example in a couple of pages' time, when we cover the gold standard of storytelling.

It requires only a few words, but establishing a rapport with the audience can greatly enhance the impact of your storytelling. So set forth, pat that dog and stroke that cat, in whichever metaphorical way you choose.

A Word of Wisdom

This is probably going to be the shortest section of the book. But I wanted to include it, because a valuable lesson of the storytelling art lies within:

- Stories are for savouring.

As we've seen, much of the impact of a story comes from the telling. So it's important not to rush. Watch one of the great storytellers in action. Whether it's a comedian, an entertainer, an actor, a journalist, a writer, a TED talk, whatever. I'm betting, for all their different styles, one factor unites them.

Each takes their time to tell the story. There's no rush, the tale unfolds as it will. At its own pace, as it were. And that just makes it all the better.

I've offered you my version of the insight that stories are for savouring. But for a far better way of remembering it, we'll turn to another of our masters of communication. The great storyteller Charles Dickens had a precious mantra, one by which he judged his novels:

- Make them laugh, make them cry, make them wait.

So should it be with the stories which you tell.

Through the Eyes of Others

We're moving towards the end of our time on storytelling now, sad to say. But! I have one last treat for you. Or two, in fact. Because, in the true tradition of the art, I've saved the best for last.

The first of our double-feature denouement is a handy way to get a message across if you don't have a tale in your personal story bank, but still need to make an important point. In which case, you can always tell a story as seen through the eyes of others.

I use a couple of these in the 'Secrets of Success' talk I give in schools. The first attribute I highlight is lateral, or creative thinking. For this, I tell the students the biblical story of the Judgement of Solomon.

If you don't know it, the great and wise ruler was faced with two women. Both claimed to be the mother of a baby. Solomon considered the issue and decreed the baby should be cut in two, with each woman given half. That, he said, was the only fair solution.

If you're feeling shocked, don't worry. The story has a happy ending.

The first woman accepted the ruling. The second begged Solomon not to carry out his judgement and instead give the baby to her rival. From this, he could tell such selfless love meant she was the true mother, and she was allowed to take the baby. Some impressive lateral thinking meant justice was done.

The second issue I explore is the power of persistence.

I could just tell the young people never to give up, because quitters never win and winners never quit. Or some such well-worn saying. But would they remember that? I rather doubt it.

So instead I tell them a brief story, and one they can relate to. It's about a website I think they will know. I'm sure they will know, in fact.

Launched in 2005, its original business plan was to become a dating site. For which the founders used the slogan *Tune in, Hook up.*

When the reaction was (perhaps understandably) poor, they even offered women $20 to upload videos of themselves . . .

And didn't get a single response (again, perhaps understandably.)

The company then switched to hosting any type of video, its first being an eighteen-second clip of elephants at a zoo. Business started to get rather better from there. Very much better. To the extent that this website now has more than 2 billion users.

So, what's the site?

I get lots of guesses. Lots and lots of guesses. All of which are usually wrong. Because it's hard for the young people to believe this website has ever been anything other than a slam dunk of a shining success.

What is it? The answer is YouTube. Yes, the mighty, first port of call for just about any video millions of people ever want to watch, YouTube.

Surprising though it may seem, the original incarnation of YouTube was far from being a success. And, most importantly of course, if the founders had then given up instead of persisting . . .

It might be hard to imagine, but we could now be living in a world without YouTube.

That's the power of persistence, as well as, courtesy of our first tale, lateral thinking. And that's also the impact which telling stories through the eyes of others can have.

The Gold Standard of Storytelling: The Teachers' Tale

And so we reach the end of our journey through storytelling. Which means it's time to introduce the gold standard of the art. Please give a huge round of applause for – because it's well worth the appreciation – the story only you can tell.

Given all you now know, if you can master this you're pretty much guaranteed to render any audience spellbound. I know, because I'm about to tell you the most powerful of the selection of stories from my personal collection. And I've seen what it can do.

You've heard the otter, and the imposter syndrome, and all about blood-thirsty Barbara, and more besides. All are examples of stories only I can tell. Because I was there, they happened to me, and only I can explain how those remarkable experiences felt.

But now we come to the most moving and memorable of the set. One which often has audiences in tears. Me too, if I'm being honest.

I sometimes struggle to get through this one, it's so profound, so meaningful, so very important to me and all that I am.

Which is quite a build-up, I appreciate. So, with all due fanfare, drum roll, and even twenty-one-gun salute, here comes the story of stories that only I can tell. I call it The Teachers' Tale:

This is the moment which made me.

I've already mentioned that I was a horrible student in my schooldays. I was often disappearing from home, being suspended from school, fighting and committing crime, and I was arrested by the police several times.

Pause for a second to reflect on that. Are you surprised? Maybe not, given the sometimes strange ways I've behaved in writing this book. But then again, thinking about my position with the prestigious University of Cambridge, running my own business, and previously working for the BBC, you might be just a little taken aback.

In which case, the question I suspect you may now be asking is: how did life turn around for me? Well, surprise, surprise, the answer comes with this story. It details a beautiful and formative intervention that transformed my life, and which showcases the gold standard of storytelling.

I was fourteen years old and walking down the corridor of my school one ordinary Tuesday morning. I was strutting along, like I did, tough guy stare on my face, growling at the world. Yes, I really was like that back then. On I swaggered, exuding attitude, when out of a classroom jumped two teachers, Nigel Warr and Jerry Lewis. You'll see why I remember their names so well in a minute.

They grabbed the horrible young me, pulled me into the classroom, locked the door behind us and closed the curtains. And suddenly I wasn't feeling so tough any more. In fact, I was terrified. These were big men. Nigel was an athlete, Jerry a rugby player, and I thought I was going to be beaten up for all the trouble I'd caused. Remember, this was the 1980s, it was a savage decade, and that was perfectly possible.

But actually, what happened was very different. They sat the scared young me on a desk in that chilly, echoey, half-lit room, which smelt unpleasantly of chalk dust and teenage kids, and gave me a five-minute grilling.

They told me how I was stupid, because I was blessed with some great gifts. I had a smart brain, I was eloquent, thoughtful, creative, people listened to me, I could lead, I could inspire, I could do so much with my life . . .

Or I could screw it all up and throw it all away, exactly as I was right on course to at that time.

Nigel and Jerry finished their bombardment by telling me they'd made their plan for this ambush because they thought I was worth it. They believed that there was good in me and I deserved a chance. So now my challenge was to prove them right, sort myself out and make something of my life.

I remember stumbling out of that classroom in a daze, absolutely stunned. It was the first time in my life that anything so deeply moving had happened to me. That two people, whom I secretly respected, thought enough of me and believed enough in me to do something like that. It was a truly extraordinary moment.

I was so touched by what Nigel and Jerry had done that I did indeed turn my life around. I started to behave much better and do reasonably well at school. I went on to university, to work for the BBC, travelling, covering incredible stories and meeting remarkable people. Then to write books, lead a course here at the University of Cambridge, and to run my own company.

And here's the punch line, the critical point. Do you know what? I don't think any of that would have happened without the brief but profoundly transformative intervention of those two men, all those years ago.

So now, whenever I teach anything, whether it's a lecture, a workshop, or even writing this book, I always remember them. I remember Nigel and Jerry and hope I'm fulfilling the wonderful legacy they left me, changing other lives for the better just as they changed mine.

And pause.

If I were telling you that tale in person, I'd now be leaving a few seconds to let the story resonate. So why don't we take just such a moment, even if we are in the world of print.

Which leads me to one more thought before we leave storytelling, and it's a confession. Even now, even after relating that story more than a few times, even after all these years, tears fell from my eyes as I wrote the words of The Teachers' Tale.

That's the power of stories. And even more so, the story only you can tell.

- Exercise: What's a story only you can tell? And how can you use it to help make an important point, one which really gets noticed and remembered?

The companion website to the book has a quiz and video for you on the splendour of storytelling. You can find it at www.cambridge.org/compellingcommunication.

Finally for this chapter, a poignant P.S. Do you remember the dedication at the very start of the book? To save you flicking back, and because it deserves repeating:

For Jess and Niamh, for obvious reasons, and for Nigel and Jerry, for reasons which will become obvious.

Jess is my wife, and Niamh, my daughter. Which makes that the straight-forward part of the dedication, although, of course, no less heartfelt.

As for the other two wonderful names I mention, I hope they now make very meaningful sense.

6

Public Speaking, Presenting and Performing

At a glance: Impressive public speaking requires a sound structure for a presentation, along with the effective use of data and slides, as well as interlacing elements of character.

A question comes to mind as we reach this stage of the book. I suspect I know the answer before I even ask. But here we go anyway:

Has the title of this chapter set your heart racing and prickled your skin with sweat?

If so, don't worry. You're far from alone. Surveys repeatedly show that public speaking is among the most daunting ordeals of modern life. But we're also well aware that professional, polished and powerful presenting is a much admired and widely desired skill.

Should that sum up your situation, if you need to be able to present well but fret you'll never be able to do so, then fear not. Help is at hand.

Come join me on this scary but critical next step of your conquest of the kingdom of compelling communication.

The Elevator Pitch

We'll begin with a gentle loosener of a concept to build up some confidence and get us into the spirit of public speaking. You may have heard of the elevator pitch, but in case you haven't, a word of explanation.

It's a very brief talk designed to engage interest. That's whether in what you do, or the work of your business or organisation. As the name suggests, it comes from this scenario:

Imagine you're at a conference. You're about to take a lift from the floor where the trade show is being held to your room. As the doors are going to close, in walks your perfect customer, business partner or investor. It's just the two of you, no one else. You have their captive attention for the time the lift takes to move between floors, which is anything from twenty to thirty seconds. Opportunity is smiling upon you like the glorious rays of the summer morning sun.

But! What if you don't have an elevator pitch to mind? Perhaps you're rather flustered by the arrival of Mrs/Mr/Ms Professionally Perfect, beautifully gift wrapped and kindly delivered by the fates. And so the scene plays out this way:

> Um, err, hello. Nice weather, isn't it? For the time of year, anyway. The conference is awfully good, don't you think? Wasn't that speaker just now super? Lovely hotel, as well. Pretty wallpaper and carpets. Great food, too. Did you try the full English breakfast? I'd thoroughly recommend it. Anyway, I was, umm, err, wondering if . . .

But then the doors open and away they go. Vanishing before your eyes, as your nonsensical babble tails off into nothingness and you quietly deflate. Your perfect customer, business partner, investor or maybe even employer has gone. The opportunity is lost, never to come again, and you'll be cursing yourself for days, if not months, and quite possibly even longer. Nasty.

Whereas! If you have a slick, smooth and appealing elevator pitch all lined up and ready to go, the outcome is very different. You come away with their business card, having made a glowing impression, and you're all set to line up a meeting for next week.

The elevator pitch is ideal for beginning our public speaking journey, as it has some important learning to offer. It's also incredibly useful to have in your mental back pocket, ready for when needed. Because if there's one thing I can guarantee in life, it's that the pitch will be required when you least expect it.

Queuing for the toilets? Yep, that one's happened to me, however odd. Staring at the departure boards in an airport? Yes, there too. Helping yourself at a breakfast buffet, and waiting for one of the chefs to bring out more of those delicious sausages you know you really shouldn't have but are going to anyway? That's another from my collection of moments the elevator pitch was needed.

So, let's have a look at a sample of a pitch, break it down, and see how it works. We'll begin with mine for Creative Warehouse, as you know the company well enough by now. I've numbered the points for ease of reference, but in reality this would be one continuous spiel:

1. We can solve all your communication problems with style and a smile.
2. We've already done so for scores of businesses, from small start ups to companies worth hundreds of millions of pounds. We can look after everything from building, writing and producing websites, to pitching for investment, to attracting impressive media coverage.
3. We're Creative Warehouse, I'm Simon Hall, Director of the company.
4. And if you give me your card we can set up a meeting to talk more.

Now let's break down the key elements which make up an effective elevator pitch.

1. The hook

Point one, and the most important. Remember yet again, modern attention spans are short. If you don't catch the interest of your victim in the first few seconds of your elevator ride together, they're likely to be engrossed in their phone and not listening.

So don't forget what we discussed about striking starts, way back in Chapter 2. Hit them with your best line to begin, summing up your story and making them want to hear more.

Even better if you can include a sense of your character as well. I did so by talking about solving your communication problems with style and a smile. Trying to produce a cheesy grin or two is very me, as you've doubtless sadly concluded by now.

By the way, although I've outlined a pure elevator pitch, it's worth noting, in practice, you'd soften the opening instead of leaping right on in. That might require a few words to establish a connection of some sort, however tenuous. Perhaps a brief preamble like: *As someone prominent in this field of work* ... or, *Given the company you run, I thought you might like to hear about* ...

That should help to ease you into a conversation, but without greatly reducing the impact of the opening line of your pitch.

2. Credibility

Any fool can make all sorts of overinflated claims about themselves or their business, as indeed they often do. So next in the recipe for our perfect elevator pitch, at point two, we need to establish credibility.

For me, it's talking about the many businesses Creative Warehouse has helped, along with the work we've done for them.

As the substance of your elevator pitch, this can often be the hardest part to write. Not because you haven't got anything to say, but quite the reverse. The danger is trying to say too much.

Remember another of our lessons from earlier in the book, the beautiful art of less is more. Just summarise your most important appeal, assets or offerings in a couple of sentences, no more.

It might be all the investment money you've raised if you're a start up business, along with perhaps an insight into your new technology. It could be the awards you've won as a service, or your impressive number of customers. If you're pitching in a personal capacity, it might be your long track record of achievements and prestigious employers. Anything so long as it marks you out as a serious player, not just a windy braggart.

3. Introduction

You should, of course, introduce yourself. It's only polite.

But you don't have to do so in the traditional way, via your opening line. So the introduction can come later, as it does in my sample pitch, at point three.

It's more important to seize the attention of the listener before anything else. Without being rude, it's unlikely your name is the most interesting thing about you. Unless it's Elon Musk reading this. In which case, would you mind writing me a testimonial for the next edition of the book, please?

4. Call to action

OK, you've done some great work, engaging the interest of your victim, establishing your credibility and introducing yourself. Now what?

The answer is to make sure that excellent impression isn't wasted. It's no use if Mrs/Mr/Ms Professionally Perfect now wanders off into the proverbial sunset, never to be seen again. Which means, at point number four, comes the call to action.

Mine is very standard and rather retro, with an exchange of business cards. But that's because I'm an old guy and it's what I'm used to. In these modern times, the call to action could be swapping email addresses on your phones, a social media connection, a coffee later at the conference, or whatever you wish. Just so long as you have the chance of a follow-up meeting to further explore opportunities.

And that's it, the art of the elevator pitch. Remember again to keep it short and simple. You've only got the time it takes the lift to travel between floors. Mine was about eighty words, which equates to around twenty-five seconds of time. If you aim for anything between seventy-five and ninety-five words, that should be about right.

Next, a challenge for you. Pick out the hook, credibility, introduction and call to action from this elevator pitch of my irrepressibly strange imagination:

Would you like all your administration hassles, from invoices, to tax returns, to travel arrangements and expenses sorted in an instant? Amazing AI Admin Assistants have done just that for hundreds of businesses and executives, and with an average rating of nine and three quarters out of ten for our service. I'm Orinoco Omnipotent, CEO of the company, and if you fancy a coffee I'll be happy to give you a free ten-minute demonstration.

Did you spot all the key elements in action? Yes, I suppose it was a trick question of sorts. The order was the same as with my patter for Creative Warehouse. It went: hook, credibility, introduction and call to action.

A pitch doesn't have to be structured that way. There are no rules in the communication trade, as we've said many times before. But the way I've outlined is a useful guide, at least until you get more confident with your elevator pitch and feel able to play around with it. Just so long as the key elements are all present and correct.

- Exercise: Finally for this section, write an elevator pitch for yourself or your business. Then practise until it flows smoothly and easily, elegantly and effectively, ready for when you need it.

    Now video the pitch on your phone and watch it back. Notice particularly how you're delivering it. Do you look and sound confident? Is the pacing right? The way you project and modulate your voice? What about your body language?

We'll build on these points as we journey further into the world of public speaking and presentations.

Building on the Basics

Now we've warmed up with a brief public speaking exercise, it's time to start looking at longer form talks.

Although it's most likely your elevator pitch will be presented to an audience of one, it's quite possible you might have to offer it to a room full of people. That's a standard request at many a networking event, and might be intimidating enough. What then, when you come to face a packed lecture theatre or conference hall, with all those expectant eyes fixed upon you, and you have a much longer talk to deliver?

Are those shivers and sweats running through you again, by any chance?

In which case, I'll stop tormenting you and we'll start work. First of all by building on the basics, how to begin and then conclude a presentation.

I know we looked at starts and endings earlier in the book. But there are some extra elements you need to remember for powerful public speaking.

Super Striking Starts

Yes, that's right. Not just striking starts, but super striking starts. We've upped the ante. Why? Well, imagine these two scenarios, which will probably account for the vast majority of presentations delivered on planet Earth come any particular day.

1. **The conference**

   How many speakers does a conference typically have? Yes, I know it depends on how long it lasts, and the duration of their talks, and other factors besides.

   But the point is that it's unlikely you will be the only speaker. Far from it. I suspect you've been in the audience for these events. It can feel like waffle after whine, blabber after bluster, as presenter after presenter does their thing. It's not long before all their messages start to merge into one and you begin to zone out.

   But, by starting in a way which really impresses and engages, you can lift your talk above the mundane and make an audience take notice. That – along with the other tricks we'll cover – can help to make your presentation the one which gets remembered.

2. **The report**

   If the first scenario set your nerves on edge, prepare yourself for a shock. This one is worse. But it's very common, not to mention important, so we need to think about it.

   Imagine you've been tasked by your employer with investigating an issue. Perhaps it's the possibility of introducing an innovation, maybe a way to react to a competitor's move, or to handle a new piece of legislation.

   You've spent months carrying out your work and it's time to present your conclusions. There are far fewer eyes on you this time. Just a handful, in fact.

But! They're the eyes of your boss, and your boss's boss, and your boss's boss's boss, and so on up the food chain, perhaps even to the very top.

These super senior people have not the time, patience or nature to sit through a rambling, ineffective or plain impenetrable beginning. You simply have to impress them from the start, or they may be offside for everything else you say.

Now is it clear why a super striking start is an essential part of your presentation? Which then raises the question: how to make sure that's exactly what you produce.

The good news is the three principles we covered back in Chapter 2 will help. You still need to set out your story from the very beginning. You should also establish your authority and character. And, critically, you need to hook the audience right from the off.

However, now we're talking presentations, rather than just words on a page, you need other elements too. This is a doctrine which will run through our work on public speaking, so I'm going to emphasise it in my usual not terribly subtle way:

- It's not just your argument an audience buys into, it's you as well.

What does that mean for how you begin your talk? To coin a common phrase: it's not just what you say, it's how you say it.

Let me give you an example based on a company I work with. They help farmers increase their yields by using image recognition technology to estimate harvests far more accurately than was previously possible.

One of the challenges we faced with their presentation is that farmers can be a difficult group to win over. They tend to be wary of change, and more than a little cynical. So we worked hard on the opening line:

- We can increase your profits by around 10 per cent on average, by cutting your use of pesticides and ensuring you employ just the right number of pickers.

We were reasonably sure that would get their attention. As indeed it did. Notice also how it fulfils the three principles of a striking start. But there was still more work to be done, because we knew the farmers would be scrutinising the presenter, in addition to listening to his words.

So we played a little trick for dramatic effect. Because we wanted to avoid the usual beginning to a presentation, when the speaker himself has to ask the audience to settle, and you have that awful hiatus:

- *Hello, hello, OK, are we ready to start? Hello! Is everyone OK to get going? Thank you.*

Instead, we had a colleague call the room to quiet. And when the farmers were paying attention, the presenter let a couple of seconds run as he looked around, calm and confident, eye contact for all, before beginning. He was also sure to stand up straight, not fidget, and smiled to warm the atmosphere, as well as demonstrate that he wasn't cowed by the moment.

OK, it was a little of the yours truly tendency to showbiz. But that's part of the game when it comes to presenting. You're putting on a performance and an audience likes to be entertained, as well as informed. So work hard on your words, but think also about how you're going to deliver them. We'll look more at that later, when we cover body language.

There's one more point to mention for super striking starts. As with elevator pitches, you should introduce yourself. But you can do so in the second, third, or even fourth line, after you've hooked the audience.

Enduring Endings Extras

Yep, I've done it again and upped the ante once more. Not just enduring endings, but enduring endings extras. That's a big ask (as well as quite a mouthful). But it'll be worth it, I promise.

So, what do I mean by enduring endings extras?

Once again, the principles which we explored back in Chapter 2 still apply. You should sum up your story, memorably and emphatically. Also, pay attention to the way you deliver the words. As with super striking starts, don't rush. Stand up straight, make eye contact with all in the audience, smile, and deliver your line with heart and soul.

But as if that wasn't enough to remember, there are two more points to bear in mind for the conclusion of a talk:

1. Call to action

Every presentation is an opportunity, which means you should consider a call to action, just as with elevator pitches. If you're pitching for investment, it might be to fund your company. Should you be in front of the board, you might ask them to support your conclusions and implement them.

If you're only at the stage of floating an idea, or carrying out an investigation, you could ask the audience to fill in a brief survey. Or visit your website to leave some feedback.

Whatever it might be, the call to action usually comes at the end of a talk. For example, with our farmers:

So, to increase your profits, cut your use of chemicals, and make your farm fit for a prosperous future, come talk to us afterwards about our range of services.

2. Ending with a bang

Many times I've seen an otherwise impressive talk somewhat spoiled by an awful ending. And they nearly always go like this:

So, that's it . . . I think. Um, yes, that's all. No, hang on, there was something else. Or was there? Err, no, no, actually I don't think so. Which means . . . yes, um. Yes, that's it.

This makes me want to SCREAM. To be honest, I could be even more forthright. But this is a polite book so I shall leave space for you to imagine. I find such endings incredibly frustrating because they're so very easy to avoid.

You don't even need to say *And that's it*, or *Now any questions*, or anything so dull or cliched. All you have to do is add a big *Thank you* to your final words.

The audience will understand, take that as their cue for wild applause, and then you can move on to questions. Simples.

The Golden Thread

Once again, the concept of the golden thread applies just as much to a presentation as all other areas of communication. As we explored way back in Chapter 1, whether it's for films like *Alien*, songs such as 'My Way', or our meandering guide to email activation, you should follow one single, clear and simple narrative.

It sometimes comes as a surprise that a speech, talk or presentation should focus on just one theme. To take a well-known example, you might ask: Don't politicians cover a series of subjects in an address?

But here we can turn to the wisdom of another of our great communicators, who was also a politician. The former British Prime Minister Harold Macmillan once said:

- If you have made three points in a speech, you have made two too many.

The most famous speeches in history tend to have a single, clear and simple narrative. Which is arguably one of the reasons they make such an impact. Take John F. Kennedy's 'Ich bin ein Berliner' address, from 1963, just months before he was assassinated. It's often held up as an outstanding example of speechmaking, but has just one, and only one, theme throughout.

Take a few minutes to look up the speech online and spot what it is. You'll find a transcript on the John F. Kennedy Presidential Library and Museum website. Then identify the various forms in which Kennedy refers to his golden thread. When you're ready, have a look at my thoughts, below.

The golden thread running through the speech is freedom. It starts with mention of freedom through reference to the fighting spirit of West Berlin. At the time, as a legacy of the Second World War, the city was divided into sectors. It was made up of the Communist East, part of East Germany, and the democratic West, which was part of West Germany (Figure 6.1). Berlin itself was located deep inside Soviet-controlled East Germany, and so was often referred to as an island of freedom in the Cold War.

Figure 6.1 Germany divided on Cold War lines. Map by David McCutcheon FBCart.S www.dvdmaps.co.uk

Kennedy goes on to compare living in Berlin to the freedom of being a Roman citizen (*civis Romanus sum*), a proud boast in those days, and contrasts that with the lack of freedom under Soviet rule. He then talks about American freedom, German freedom and the indivisibility of freedom. Summing up his story memorably and emphatically, Kennedy concludes with a reference to freedom through the perspective of being a citizen of Berlin.

Whichever way Kennedy might refer to it, the audience is left in no doubt. The speech is an exploration of freedom, a celebration of freedom and a commitment to freedom.

That was particularly important as Berlin was on the frontline of the Cold War. The Berlin Wall had been erected by the East two years before Kennedy's speech. It divided the city and prevented East German citizens from escaping. The President left the citizens of West Berlin, and indeed the world, in no doubt about America's dedication to defending them and their precious freedom.

On a rather less geopolitical, historic and significant note, I've mentioned the 'Secrets of Success' talk I give in schools a couple of times. There, the golden thread is spelled out loud and clear in the title. I cover six qualities, all of which are important for doing well in life. The presentation begins with thinking, moves on to teamwork, then dealing with doubt, next comes persistence, then lateral thinking and finally hard work.

As someone who's given the talk many times, I can vouch for this. The clear and simple golden thread which runs through the presentation is a critical factor in making it work well.

Storytelling

I have a gold star award for the finest presentations. To be thus honoured, they have to include a range of features. Many are new tricks, which we'll examine a little later, when we come to the next chapter. But one element that I always try my utmost to include is our old friend storytelling.

Why? Well, for very much the same reasons we explored previously. Storytelling can add humanity, impact and memorability to a talk.

For example, one of the companies I work with is called Boutros Bear. They help people who have suffered serious illnesses, such as cancer, on their journeys to recovery.

Figure 6.2 Sheila Kissane-Marshall

When pitching the business, the founder, Sheila Kissane-Marshall (Figure 6.2), can talk for hours about the importance of their work. She can quote facts galore about how many people suffer a chronic illness in their lifetime, and the costs to the economy, let alone the personal suffering. As she does, an audience will listen, nod along and be sympathetic, understanding and supportive. I know because I've sat in a lecture theatre to hear Sheila speak.

But there's one moment in her presentation which is special. It always stands out because it transfixes an audience.

When she gets to this, I notice the people around me start to lean forwards. Their eyes are set on Sheila, instead of occasionally roving around the room or glancing at their phones. All passing thoughts of what to wear for that event tomorrow, or where to go on holiday, or that awkward meeting are banished. Sheila might as well be in a spotlight and the audience under a spell.

What is this moment of extraordinary connection? Yes, you guessed. It's when Sheila tells a story. And not just any story. This story.

> It was a few years ago I received my diagnosis. And it came, as the saying goes, like a bolt from the blue. It sounds like a cliché, but it really is like that.
>
> I had breast cancer. And not just any old boring or usual form. Oh, no. Mine was a rare and aggressive type. Bad news upon bad news, in other words. Things weren't looking good, to say the least. And I had a husband and two young children. You can imagine what was going on in my mind at the time.
>
> Anyway, I listened to my options and I went through the treatment. I won't make you feel uncomfortable with the details, but there was the chemotherapy, and the surgery. And it was gruelling and emotional. On it went, for what felt like months. Some days, to be frank, I wondered what the point was anymore. But I managed to get through it, much due to the brilliant care I received from the National Health Service. And so it was time for me to begin my recovery.
>
> But now came the problem. I knew I had to eat well. I also had to try to build up my strength and keep myself fit. I had to look after my emotional and mental wellbeing, too. But where was the support to help me start living again?
>
> There were bits and bobs, here and there. But nothing comprehensive and coordinated. I got frustrated with trying to find help, so instead I decided to help myself. I created my own nutrition, fitness and wellbeing plans. And they worked. I started to get better, I'm happy to say. As I did, I realised it wasn't just me going through this experience. There must have been thousands and thousands of others struggling in similar ways.
>
> But I also knew I had an answer for them. So I set up the business, and I'm proud to say we're doing well, supporting so many people in their battle to recover from serious illness.

OK, take a few seconds to compose yourself. I know how you feel. I've heard the story a few times and it never fails to squeeze my heart.

That, of course, is another example of the story only you can tell. And once again, it's an insight into the power of storytelling.

You might not have a tale which involves you personally. But I'm willing to bet you have one you could tell from the perspective of your customers, colleagues or business partners. And such anecdotes can help to make your case in a presentation far more effectively than mere facts and figures, however important they may be.

Here are just a few examples of the kind of stories you might use. I've heard similar as part of talks to help persuade an audience of the merits of an argument, and they worked:

- Why are we looking at this new service? Because there's so much demand for it. Listen to a couple of the insights customers have given us about how it could help them . . .
- We're examining this new technology because every time we try to link up with a partner's IT system, it all goes wrong and causes endless hassle. Take this one case in particular, which caused serious disruption to our operations for the best part of a week . . .
- What's the number one frustration in our company? This might surprise you, but it came through loud and clear when we carried out an all-staff survey. Here are a couple of examples in the form of colleagues' stories of hell in trying to get backing for a great idea . . .

Another nifty trick on the storytelling front is to conjure up visions of the future. I've seen this used to good effect in presentations as well:

- Imagine a tomorrow where we've introduced this new IT system. There are no more maddening frustrations in the office, when we spend hours battling with the computers rather than having them help us. We free up more time to focus on our work. We become more productive and profits grow. Bonuses rise too. Staff are happier, better paid, and retention rates rise significantly. Customer service also improves. Now contrast that with the current situation and where we seem to be heading . . .

The stories you can relate as part of a presentation are limited only by your imagination. Which, happily, means they're limitless. But whatever type you tell, just make sure you tell them. You won't be eligible for a prestigious and highly coveted Hall Gold Star for a talk without a story in there somewhere. And I know that would be devastating for you. Ahem!

To conclude this section, one final point about stories in presentations. I'm sometimes challenged on whether recounting an anecdote is good use of the precious time you've been allocated for a talk.

My answer is always an emphatic yes.

Remember Sheila's story? Or, more accurately, how could you forget it?

That tale of pure and heartfelt humanity is just over 300 words long. It takes her about a minute and a half to tell. And is it worth that time in the presentation?

Oh yes. A thousand times and more yes, in fact. The impact the story has is striking.

Once again, the reason comes back to the emotional power and memorability of stories. After all, what will you remember? My summary of Boutros Bear and the nature of their business? Or Shelia's story recounting how the company came about?

Character

On, then, to the final basic we need to build on to help us with public speaking. Once again, doubtless because of my love of storytelling, I've saved the most important for last. Because arguably nowhere is it so critical that character and content work in harmony than when giving presentations.

As I've said before, and will say again here, Churchill-style, to ensure it gets the tremendous whack the point deserves:

- It's not just your argument an audience buys into, it's you as well.

To whet your appetite a little more for this section, a teaser. We're going to work our way to revealing the golden secret of success for using your personality to produce truly powerful presentations.

So to business. Here I'm going to be traditional Cambridge and set you a research, compare and contrast exercise. Don't groan, please. It'll be simple, brief and worthwhile, I promise.

First, the research element. Look up online videos of these three renowned, but very different, orators, giving three celebrated speeches:

- Martin Luther King, 'I Have a Dream'
- Ronald Reagan at the Brandenburg Gate
- Margaret Thatcher, 'The Lady's Not for Turning'

You don't need to watch the whole of the addresses, although feel free to do so if you have the time. King, Thatcher and Reagan are all masters of the craft of public speaking in their different ways, and well worth studying. But take in just enough so that you understand the theme, or golden thread, of each speech. Then, most importantly for our purposes here, scrutinise the character of the speaker.

Use the approach we discussed way back in Chapter 1. Try to summarise the personality of each in a handful of words. Take a few minutes to think before we compare answers.

So, what did you come up with? Although we might disagree on our exact words, these were my thoughts:

- Martin Luther King: passionate, fiery, principled, determined, strong, charismatic, courageous
- Ronald Reagan: avuncular, thoughtful, calm, gentle, resolute, trustworthy, measured
- Margaret Thatcher: strong, steely, determined, hard, principled, steadfast, daunting

Whatever you might think about the politics of the three, I suspect we can agree that all were highly effective speakers. But equally, all had very different styles. So, what's the key to using your character effectively when presenting?

The answer comes back to another critical concept we discussed in Chapter 1. Yet again, it's all about authenticity. Whether you agree with them or not, you never doubt that King, Thatcher and Reagan believe in what they're saying. They let that come across loud and clear in the way they speak and their words are all the more effective for it.

So it goes for you when the time comes to speak to thousands of people. Or just a roomful, or even only one, as is often the case with the elevator pitch.

Are you passionate about this subject? Then let it come across. Are you convinced what you're talking about is the way forward? Then show that. Do you have the strength and determination to push through the change you're advocating? Then leave us in no doubt.

If you can get your character and content working in tandem, then you'll always have a top team onside to help power up your presentations.

- Exercise: Think about a presentation you might have to give. How can you be sure to show your character when you speak?

The Slippery Slope of Slides

Soundbite alert! But that title reminds me: don't forget to include a soundbite in your presentation, if you can. Although, as previously discussed, only one, and probably for your most important message. An audience can grow jaded and switch off if you scatter too many soundbites around.

We're moving towards the end of this chapter, which leaves a couple more topics to cover. The material we've discussed so far should allow you to put together a strong talk. But, until now, we've dealt only with words. So the time has come to look at your visuals, because I've seen many an otherwise good presenter trip up and stumble down the slippery slope of slides.

The happy news is that we've already covered the principles we need to ensure our slides are both impressive and effective. Remember the lessons of the angle, simplicity and brevity, not to mention the magical marvel of less is more? Let them be your guides. Because there is one golden rule to bear in mind when you're creating the visuals for a presentation:

- The audience is either listening to you or reading the slide, **but not both.**

So, how does that mantra feed into creating successful visuals? It means your spiel and the slide have to work together in perfect harmony, strawberries and cream style, to quote a very English example.

Happily, that requires we immediately eliminate one of the most common fails of slides. I see this so often, and it always makes me wince. Sometimes it actually makes me want to cry out to be honest, but I'm polite enough to refrain. Usually.

What is this horror show? Why the big build up? Well, how many times have you been to a presentation and witnessed a visual like Figure 6.3?

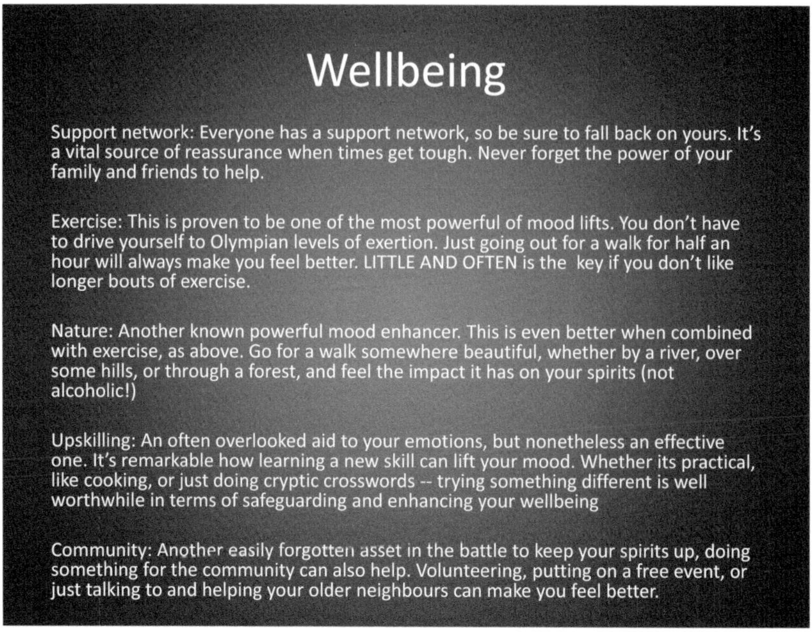

Wellbeing

Support network: Everyone has a support network, so be sure to fall back on yours. It's a vital source of reassurance when times get tough. Never forget the power of your family and friends to help.

Exercise: This is proven to be one of the most powerful of mood lifts. You don't have to drive yourself to Olympian levels of exertion. Just going out for a walk for half an hour will always make you feel better. LITTLE AND OFTEN is the key if you don't like longer bouts of exercise.

Nature: Another known powerful mood enhancer. This is even better when combined with exercise, as above. Go for a walk somewhere beautiful, whether by a river, over some hills, or through a forest, and feel the impact it has on your spirits (not alcoholic!)

Upskilling: An often overlooked aid to your emotions, but nonetheless an effective one. It's remarkable how learning a new skill can lift your mood. Whether its practical, like cooking, or just doing cryptic crosswords -- trying something different is well worthwhile in terms of safeguarding and enhancing your wellbeing

Community: Another easily forgotten asset in the battle to keep your spirits up, doing something for the community can also help. Volunteering, putting on a free event, or just talking to and helping your older neighbours can make you feel better.

Figure 6.3 A text-heavy slide

Not content with having filled the screen with a bombardment of words, the speaker then proceeds to read exactly what's written before you, line by tedious line. Aaaarrrrggghhh!

In such situations, I often wonder why I bothered to come to the talk. Surely it would have been easier for the presenter to email the slides out to the audience and we could then read them at our leisure.

Look around the room the next time you're placed in such an unfortunate position. At best, you'll notice people reading the slide well ahead of the speaker, then returning to their phones to check their emails and messages. At worst, they'll be far away and elsewhere, in a land of more pleasant imaginings.

So, how do we make sure we keep the audience engaged and avoid such nightmares on slides street? This is where we come to another useful guideline. I don't entirely agree with it, hence using the word guideline, rather than rule. But it's a simple, memorable and useful thought to bear in mind:

- Don't put more information on a slide than you would see on a T-shirt.

I like this concept because it's easily visualised. Most T-shirts have a picture and a few words. So should it be with slides. Which, coming back to our wellbeing example, gives us a far more appealing alternative (Figure 6.4).

This time, instead of assaulting the audience with words, the presenter could reveal the slide and say: *I'd like to talk next about the subject of wellbeing, something which is so important in our busy modern lives.*

Now the slide and commentary are working in harmony. The audience understands what's being discussed from the visual and its title, as well as the words being spoken. They don't have any option to start reading the slide instead of listening to the presenter. And they get a lovely image to help keep them engaged.

But what about the rest of the information the speaker wants to get across? All of that mass from the wordy slide. Well, animations exist for

Figure 6.4 A text-light slide

a reason. Thus the presenter comes to their point about the importance of having a support network. And so they trigger the animation (Figure 6.5).

The speaker then says: *Everyone has a support network, so be sure to fall back on yours. It's a vital source of reassurance when times get tough. Never forget the power of your family and friends to help.*

From there, each point is covered by a new animation. The audience has nowhere to go except listening to every element that's being explored as the story unfolds. That's step by step, through the subheadings about exercise, nature, upskilling – or learning new skills – and community (Figure 6.6).

How much better and more effective was that, compared with the blizzard of words which hit us on the first and entirely lamentable slide?

Notice also how clarity of message comes into play. Each slide should have only one angle. Anything you talk about follows the golden thread

Figure 6.5 A text-light slide with subheading

Figure 6.6 A text-light slide with a series of subheadings

which that determines. With the visual above, the angle is wellbeing, and the subheadings encompass the various strands.

If the angle was how to start a talk, that might also be the title. The image could be of a presenter at a podium. The three points would be, as you know by now: Set out your story from the start, show your character and authority, make the audience want to find out more.

The subheadings, or bullets, could be summaries of the three points, animating in turn. Those areas would be chatted through by the presenter. And the whole slide would then look something like Figure 6.7 (excuse the scary lecturer).

Incidentally, I find this technique of titles and subheadings is invaluable in guiding me through a talk. They're helpful prompts, reminding me of what I'm going to say. It's like having my notes up there on the screen.

Figure 6.7 A text-light slide with a series of subheadings

Figure 6.8 How to start a presentation slide. Taken from the Compelling Communication Skills course, reprinted with kind permission of Cambridge Advance Online © University of Cambridge.

OK, now we've covered the principles of how to put together slides which look smart and work well, it's time for one of my challenges. Don't sigh, I think you'll like this one.

The game is called Good Slide – Bad Slide. Funnily enough, that's exactly how it works. I show you a slide, you decide if it's good, bad or somewhere in between.

Are you ready? Then here we go. By the way, don't worry about whether you like the graphics, fonts, colours or any other design features. Just focus on the effectiveness of the slide. So, your opening question, on Figure 6.8: good slide or bad?

What's your verdict on that? Good or bad?

I'd say good. It might not be inspired in terms of the image or design, but it tells an audience clearly what's going to be discussed. It also leaves them no room to read anything else on the slide. In short, it follows the T-shirt rule and works because of it.

So, on we go with our jolly game: Figure 6.9.

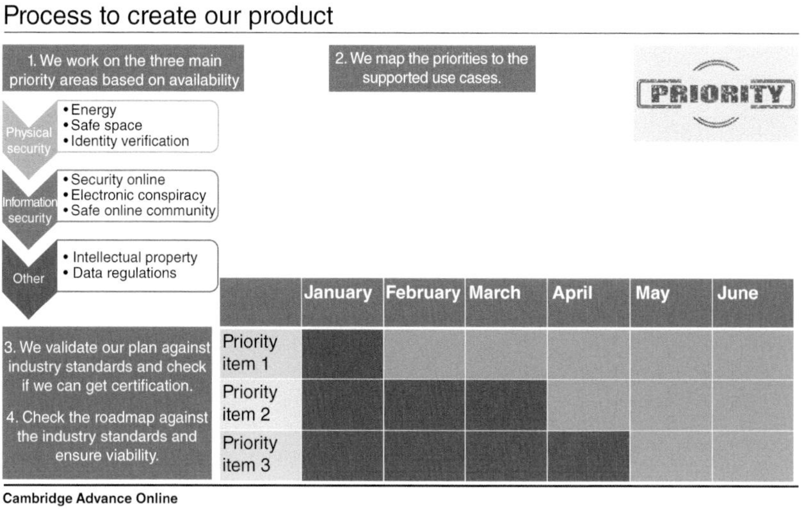

Process to create our product

	January	February	March	April	May	June
Priority item 1						
Priority item 2						
Priority item 3						

Cambridge Advance Online

Figure 6.9 Process to create our product slide. Taken from the Compelling Communication Skills course, reprinted with kind permission of Cambridge Advance Online © University of Cambridge.

What about this slide? Have a think for a moment.

Here, as it is, I'd say bad.

The angle is confused. Is it about the process to create our product, or the timeline? There's also a lot of text, where subheadings would work better with the accompanying words being spoken by the presenter.

So, how to save this slide, if the information was important to convey. What would you do? Again, have a brief ponder before I offer my suggestion.

Personally, I would turn this slide into two. The first for the process, the second for the timeline. Cutting the amount of text to the bare minimum and animating subheadings to cover the key points for each slide would also help.

In summary, this is a flagrant breach of our guiding principles of less is more, and keeping it simple. Naughty slide!

So, on to our next contender. What do you think of the slide in Figure 6.10?

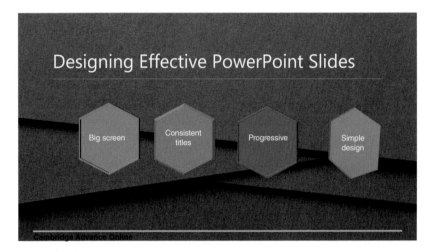

Figure 6.10 Designing effective PowerPoint slides slide. Taken from the Compelling Communication Skills course, reprinted with kind permission of Cambridge Advance Online © University of Cambridge.

I'd say pretty good here, so long as each of the hexagons was animated to appear in turn and the words on them were bigger and clearer. Again, it might not be inspired in terms of design, but the slide is simple and effective. The audience is clear what they're hearing about and have nowhere to go but listen to the presenter. This passes the T-shirt test.

Just a couple more before we finish our fun. Next, your verdict on the slide in Figure 6.11?

I'd say bad. First of all, the slide raises a basic point, which we should mention: The simple issue of readability. A visual fails by default if it can't easily be read.

Also, this slide is yet another to fall into the familiar trap of too much text. Bullet points would help, with the rest of the words being spoken by the presenter. This is very subjective, but it also feels to me as though there are too many points being made. I tend to prefer three or four. Once more, let simplicity and brevity be your guides.

OK, next to our final slide on which to pass judgement, Figure 6.12.

How to predict questions for the Q&A

- When you've got a presentation to give, run through it with some family and friends.
- Not only can they give you helpful feedback, you can ask them what questions they would raise.
- You can then work on preparing good answers.
- And when you've done that, if it's a work presentation find a couple of colleagues you trust and do the same with them.
- That will all help you prepare for the Q and A, and mean you're much more likely to perform impressively.

Cambridge Advance Online

Figure 6.11 How to predict questions for the Q&A slide. Taken from the Compelling Communication Skills course, reprinted with kind permission of Cambridge Advance Online © University of Cambridge.

How to make a good first impression

BE ON TIME	DRESS TO IMPRESS	BE PREPARED	CONSIDER NON-VERBAL CUES
Too early is better than too late.	Take care of your clothes and your overall appearance.	Do your homework and practice.	Be friendly and confident.

Cambridge Advance Online

Figure 6.12 How to make a good first impression slide. Taken from the Compelling Communication Skills course, reprinted with kind permission of Cambridge Advance Online © University of Cambridge.

Here, I'd say largely good. The slide is clear, and if each of the four points was animated to appear then the story would be easy to follow. The only caveat is that there's probably too much text. The words below the headings BE ON TIME, DRESS TO IMPRESS etc. could be removed and instead spoken by the presenter. That way, this slide would also pass the T-shirt test.

- Exercise: Look at the slides in a presentation you've given. Would you redesign them now, on the basis of what we've explored?

Character in Slides

We've talked repeatedly about the importance of finding your unique voice in order to become a compelling communicator. But it might surprise you to know that your character can also emerge in your slides.

Take a look back at the couple designed by me, on wellbeing and how to start a talk. The pretty wellbeing one featuring the person on the bench I mean, not the version which comes across as a mess of words. Is there anything unusual you notice about this pair of slides? Have a glance at another of my visuals, Figure 6.13, to help.

You might have noticed that I fill the entire screen with the image and then add text on top. That's part of my style, or character with slides. I'm a keen amateur photographer, so delight in collecting pictures to use in my presentations. I love the photos I take and want to make the most of them. So I remove any boundaries and use all the available space.

Some communication advisers say you should never put text over pictures. I understand why. They worry about the legibility of the words, which should always be the priority. But I use images where I can fit in easily readable text, so this trick works well for me.

The technique has another advantage. It forces me to be disciplined with the words I put on a slide. There's simply no room for lots of text when you're overlaying photographs.

This is just my style. It might not necessarily be yours. But it's worth playing with the functionality of whatever system you use to create presentations in order to develop a character of your own.

Figure 6.13 Character in slides

It might be a small point, but it can still make a difference to how your talks are received. And any advantage to help you make a good impression is worth taking. I often get compliments about my use of slides, and that never fails to make me smile.

We'll be looking more at photography later in the book, by the way. It's an essential part of your communications toolkit, relatively easy to master in our smartphone era, and much fun as well.

The Dos and Don'ts of Data

You may have noticed a significant missing link in our discussion of visuals thus far. Do I sense you thinking: *This simplicity and brevity, with putting bullet points over pictures, is all very well. But what about when I need to use data?*

Good point. But fear not, I haven't forgotten. Data is critical.

So, finally for this chapter, given the importance of facts and figures, let's have a look at the dos and don'ts of data in slides.

Happily, there's yet another simple rule to help us. And, would you believe it, once more it comes back to the principles of simplicity, brevity and clarity. What a truly wonderful trio they are. When creating a slide using data, always ask yourself this question:

- What's the single, simple point I'm trying to make, and what's the MINIMUM amount of information I can use to make it?

There's a dangerous temptation with data. You've got a bucket full, so you're going to use it in order to impress an audience, right? They're bound to be awed by all those statistics, surely?

Wrong, wrong and wrong again. Just like with that awful word storm slide on wellbeing, people will stare at a screen full of data, try to puzzle out what you're talking about, and so stop paying attention to you. And that's the best case scenario. They're equally likely to be left with no clue whatsoever about the point you're attempting to make.

Instead, remember the beauty of the KISS. Keep it simple, silly. What's the one point you're trying to make? And what's the minimum amount of data required to make it?

Here's an example. Imagine I was selling Creative Warehouse, and I'm pitching the company to a room full of potential buyers. I've got lots of data about the various projects we're working on, from websites, to videos, to media campaigns, plus customers, revenues and profits. I'm a data diva, make no mistake. Just look at it all (Figure 6.14)!

I could pop that in front of the audience and talk them through it. But hang on. How much would they take in? Might I be in danger of trying to say too much? After all, how long is it taking you to work out what's going on as you follow the various lines, try to discern what they represent, and the sort of figures I'm attempting to convey?

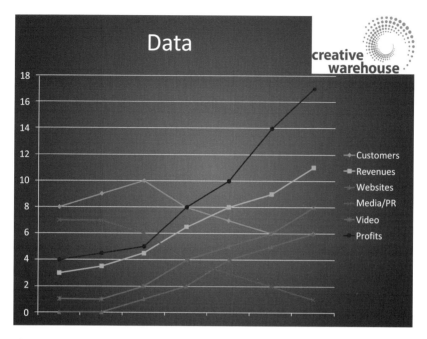

Figure 6.14 A data-heavy slide

A rethink is required. These are potential buyers, which means I need to make the company look as appealing as possible. So, what's the key point that I want to establish?

I'd say it's this. I've reduced the number of customers we have, because some weren't, frankly, very interesting. Plus they didn't pay well. Instead, I've focused on the most interesting clients, who are far more rewarding to work with. And I mean that both professionally and financially.

The result has been less pressure for our team, which has made them happier and more creative. The work we're doing is also more fulfilling. The customers we've retained are receiving a better service, which they appreciate. And our profits have gone up.

That's what I want to say, the single, simple point I need to convey. Fewer customers, bringing benefits all round. So, what's the minimum amount of data I can use to make this clear? Perhaps as in Figure 6.15.

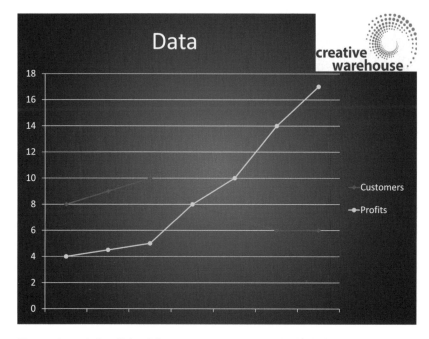

Figure 6.15 A data-light slide

How much easier to take in is that than the first version? Everyone gets it in an instant. Customers deliberately down, profits happily up. A message which is simple, appealing and memorable. Splendid!

By the way, notice there's usually no room for background images when dealing with data. They can over complicate a visual, and audiences have enough work to do understanding the message. Slides can't be pretty all the time, sadly. Practicalities come first in presentations.

Now let's put the principle of the single message and the minimum amount of data into action. It's exercise time again. Imagine that I'd like to expand Creative Warehouse. We currently operate in the east of England. But I want to find another region of the UK to grow our business.

I've done an analysis of all the competitor companies across the nation, region by region. They range from media and PR, to web and design, along with video and strategic communications. Figure 6.16 shows what I've found.

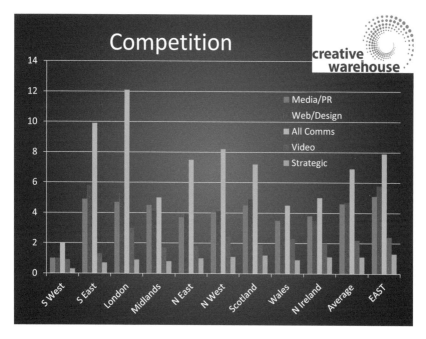

Figure 6.16 A slide containing a large range of data

I've got to present this data to my team, to convince them that the south-west is the region to target. That's logical. It's where there's least competition. But I'm not happy with the slide I've produced. It feels cluttered and challenging to interpret.

Can you help me simplify it, so the team will immediately understand that the south-west is the place to go? Remember to keep in mind the single point you're trying to make, and to use the minimum amount of data needed to do so.

Sketch out some thoughts, then have a look at my suggestion, Figure 6.17.

Did you come up with something similar? By stripping away the categories of communication companies and focusing only on the totals in each region, the graphic becomes much simpler and easier to digest. It's clear at a glance that the south-west has the least competition, so that's the region to target.

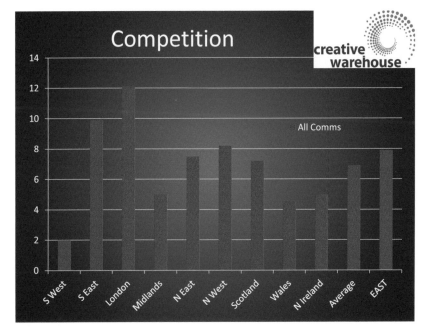

Figure 6.17 A slide containing a limited amount of data

- Exercise: Have a look at some slides you've produced which use data. Could you improve them on the basis of making one single point, using the minimum amount of information needed to do so?

The Killer Fact

The killer fact is your headline data. As with the exercise about where to expand Creative Warehouse, it's the one statistic you think will cut through and make an impression above all others. Once identified, you'll probably find yourself using it repeatedly until your argument is won. It's that powerful.

For example, take the company which helps farmers increase their yields, which I mentioned earlier in the chapter. We had lots of facts to choose from. They included reducing the workforce, increasing productivity, time saving, positive environmental impact and more besides. But from all those, we chose one key, simple and striking fact:

- We can increase your profits by 10 per cent on average.

We explained why, of course. By optimising staffing levels, and cutting use of pesticides through far more accurate estimates of yields. But we didn't throw around statistics to illustrate those points. We didn't want anything to clutter that single killer fact. Which, we thought – rightly and happily, as it turned out – would get the most attention and attract the most new customers.

If the farmers wanted the data which lay behind our headline claim, we could provide it. We often did, in the question and answer session at the end of the presentation. More on that in the next chapter. But using that sole killer fact was highly effective in terms of making our case.

How then do you choose which fact to wield from all the data at your disposal? I find putting yourself in the place of the audience helps. What would be most likely to impress them? Making more money? Cutting bureaucracy? Enhancing the environment? Offering a significant competitive edge?

With the farmers, it was the profits. They're business people, after all. With Creative Warehouse, when talking about our public relations work, I sometimes say:

- Stories we place in the media average about £15,000 worth of coverage.

Unsurprisingly, that usually does the trick and gets an audience interested.

Here's a quick killer fact exercise, based on a company I work with. It uses artificial intelligence to predict demand in hospital accident and emergency departments, and so make them more efficient.

Imagine you had the following statistics available and you're presenting to a hospital's board of directors. Which would you choose as your killer fact?

Our trials show we can:

1. Reduce wasted doctor and nurse time by 20 per cent
2. Create financial savings of 15 per cent
3. Cut patient waiting times by 40 per cent
4. Reduce abuse of staff by 20 per cent
5. Increase patient satisfaction levels by 35 per cent

Tricky, isn't it? They're all impressive figures. But, for the board of directors, I'd choose point 3. For such a broad audience, all concerned with the hospital's performance and reputation, I suspect that would be the most effective in making an impact and getting remembered.

Your killer fact can change, depending who you're talking to. Always adapt for your audience. If we were presenting to the finance director, I'd choose point 2. Experience tells me the bottom line matters most to them. We could always introduce the other advantages later.

But, whoever you're addressing, strategically wielding a killer fact can help to make your presentations far more effective.

- Exercise: Think about a talk you've given which uses data. What should be the killer fact? Can you strip away most of the other information to ensure it stands out?

A Lifesaver

I have one final sunbeam of wisdom to offer on the subject of slides. And this is where the principle of having a single point to make, and using the minimum amount of data required, could be a lifesaver. It's such an important message that it deserves highlighting in my familiar manner:

- You should still be able to deliver your talk effectively even if the slides fail.

Think about that for a moment. It's a common nightmare. You're about to give your presentation to a high powered group of people. It's an important moment. You've worked hard at your performance. You're ready to go ...

And the presentation fails. Just like that, as they sometimes do. It simply refuses to work. No matter what you try, or the efforts of the support team, the slides refuse to cooperate.

Disaster.

Or perhaps not. The audience is expecting you to admit defeat. At best, perhaps the presentation can be rearranged for another time. At worst, this wonderful opportunity is lost. But instead, you smile, make a joke of the IT failure and say:

> It's OK. I can still tell you everything you need to know without the slides.

The people you're talking to are certainly going to be interested. And they'll definitely give you a chance to live up to your promise. Believe me, I know, because this has happened to me and others I've worked with.

But how? How can you still tell your story without your precious slides?

The answer is the old-school flipchart. My tip is to always have one standing by, even if, on almost every occasion, you won't need it. The one time you do it will save your life. Professionally speaking, anyway.

Look back at the sections on slides and data. I hope you'll draw an important conclusion, which is this. By simplifying your visuals, you could still give your talk even if the IT fails.

In fact, that's an important indicator of whether a presentation is a good one. Can it still make sense without the slides?

So, revisiting the examples we've discussed: If it's wellbeing you're talking about, you can introduce the topic and chat through the five subject areas: support network, exercise, nature, upskilling and community. You can note those headings down on the flipchart to reinforce your point.

OK, the audience might miss out on the pretty picture you'd planned to show them. But that's nice to have, rather than essential. Critically, you would still be able to convey the important points.

So far, so good. But it's when you need to talk data that simplicity, and the beauty of KISS, really come into their own.

Imagine the selling Creative Warehouse scenario, and the slides failing when I came to outline the point about reducing the number of customers but increasing profits. I would struggle to convey what I was trying to say if I stuck with the original slide, featuring all those lines showing the number of video projects, websites etc. we were working on.

But with the simplified version, the one featuring just two lines, customers and profits, suddenly it becomes far easier. I can draw a rough graph on the flip chart and make a joke about my poor artwork. I might impress the audience with my ingenuity, improvisation and persistence, which would be no bad thing. But, far more importantly, I still get the point across. Number of customers down, profits up. Job done.

Have the flipchart tip on me. I hope you never have to use it. But if you do, it might just prove to be a lifesaver.

- Exercise: Run through a presentation you've given. With the help of a flipchart, could you still deliver it effectively if the slides fail? If not, what does that tell you?

Powerful Public Speaking and Presentations

Stand by for a shock. I hope you've realised you are now a good presenter, given all that we've learned in the previous chapter, and indeed its predecessors. But next – if you're ready for this – we're going to reach for the sky and shoot for greatness.

Yes, I really do mean that. I told you to prepare for a shock!

In this chapter, we'll explore the tricks which lift a presenter to the hallowed ground of excellence. There are three critical insights in particular that can take your talks to the top level. And, with another of our well-deserved fanfares, they're where we'll begin.

Interactions

Think back on the most boring presentations you've ever suffered. What one theme runs through them? I'm talking about something I suspect each speaker had in common. Take a few seconds to reflect.

In the meantime, to help focus your thoughts, I'm going to tell you a brief story. After all, stories are the best way of getting a point across. Wouldn't you agree, given what we've previously discussed?

One of my best friends definitely isn't called Stuart. But that's the name we'll use for our purposes here. Because this is a story of sadness.

Codename Stuart was very keen on a woman he met at the gym. We'll call her Erica. Week upon week he would exchange conversation with her, building up the friendship, before finally he found the courage to ask Erica out. Happily, she said yes. And so the date was set for the next day.

Stuart was in a state of great excitement. The more he'd got to know Erica, the more he liked her. She was beautiful, he told me, clever, funny, successful, just perfect. He bought a new shirt for the night, some special cologne, and all was set fair for the big date.

Like a good friend, I called him the day after to find out how the evening had gone. *Great,* Stuart replied. *I told her all about my job, and my hobbies, and the music I like, and the films, and the books, and my life, and my family, and my friends, and my travels, and what I'm going to do in the future, and all that.*

Right, I replied, although I think I said, *Riiiigghhht* to be more accurate, because a heavy concern was already settling in my heart. *And what did you find out about her?*

Stuart thought for a few seconds, then said, *Well, um, not a lot I suppose.*

Are you thinking you know what's coming next? I suspect so. And I'm guessing you're right.

So, I said, *When do you see her again?*

Well, that's the odd thing, poor, forlorn Stuart replied. *I've sent her a few messages, but she hasn't replied.*

Now relate that story to your reflections on the most boring presentations you've endured. And, critically, the theme which unites them.

I'm imagining it's that the speaker went on, and on, and on, and on, and then on some more, and then more and more, and then more and more besides. In other words, they just talked at you, blah, blah, blah fashion, without you having any chance to interact, or think, or pause, or reply, or respond, or take in the words, or feel in any way part of the performance.

Just like poor Erica, in fact.

The lesson being that monologues are dull, but dialogues far more interesting. Indeed, if searching for a soundbite to do some more busy hammering home of the point, I might write:

- Monologues are monotonous, but dialogues delight.

Which means trick number one for becoming a great public speaker is to incorporate interactions into your presentation. In other words, make the audience feel part of the show rather than just passive spectators.

So, how do we do that? First, let's look at a masterclass of the technique in action. I'm going to take you deep into a memory of British politics. Before we head off, please remember this. I'm making no partisan point here. Put all ideology aside. I just want to focus on the way the speaker addresses the audience. I'm not commenting on the politics in any way.

I'm going to ask you to look up *Geoffrey Cox, Attorney General – Speech to Conservative Party Conference 2018*. You should find it on the Conservative Party YouTube site. But before you view the address, a word of context to understand the impact it had.

Prior to this speech, Geoffrey Cox was relatively unknown. Afterwards, he featured in much of the UK media, was widely praised for the address, and was even spoken about as a potential future Conservative leader. That was quite a turnaround in his fortunes. And all because of these twelve minutes on stage.

For our purposes, watch what he does to turn what might have been an average and ordinary monologue into a far more captivating dialogue with the audience. See how it brings his words to life, electrifies the crowd, and makes an impression which echoes far beyond the conference hall.

By the way, the start, when Cox talks about so many people coming to see him, the Attorney General, is a joke. He's there as the warm up act for the star, the Prime Minister, who is to follow.

In terms of Cox's speech, yes, of course, the content and his character are important. We already know to expect that. But what an impact making the crowd feel part of the performance has.

If there's one single trick you can use to elevate your public speaking towards true excellence, it's incorporating interactions. There are many ways of doing so. But here are some favourite methods of mine:

1. Silence – let the words settle

Silence is probably the easiest yet most effective way of making an audience feel you're engaged in a conversation, rather than talking at them. All the greatest public speakers use the trick. Remember back in the last chapter, when we watched Martin Luther King, Ronald Reagan and Margaret Thatcher in action? They all left gaps for the audience to absorb their words.

To use silence successfully you have to watch the crowd, just as they're watching you, and allow them space to react. I know it's yet another trick to think about, but it's critical. Look back at King, Thatcher and Reagan again. See how the masters do it. If the audience sigh, or laugh, or clap, let them finish before continuing. Geoffrey Cox does this to great effect too.

You also have to overcome the evil influence of nerves when deploying silences. Of course you'll be nervous when delivering a talk. I am, and everyone I've ever worked with is. Nerves exist for a reason. They're to fill your body full of adrenaline, ready to perform at your peak. But they also tend to make you speak faster, to get this scary moment over and done with ASAP, if not sooner.

Beware of that. Control the nerves and pace yourself. Your performance will be far more effective for it.

It's also a good idea to target areas of your talk which are particularly important. Be sure to pause after those sentences. That's a subtle but strong signal that the audience should notice what you've said and take it in. It also helps to make them feel part of the show, giving them time to think, and so turning your monologue into a far more powerful dialogue.

It might take you a while to develop the confidence to leave pauses. But persevere. Because, as we've seen, it's a trick which is very well worth mastering.

2. Questions

You'll have spotted that Geoffrey Cox raised rhetorical questions in his speech. That's a useful strategy when there are too many people in the audience for them to be shouting answers at you.

But, when you're dealing with a smaller group, you can pose questions as an effective form of interaction. When I'm speaking, I use some that I've asked you in this book to break the ice and engage an audience. If I'm talking about storytelling, I might ask: *What percentage of our day to day conversations are taken up with stories?*

The group would offer guesses, and just like that we've got a dialogue running instead of a boring old Hall monologue.

But beware, when asking questions, to make sure they're focused. You need to keep control of the discussion. If your question is too broad, such as, *What's your favourite story and why?*, then the answers could last for quite a while. You're looking for brief responses, so you can hear a range of views, all quick fire, and then reveal the answer.

3. Polls

This is particularly useful when dealing with larger audiences. For example, I tried the trick when I was chairing a debate about artificial intelligence. Because scores of people had come along, I asked:

Who thinks artificial intelligence offers great opportunities for humanity? Hands up please. Now who thinks it could be a real threat to us? Finally, hands up who thinks it could be both.

That improvised poll worked well in warming the atmosphere, giving a sense of people's opinions, and making the crowd feel part of the show. Most people agreed with the final suggestion, by the way.

4. Show and tell

I often use show and tell as it's highly effective at drawing an audience into a performance. If one of the companies I work with is pitching its technology, we'll generally show it off. Even if the gadget in question just looks like a small silvery box, people love to get a sense of its physical reality.

See this cube? It might not look much, but in a couple of years it will ease your stress and anxiety in an instant, just by holding it.

You can see the audience leaning forward to look, and so becoming part of the show.

When I teach writing, I'll often hold up a pocket notebook and say, *From this, came one novel, nine blogs, three short stories, two lecture courses, and about a thousand social media posts.*

Everyone might wonder what I'm talking about, but I can guarantee they'll be engaged with what I'm saying. The point being that no content creator worth the name should ever lose an idea. They're precious, the foundation of all we do, so always keep a notebook with you.

5. Pause for thought

This is a variation on silence, but worth mentioning separately because it can be so effective. After telling a story, or revealing an important point, say: *Just think for a few seconds about what that means.*

I often do it with my imposter syndrome story, when I've delivered the punchline. That moment of realisation, when everyone understands the syndrome is part of us all. Asking the audience to reflect on what we've just discovered makes them feel part of my talk, as well as reinforcing the point.

The trick can also be useful when you're pitching a new idea. Imagine you've got a proposal to make your company 10 per cent more efficient. *Just think what that will mean*, you might say. And after a suitable pause, reinforce the point: *Better customer service, less pressure, happier staff, more profitability . . .*

6. Humour

Humour is wonderful for engaging an audience, so long as it's in keeping with your character. Which means it's a favourite trick for me, however cheesy.

For instance, sometimes I'm asked to teach public speaking at companies where I get a strong sense my arrival is less than popular. You know the kind of thing. A room full of people with their arms folded, staring out of the window and yawning theatrically. On such occasions, I might say, *Who wants to be here and who was told they had to be here?*

That usually prompts at least a few begrudging smiles and gives me a chance of making progress with the group.

To end this list, another example, just because I know you love my humour so much. When I'm teaching presentation skills, and we get to interactions, I sometimes ask the audience, *Who needs rhetorical questions?*

Oh, the laughter which naturally gushes forth!

OK, enough of my idea of comedy. What I've set out above is not a comprehensive list of how to create interactions. I have no doubt you'll be able to come up with plenty of ideas of your own, which may well work better for your individual style. But just so long as you start to incorporate interactions into your talks, you'll quickly find yourself making much more of an impact.

- Exercise: Look back at a presentation you've given. Can you find scope for introducing some interactions?

Signposting

What have signposts got to do with advanced public speaking insights, you might understandably ask. Well, this strange sounding concept is remarkably useful for a presenter.

Signposts in a talk fulfil exactly the same function as they do in a town or city. They offer directions and point out areas of particular interest.

The joy of signposting is that it requires only a few words, but can have a powerful effect in retaining and reinforcing an audience's interest. So, as the second of our trio of top tips for truly excellent public speaking, let's explore signposting in action.

Here's an example. Imagine I'd written a brief summary of how to put together a talk:

> The start is the most important part of a presentation, the end the second most important. The content should follow the narrative you set out at the beginning and never deviate from it.
>
> Only say what you need to and stop, a technique known as less is more. That also goes for slides. Keep them simple. Data is an area where less is more is very effective. Using your character helps to engage and impress an audience.

That's OK. It covers some of the main points to bear in mind. It sticks to the golden thread, doesn't use long or complicated words, or jargon, and it's brief, according to our sacred less is more mantra.

But there's a but. Something's not quite right. Do you sense what it is? Imagine me speaking that passage out loud. What's missing?

The answer is signposting. And here's the clever part. You probably use the trick already, but without realising it. Except now, we're going to examine how it works and make sure we incorporate it in our talks.

So, here's that passage again. The content is exactly the same. But notice, with the addition of a few words of signposting here and there, it becomes much more engaging.

> Let's begin with a bang by revealing the most important part of a presentation . . . the start. Then we'll unveil the second most important part, which is the ending. Moving now onto the content. That should follow the narrative you set out at the beginning and – importantly – never, ever deviate from it.
>
> Next, there's a critical principle which runs through the whole of public speaking . . . a technique known as less is more. It's wonderful as it works with words, and also slides. The technique is particularly effective when dealing with data. In fact, it's arguable that if there's one thing you remember in presentations, let it be the art of less is more. Finally, a small but important point: using your character always helps to engage and impress an audience.

I've probably overdone the signposting just to make the point. You know me. Subtle as a snakebite. But, importantly, do you have a sense of how much more engaging that passage is now?

The addition of signposting has brought it to life. Every single signpost reinforces the audience's attention, either by telling them something new is coming, or by highlighting a point of particular interest.

In fact, why don't we enjoy (hmmm!) another of my challenges. Work back through the passage and see how many examples of signposting you can count.

When you're ready, have a look at my answer, below. The geographical signposts are in italics, guiding an audience through the talk. Those emphasising key points are in bold:

> *Let's begin with a bang* by **revealing the most important part of a presentation** ... the start. *Then we'll unveil* **the second most important part**, which is the ending. *Moving now onto* the content. That should follow the narrative you set out at the beginning and – **importantly** – never, ever deviate from it.
>
> *Next*, there's **a critical principle** which runs through the whole of public speaking ... a technique known as less is more. **It's wonderful** as it works with words, and also slides. The technique is **particularly effective** when dealing with data. In fact, **it's arguable that if there's one thing you remember in presentations**, let it be the art of less is more. *Finally*, a **small but important point**: using your character always helps to engage and impress an audience.

I make the total thirteen. And yes, on reflection, I definitely did overdo the signposting. But only for dramatic effect. Critically (spot the signpost there?), I hope that brief example gave you a clear sense of how the technique works, and how useful it can be.

You might have spotted that I've used signposts repeatedly throughout the book. *To start this chapter, in conclusion for this section, a key point is that* ... etc. Yes, they're yet another treasure of your compelling communication vault which can be used across the various forms, from writing, to storytelling, to public speaking.

Finally for this section, a few thoughts about the kind of signposts you might use. Once more, this list is far from exhaustive. You'll develop favourites of your own, which work for your particular style. But these ideas could be useful:

- **Milestones**
  Probably the most standard geographical signpost in a talk. Phrases such as *To begin*, or *as we reach the midway point*, or *moving now to a conclusion* ...

- **New development**
  Useful as a page turn in a presentation and often accompanying a change of slide. You'll typically find yourself using words such as *Turning now to the economics of the plan*, or *So how do we go about putting this into practice?*
- **Drill down**
  You've introduced a concept, but now it's time to explore the point in depth. So you might say: *Looking in more detail at that* or *Let's delve into the mechanics of this idea.*
- **Trumpet fanfares**
  This is my favourite form of signpost to highlight an important message. I often use the phrases: *Now an absolutely critical point . . .* or *If you remember only one thing from today's talk, let it be this.*

  Fanfares are particularly valuable for your key message in a talk, to make sure the audience gets it, loud and clear.
- **Conclusion**
  A classic trick when storytelling. Remember what Charles Dickens taught us, about making an audience wait for the punchline? This is a lovely way to further enhance the anticipation. You might use words such as *And then came the moment of truth . . .* or *So, how did the story end?*
- **Reverse signposting**
  Another favourite of mine to ensure your key message is imprinted upon the minds of the audience. I'll often signpost into it, then, after making the point, signpost backwards, to double emphasise it. The concept is similar to the pause for thought we explored during the section on interactions.

  For example, with the imposter syndrome, as I might relate the story: And that was it, the moment of truth. The syndrome is part of us all. *Just stop and think about that for a moment . . .*

  A signpost into the most important point and then a reverse signpost to really hammer home the message. That's what I call true Winston Churchill style.

In summary for this section (see what I did there, again? – OK, enough now), signposting is a more subtle technique than interactions and is likely to be used more often. But the key point is that it can greatly enhance an audience's engagement with your presentation.

- Exercise: Look back on a presentation which you've given. Does it include signposts? If not, would it be improved if you incorporated some?

Magic Moments

And so we come to the third in our trio of terrific tricks for splendid speechmaking. Yet again, and once more, I've saved the best for last. Magic moments are my absolute favourite.

I always try to get one of these into every presentation I give, or consult on. They're usually the highlight of the show, a moment which lives on in the memory. Or, to put it another way, a magic moment. Hence the name.

Here's an example. When I'm teaching communication skills, I always cover the concept of less is more early in the session. It's so important, after all. I could just outline the principle, and perhaps put it into action with an exercise. But I have a trick I use to make sure the group remembers it, and indeed me. Because that helps to spread word of my work, how I teach, and tends to secure me more invitations to interesting opportunities.

I explain to the audience that humans can take in only so much information, so we have to be selective with what we communicate. Then I ask for a volunteer. *Someone who can catch.*

That in itself raises anticipation that something interesting is about to happen. It's a very effective signpost.

The volunteer comes to the front of the room, and, from my bag, I take a dozen brightly coloured ping pong balls. I wait for a second, then throw the balls at them, all at once. The poor victim invariably only manages to catch one or two. So we retrieve the balls and repeat the exercise. But this time I throw them one by one, slowly and carefully.

The result now, of course, is very different. My volunteer usually manages to catch all the balls. There's much laughter and enjoyment of the exercise. But critically, the point is made and remembered by the group.

On many occasions, people have approached me at networking events, or conferences, or just in a bar, and said: *You're the one who threw the balls to demonstrate the less is more thing. I've never forgotten that.* Likewise, when I've been booked to teach by a new client, they'll sometimes say, *You will do your balls trick, won't you?*

Both of which tell me the magic moment has worked in exactly the way I intended.

Let's enjoy a few minutes of the technique being put into marvellous effect. Look up *TED Talk, Julian Treasure.* You should find a video called 'How to Speak So That People Want to Listen'. It's less than ten minutes long and worth watching in its entirety. But if you're pushed for time, just get a sense of the subject from the first minute or two. Then wind on to seven and a half minutes in.

I won't spoil the surprise, but what a lovely magic moment it is. You can see from the reaction of the audience the impact it has.

That talk is one of the top rated of the excellent TED series, with millions of views. I wouldn't be at all surprised if the magic moment was an important contributor to its success.

So, how do we go about creating magic moments? Again I'll offer some of my thoughts, but once more feel free to harness your creativity and come up with other ideas:

- **Try it out**

  Way back at the start of the book, I mentioned a researcher who grew synthetic meat in her laboratory. For her magic moment, we bought some traditional beef from a supermarket, put it next to her version, then asked some of the audience to join us on stage to see if they could taste which was which.

  It was a wonderful magic moment, with the volunteers pulling a lovely range of expressions as they sampled the two dishes. The rest of the audience watched in delight. The point was also well made: the volunteers couldn't tell the difference between the two.

If you've got a product, or innovation, which can be tested by the audience, trying it out is a potentially enchanting magic moment.

- **Spring a surprise**

I worked with an academic on a talk about the interconnectedness of modern society. How if you remove one link from the chain which keeps life running, everything else can rapidly collapse. A particular point she wanted to make was the way we take so much of the technology around us for granted.

At that point in the talk, without warning, we killed the power in the lecture theatre. All the lights went off, as did the screen. Suddenly, everyone was sitting in pitch darkness. You should have heard the gasp.

The magic moment lasted only a handful of seconds before the lighting was restored. But it certainly made the point about how we feel when a fundamental technology which we rely on, such as electricity, is abruptly taken away.

My trick with the balls is another version of springing a surprise. Most people expect training courses to be relatively dull. By playing this game near the start, I engage the group and make it clear our time together will be entertaining, as well as informative. In show not tell style, naturally.

- **Raising the curtain**

People are fascinated by worlds of which they have no experience. So raising the curtain on what happens in them can be an impressive magic moment.

One company I work with makes medical devices which help the body heal after surgery. They take the form of tubes, patches or lattice structures to support the regrowth of skin and muscle.

Most people would never see them, given their purpose. So it proves a fascinating moment when we hand around some samples in a presentation. You can see the audience touching them – albeit warily – to experience how the devices feel, and bending them to test their strength and flexibility.

- **Unseat the audience**

Getting the crowd on their feet to take part in an interaction is another effective form of magic moment. Julian Treasure demonstrated the technique beautifully in his TED Talk.

I worked on a lecture about the contagiousness of airborne diseases, a very important topic after the Covid-19 pandemic. There were 200 people in the audience and we wanted to illustrate the point about how very infectious these illnesses could be.

So, fifteen minutes into the presentation, the academic stopped and said, *Just to demonstrate the contagiousness of some of these diseases, imagine I had one. I've been talking to you for a quarter of an hour. Would you like to know how many of you would probably have been infected?*

Naturally, the audience did. So he invited them to stand up and look under their chairs. Around a third had a piece of paper with a charming large red cross printed upon it.

The point was made, and powerfully, as the magic moment did its work.

- **Storytelling**

I include storytelling because it can provide a less showbiz style magic moment, which is sometimes most appropriate for your talk. The power of storytelling certainly means it qualifies, as we've discussed.

When I teach communication skills, and we come to magic moments, I ask the group to identify one from the session so far. It's interesting that most will refer to the balls trick, but quite a few will say storytelling as well. The tale I tell of Nigel and Jerry, or the imposter syndrome, always makes a mark.

So if your presentation is a more formal one, or you can't think of a different magic moment to try, storytelling is an option to ensure you're remembered for all the right reasons.

- **Audiovisual oddities**

The Internet provides a vast expanse of material which you can harvest to illustrate a point. The video of Martin Luther King speaking, for example, is arguably a magic moment when I teach presentation skills. It never fails to send tingles down the spine of a group and they certainly remember it.

As a tease, I'll tell you that we're going to enjoy a favourite audiovisual magic moment of mine when we get to the section on body language. That's coming soon.

If you choose a video, remember to rehearse well and make sure it works in advance of your performance. The embarrassed wait and panicked fiddling around with the technology in front of an audience can otherwise prove agonising.

As with all the magic moments we've discussed, your audio or video must be relevant to the subject. It sounds obvious, but I've seen some presenters use videos which seemed to be included just because the speaker liked them. And guess what the audience reaction was? Far from impressed, to put it mildly.

Finally for this section, I don't want to sound like a grumpy old teacher, but I do have a couple more words of warning.

I hope you've liked and been persuaded by the idea of magic moments. But you won't be able to get one into every talk. Some presentations simply don't lend themselves to the trick. For example, I've worked on very serious academic or political speeches which had to be delivered absolutely straight. Trying to fit in a magic moment would have jarred. Context is critical, as with so much of life.

Also, don't try several magic moments. Less is more, once again. Like soundbites, if you use too many it feels superficial, all show rather than substance, which can turn off an audience. One is usually plenty enough.

I mentioned earlier that I award a prestigious gold star for presentations which hit the absolute heights. To win one, the talks have to tick off a range of features. Interactions, signposting and magic moments are some of the most important to include if you're chasing my esteemed accolade. Good luck!

- Exercise: Can you think of a magic moment which would work for a presentation you might have to give?

Body Language

We've touched on body language previously, but now it's time to explore the subject in more depth. Because, when you're presenting, we might hear what you say. But we also want to know we can trust you and believe in you, your research, analysis and conclusions.

Much of that comes from good content. But plenty also comes from a sense of you. And body language is a key element in establishing your credibility.

For a little variety, and because I've just teased you with the prospect, let's begin this section with a masterclass in body language. The moment has come for one of my favourite performances in the history of pop music.

Look up *Queen, Radio Gaga, Live Aid*. You should find a four-minute video. But *before you enjoy it*, remember this:

It was a truly global event. There were more than 70,000 people at Wembley Stadium, London, back in July 1985, watching live. The television audience for Live Aid numbered over a billion. The concert had been much talked about and even more anticipated for months.

That might give most of us a shudder or two, if we were stepping out onto the stage. To say the least. But did Freddie Mercury show a shred of nerves? Was there a hint of hesitation? Or was his body language and performance such that you couldn't help but become absorbed in and uplifted by this glorious moment?

Now you've had the big build up, watch and enjoy.

So, having been richly entertained by that Mercury masterclass, let's explore the lessons of positive and powerful body language in public speaking.

- **Start with a smile**

  This is such an easy win, yet so often overlooked. But I'm not surprised. When you start a talk, you're usually concentrating furiously on what to say, not to mention battling to keep the nerves at bay. Which tends to make you scowl with the exertion of focusing hard.

  Do your best to avoid that. If you can start with a smile, you'll be amazed at the difference it makes. It's almost as though the room warms a degree or two. You'll notice people smiling with you, which eases the atmosphere and makes for a much better beginning to your performance. After all, you never see Freddie Mercury scowling at his audience, do you?

  Smiling from the start also fills you with energy and helps you to relax. Try it. For a little trick, it can make a big difference.

  Smiling occasionally throughout your presentation also tends to make a positive impression. Not all the time, of course. This is probably a serious subject you're talking about. But a few upbeat expressions can help ensure your talk is well received.

- **Own the space**

  You'll usually be presented with a lectern or table from which to present. I have a very simple piece of advice about what to do with that.

  Junk it. Shove the thing to the side. Just get it out of the way.

  Why? Because, ideally, your presentation should come across more as a conversation between you and the audience. It's why we introduced interactions and the concept of moving from monologue to dialogue. A lectern, or table, is a barrier between you and the crowd and an impediment to establishing a rapport.

  Far better to wander the stage, Mr Mercury style, and be able to get closer to your audience. That also demonstrates confidence, which helps establish your authority and credibility. Hiding behind a lectern has the opposite effect.

- **Eye contact**

  This insight is simple squared. How do you feel about someone who won't make eye contact when you talk to them? You're hardly going to trust them, are you?

  In order to make eye contact with the audience, you're going to have to learn your lines. Which might be a pain, but is well worth doing for the impact it has. You'll always make a better impression if you're fluent with your spiel.

  Yet again, we bow to Freddie for wisdom. Do you think his performance would have been so stunning if he was singing the lyrics of 'Radio Gaga' from a sheet of paper?

  I know many people worry about going blank, or getting lost if they don't have their notes to hand. But I have a solution which can help. Get yourself some cue cards (Figure 7.1).

  Jot down the bullet points for each slide, as above, and they'll serve as a prompt if required (excuse the mad writing, please.) They also fit easily into the palm of your hand. The odd thing about having cue cards is that, if I know they're there, I don't need them. That's a quirk of human psychology, I suppose.

  Working from bullet points has the added advantage of ensuring your talk is conversational, as it should be. Far better for an audience to feel you're

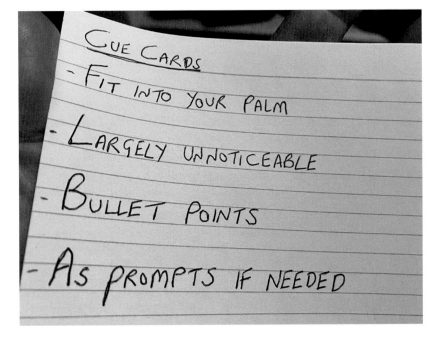

Figure 7.1 A cue card with bullet points

chatting to them, rather than lecturing. Note the points you have to make, then talk about them in your own individual style.

Don't worry if you have to glance down at your cue cards. It'll only be for a second and the audience won't notice. No one maintains eye contact throughout the entirety of a conversation. So long as you spend most of the time looking at the people you're talking to, all will be well.

- **Posture and openness**
  It's easy to be intimidated when giving a presentation. They're usually big moments, which brings pressure and stress. The danger is that hunkering down into yourself is a natural reaction when you feel you're under scrutiny.

  Don't let that happen. Stand up straight and keep your stance open. By which I mean don't fold your arms in front of your body, or put your hands in your pockets. Keeping your arms largely by your sides, with occasional gestures, is good.

And yes, before you ask, it is absolutely fine to gesticulate. That's a normal part of conversation. Hands can be very expressive, particularly when conveying passion. So long as you don't wheel your arms around as if you were a windmill, you'll look natural, engaged and authoritative.

I know this is all a lot to think about when presenting. But if you can get the hang of positive body language, it will mean your talks make a much stronger impression. You might also find that you feel more confident when performing, too.

- Exercise: Find a talk you've given previously and go back through it, thinking carefully about your body language. Now it's time for another of my dreaded recording yourself challenges. Prop your phone up in a corner and video your performance to see how you're doing.

Nerves, Redundancies and Authority

We're moving towards the end of our time looking at public speaking. But, before we finish, I want to share a series of briefer tips which will all help to make you an excellent presenter.

Firstly, you're unlikely to become a master of the art if you struggle dreadfully with nerves. Which isn't to say nerves are bad. They're just your body's way of getting you charged up and ready to perform, as we discussed when we were talking about interactions. However, it'll doubtless be useful to explore a way to control nerves.

This technique is simple, which is splendid, because we like simple. It has two other advantages, as well. It can remove umm, err, those annoying, umm, redundancies which umm, err, sometimes litter our talks, and which umm, undermine our credibility, and umm, waste time. OK, yes, point made, enough now. This insight also helps deepen the voice and so enhances your authority.

What's not to like about that splendid set? So, what's the trick, I can hear you crying out. Stop teasing me!

OK, here we go with the big reveal. The answer really is simple:

- Slow down.

Yes, that's it. That's all, that's the secret. Just that. But so you remember it, in my emphatic and ever hilarious fashion:

- Slooooowwww ... dooooowwwwnnn.

Resist the shallow gasps of air we tend to snatch when we're nervous and instead breathe more deeply. It may sound too good to be true, but on this rare occasion it's not. Slowing down can have a remarkable impact on the quality of your presentations.

It helps get more air into your body, which calms the nerves and makes your voice stronger. It also gives you more space between the words to think about what's coming next. That should eliminate those irritating umms and errs.

Remember watching the videos of Martin Luther King, Ronald Reagan and Margaret Thatcher in action? All took their time. None ummed and erred. All had voices which rang with authority, albeit in their own distinctive ways. And none appeared nervous in the slightest.

Mrs Thatcher is a particularly interesting case study. In her earlier days she was perceived as shrill, which was offputting to voters. She knew that could be a big problem, so took lessons from a voice coach to make herself sound more appealing.

You don't have to slow down a lot. Just 10 to 15 per cent will be fine. When you first try this, you'll feel you're speaking unnaturally slowly. But it won't come across that way to the audience, I promise.

To reassure you, try yet another of my cringeworthy recording yourself exercises. Take a video presenting at your normal speed. Then do it again, but speaking a little slower and breathing more deeply. Keep working at it until this becomes your standard presenting pace and delight in the difference it makes.

Timings

The first principle of timings goes back – yet again – to our faithful old friend, less is more. Only say what you need and stop. If you've got fifteen minutes, but require just ten, then end at ten. So long as you've covered everything necessary, you've done your job.

After all, how many times have you come out of a talk and heard people saying, *I wish that went on for longer.* Whereas the reverse is all too often the case.

On a couple of occasions I've worked with companies on pitches for investment and we've used the less is more trick to fine effect. We had half an hour to present our case, but started by saying, *We've got thirty minutes for this, but it's such a great innovation we're only going to take fifteen. That's all you'll need to understand its potential.*

Happily, the technique worked. It hooked the investors from the start, we said all that was required and got the support we sought.

Often you'll be given a strict time limit for a presentation, which can be ruthlessly enforced. The most extreme example I've seen involved trumpeters blaringly interrupting anyone who had the cheek to trespass even a second over their allotted time. That was entertaining for the audience, but awful for the poor speaker who was painfully cut off in mid flow.

If you've got a hard deadline, it's important not to attempt to fill every second. I always recommend leaving 10 per cent leeway. If you're given five minutes, prepare four and a half. If ten, plan and rehearse for nine, and so on.

Why? Well, because something will always go awry in a presentation. That's life. A phone will ring, and you'll have to pause for a few seconds to let it quieten. You might lose your way briefly and have to gather your thoughts. A slide may stick, taking up more time.

If you're hard up against a count, and have to accommodate an interruption, you'll be sharply aware of it. At best, you'll start to go faster to try to make up the lost time, which will undermine your performance. You may get flustered and start stumbling. All because you're suddenly under pressure to beat the deadline.

Whereas, if you've got leeway, you'll know you have time in hand. You won't flap, and can retain your cool and keep presenting calmly and effectively.

Online Presenting

I have good and bad news about online presentations.

The good news is that almost everything we've discussed so far applies just as much to the virtual world as the real. You need striking starts, emphatic endings, a golden thread of a strong narrative, and pretty much all the other tricks and techniques.

Before you ask, yes, I do even mean body language. When I'm presenting online, I usually stand up and recommend you do so too. It gives you far more energy and authority than sitting down.

The bad news is that online presenting is considerably tougher than doing so in good old fashioned three dimensions. There are far too many distractions on offer to a virtual crowd. Looking at their phones. Answering emails as they half watch your performance. Filling out their expenses. Playing with the cat. Etc., etc.

My solution is to make sure your talk is absolutely jam packed with interactions. I take the lead from a screenwriter friend, who works on a range of TV shows. He has a rule that almost without exception, no scene should last for more than about ninety seconds, in order to prevent viewers from getting bored. The constant variety keeps them engaged.

So when I'm planning my presentations online, I map them out as in Figure 7.2. (Again, excuse my eccentric handwriting.) I try never to speak for more than about ninety seconds without an interaction of some kind:

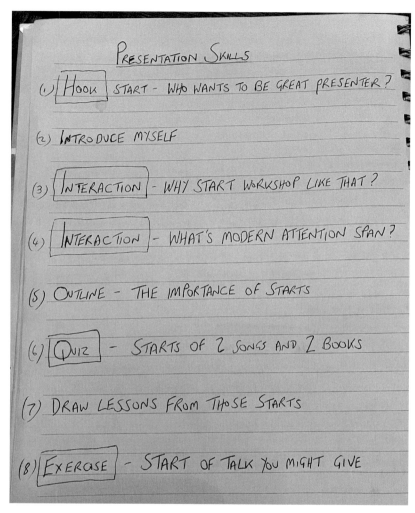

Figure 7.2 A presentation plan featuring multiple interactions

As you can see, it's interactions overload, but very deliberately so. There's the big hook of an opening, rapidly followed by a couple of questions. From the start, I want to set out a clear understanding that it's going to be a quick fire, highly interactive workshop.

When we get to the content, I introduce a topic, then immediately ask a question. Sometimes I set a quiz, like here, identifying the opening lines of famous books or songs. You know my ways by now.

In other workshops I might ask for opinions, as in *Which TV show is your favourite from a storytelling perspective?* Then I'll carry out a poll. *Who thinks* The Sopranos *is the best box set? Who thinks* Breaking Bad? *Who thinks something else?* Then we can have a discussion, and on it goes. If I'm teaching, I can set a brief exercise and ask the group to share their answers, as above, with the opening line of a presentation they may have to give.

Whatever it might be, I make sure the session is full to bursting with interactions. That way I've found I get much better results, and can strongly recommend it as a strategy for when you're presenting online.

- Exercise: Look at a presentation you've given. If you had to do so online, can you incorporate frequent interactions to make it more engaging?

The Question and Answer Session

Picture the scene. Your presentation is done, and done well. All the hard work was worth it. You've taken note of everything that strange Hall chap suggested, and – to your great surprise – it actually worked.

Your talk was fluent, informative, entertaining, and went down a treat. The applause lasted a gratifyingly long time. Now, at last, you can relax, warm and happy in the knowledge of a job well done. Right?

Wrong! Wrong, wrong, wrong and wrong again, plus some more wrong for added measure. But I bet you knew I was going to say that, party pooper, tough taskmaster and general grinch that I am.

I'm afraid to point out that your job is only half done. Because now it's time for the question and answer session. And that's as much part of your presentation as the formal talk.

I've often heard people say you can't prepare for the Q&A. But that's wrong as well. You very much can. If you do, it'll add beautiful icing to the delightful cake of your performance. And here's how to go about it.

When you've put your presentation together, and practised it, ask some trusted family and friends to give you feedback. But, importantly, not only on what you've said. Ask them to think about what questions they would raise afterwards. What occurs to them is also likely to occur to the audience when you give your talk for real. So take note of what they say and prepare some answers.

Then, when your confidence is building, ask some trusted colleagues to watch your presentation. Again, they can offer feedback on the performance, but don't forget to ask what questions they would raise, too. Take those on board and also prepare some answers.

I've gone through this exercise with lots of presenters now. It's interesting how the same questions are raised by both family and friends, as well as colleagues. Would you believe it, they then come up when the talk is given for real, and so can be dealt with smoothly.

Two Tricks of the Q&A

There are a couple of extra tricks you can incorporate into the question and answer session to make yourself look super smart, perfectly prepared and splendidly slick, if you'll excuse the soundbite.

Some of the questions you're expecting will probably require data or visuals. So prepare them, then pop them below the black line which marks the end of your slideshow.

When one such question comes up, you can summon the relevant slide and talk through your answer. I've never seen an audience fail to be impressed by this. It's an elegant and thoughtful way to mark you out as a master of your brief. We used this technique with the company that increases farmers' profits, which I mentioned in the previous chapter, and it worked nicely.

The other lovely trick makes sure the questioner feels heard, affirmed and that their point is addressed. For this, you can use the art of active listening, as discussed way back in Chapter 1.

Face the person, maintain eye contact, and also use body language to show you're truly hearing what they say. Nod and smile if they make a good point. Don't interrupt, but feel free to ask a question if you need to clarify something, then offer your answer. That all demonstrates appropriate engagement and respect.

Even if the questioner says something you disagree with, don't worry. You can still use active listening to acknowledge and appreciate them, then bring the discussion back to where you want it to be. We'll cover how to do that when we get to the chapter on 'Mixing It with the Media', and the cunning art of bridging.

- Exercise: Predict some questions which could come up in a talk you might have to give, and then rehearse your answers.

The companion website to the book has a quiz and video exercise for you on public speaking, presenting, and – particularly in this case – performing. You'll see what I mean when you have a look! You can find the site at www.cambridge.org/compellingcommunication.

The Golden Secret of Success in Presentations

And so to the last word before we leave the scary land of public speaking and presentations. Although, given all that we've worked through, I hope it's not feeling quite so daunting now? Because I can promise that if you take in what we've discussed, you'll have everything you need to become a powerful and polished presenter.

There is, however, one final point to mention. This is the last I'm going to ask of you on the subject, for reasons which will become obvious. It'll take more of your precious time, but this, above all else, is absolutely critical. Because we're going to leave public speaking by revealing the golden secret of success.

In fairness, this is also the golden secret of success for so much of life. But it always seems particularly relevant when we're talking presentation skills.

OK, so you've had the classic Hall storytelling build up. Now on to the action, and the unveiling.

To reveal the secret, we'll borrow from the wisdom of another of our iconic communicators. Certainly one of the greatest athletes humanity has ever seen, indeed perhaps 'the Greatest', as he often styled himself. The boxer Muhammad Ali:

- The fight is won or lost far away from witnesses. Behind the lines, in the gym and out there on the road, long before I dance under those lights.

That's it. The golden secret. Hard work. Prepare and practice. Prepare and practice again. Then prepare some more, then practice some more, then practice some more, then prepare some more, then again and again.

As the old saying goes: it's not what you wish for, it's what you work for.

Muhammad Ali was a great showman, a wonderful athlete and a magnificent communicator. So if even he extols the virtue of hard work, you know just how critical it is for success.

The Online World

At a glance: Establishing a positive presence online requires an effective bio, style of writing and strategy for posting, along with the use of tags, hash tags, links, photos and videos.

Many find it uncomfortable or intimidating, but we're all aware of its power and importance in modern life. So for our next chapter, it's time to think about social media and the online world.

Before you groan and roll your eyes, give this a chance. An online presence is an important component of your compelling communication toolkit. Rather than just a chore, or simply an irritant, it can actually be fun. And yes, I really do mean that. Plus you already have much of what you need to know to take to the online waters as elegantly as a swan gliding across a lake.

If it helps, I'm happy to confess I'm no great fan of social media. It arrived on the main stage of society when I was still with the BBC and I initially greeted it with due disdain. Like a true grumpy old guy, here's just another fad, I thought.

How touchingly naïve. Not to mention misguided, or simply plain wrong. But then social media just grew and grew. Dear Auntie Beeb, the kind and caring corporation, trained me to use it and I saw the advantages.

If you've got something to say, social media can carry your message around the world remarkably quickly. OK, it can equally blow up in your face if you get it wrong. We've all seen the horror stories. But hopefully, with the assistance of this chapter, you'll be able to establish an appealing and effective online presence without mishap.

Figure 8.1 Bluebells (Simon Hall)

One word of context before we plunge in. Given how fast the field changes, we won't be taking a detailed look at the current platforms. Instead, we'll consider the broad, strategic use of social media and the online realm.

And in case you're still groaning and rolling your eyes, not to mention tempted to skip this chapter, here's a taster and a tease. We also get to explore smartphone photography. Which you will enjoy, I promise. Not least because you'll be able to produce pictures as pleasing as Figure 8.1.

The Golden Rule

Yes, I know, I like my rules and secrets made of gold. But there are certain critical principles in so many of the areas we've discussed that I think the words are justified. So here's what's vital to bear in mind when you're posting online.

Rivalry for attention is even more intense than in the real world. Much more so, in fact. If you doubt me, just spend a few moments on one of the main social media platforms. How many new posts appear each and every minute?

Lots is the answer. Lots and lots. And lots more. Which is essential to keep in mind when you're online. Pretty much everything has to be short, sharp and simple.

This is the toughest battle for interest you'll face. Scrolls are bottomless. Unlike in the real world, no one is sat in a room and having to pay at least some attention to your presentation. Or dutifully cast an eye over your report. If you don't grab the attention online in an instant, your post is likely to be buried under a mass of competitors and forever lost.

Fortunately, as I mentioned earlier, you already have the skills to deal with this problem. Online, you have two best friends. One is photos and videos, which we'll come to later. The other is the inverted pyramid structure, our old ally from back in Chapter 3, on the tricks of the writing trade.

It's not just critical, or essential, but critically essential to put your most interesting and important information right at the start of a post. Take this example from a post of mine (Figure 8.2). It was on LinkedIn, the business platform, but that doesn't matter. It's the content I want to focus on.

See how the most important or interesting information comes first? I could just have started the post by saying I've written a new blog. But yawn, yawn, that happens all the time. Millions of people write blogs. Who would care?

So instead I've found something more interesting to say, which I hope will hook a reader. Then I go on to explain what I'm talking about.

That's the art of the inverted pyramid structure, this time as applied online. Notice also our much loved less is more in action yet again. I just say what I need and then stop.

Simon Hall • You
Course Leader, Compelling Communication Skills, University of Cambrid...
8mo • Edited • 🌐

What have I got in common with the legendary footballer, Pele?

And indeed, one of the most famous solos in pop music?

The answer is that both could feature in my biography...

Depending on whether you should include fun facts or not.

For the answer to that question, see my new blog: https://lnkd.in/dtVgxWVt

Figure 8.2 LinkedIn post by the author

Now an exercise for you. Imagine I'm holding a free webinar to help the world improve its writing skills. I'm kind like that, as you know. Here's what I want to say. How would you order it to make sure the post gets the attention it surely deserves? I've numbered the points for ease of reference.

1. I've noticed a lot of people struggle to get their message across when writing reports, briefings and emails.
2. It greatly frustrates them, as well as their managers and colleagues.
3. I've got more than thirty years of experience writing at the highest level, mostly for BBC News, as well as authoring almost twenty books and hundreds of articles.
4. I also teach writing skills at the prestigious University of Cambridge, in government and for private business.
5. So why not join me for this free, hour-long webinar.
6. I can show you how to write in ways which impress, influence and inspire.

What did you come up with? Most importantly, which point would you put first, to make sure you attracted the attention of a casual scroller? When you're ready, here are my thoughts:

I would say line 6 comes first. After that, the most attention grabbing detail of all, the order is less critical and more debatable because you should already have hooked a reader. But I would probably then go on to points 1 and 2, then 5, and finally 3 and 4.

Don't worry if your order isn't exactly the same as mine. It's always arguable as you move down the inverted pyramid. Just so long as you put the most important and striking detail first, you should have done your job and secured a reader's attention.

There's one more point to notice here. Layout is as important online as in the real world. Imagine that post about the webinar presented this way:

> I can show you how to write in ways which impress, influence and inspire. I've noticed a lot of people struggle to get their point across when writing reports, briefings and emails. It greatly frustrates them, as well as their managers and colleagues. So why not join me for this free, hour-long webinar. I've got more than thirty years of experience writing at the highest level, mostly for BBC News, as well as authoring almost twenty books and hundreds of articles. I also teach writing skills at the prestigious University of Cambridge, in government and for private business.

I suspect you'd be tempted to skip over that foreboding block of text, wouldn't you? Once again, a lovely layout is an easy win in making your content more likely to be read.

Remember, most posts will be viewed on a phone. Small screens particularly dislike big chunks of text. So, contrast that version above with the one below:

> I can show you how to write in ways which impress, influence and inspire.
>
> I've noticed a lot of people struggle to get their point across when writing reports, briefings and emails. It greatly frustrates them, as well as their managers and colleagues.
>
> So why not join me for this free, hour-long webinar.

I've got more than thirty years of experience writing at the highest level, mostly for BBC News, as well as authoring almost twenty books and hundreds of articles. I also teach writing skills at the prestigious University of Cambridge, in government and for private business.

Which of the two versions looks more appealing, and thus likely to actually be read? I hope that's a classic no brainer of a question.

- Exercise: Think of a social media post you might write. How would you structure it, in terms of both information and appearance, to give it the best chance of getting noticed?

Interactive Posting

The algorithms of the various social media sites all seem to function in slightly different ways, with inner workings which are opaque, to say the least.

However, like scientists, we can experiment with them, to see what happens with different sorts of posts. And there's one feature which comes up time and again in helping to spread your message far and wide and build up your online network.

- Posts which attract lots of interactions, whether likes, shares or comments.

That gives scope for deliberately writing in ways which encourage people to interact. Think back to the fun facts post I showed you in the last section. That could easily have incorporated an interaction. All I needed to add was:

- *By the way, do you have a fun fact included in your bio? If so, I'd love to hear. Please post it in the comments.*

Figure 8.3 shows a good example of an interactive post from a Storytelling page I follow on LinkedIn.

The post encourages comments, and quite a few people have contributed their thoughts. That helps it to spread across the platform.

 **Storytelling**   • • •
137,931 followers
6d • 🌐

Creating a scene with a twist can be a difficult task. It requires a balance of tension and suspense to keep readers engaged. This article provides tips and techniques to help you craft a scene that will surprise and satisfy your readers.

Have you read or watched any scenes with twists that made you gasp, laugh, or cry? What elements made them so memorable?

How do you balance the tension and suspense in a scene with a twist?

Collaborative article • 3 min read

👍👏💡 57   11 contributions • 3 reposts

👍 Like   🔁 Repost   ➤ Send

Figure 8.3 LinkedIn storytelling post

Here's another example, Figure 8.4, this time from Twitter, or X as we now seem to call it. Again, it attracted lots of likes, comments and shares.

I wouldn't try to encourage interactions all the time. People quickly get wise and zone out if you overdo it. But used strategically, every few posts, the trick can be effective for getting traction with your posts and building an audience.

Your Bio

Isn't that just social media in a snapshot? The word biography is too long for the medium, so it has to be abbreviated. See previous thoughts on the golden secret of success online. Short, sharp and simple are our watchwords.

Having established the principles of how to post, you might expect us to get on with doing so. But whoa there. Hold those horses.

Tilly
@TillyLovesBooks

…

I'd love to know if anyone has read/is reading anything truly brilliant this bank holiday weekend?

I just finished The Last Bear which was such a gorgeous MG read and now I want to cuddle a polar bear 🐻 😁

Figure 8.4 Twitter/X reading post by Tilly

We have a couple of basics to get right first, to make sure you're fit and dandy to strut your virtual stuff. Which means paying attention to the bio, and how to make yours work. As a rule, there are three elements:

- **The words**

  Curiously enough for such a short piece of writing, this can be tricky. Firstly, because you have so very few words to play with. The mainstay of which should focus on how you want to be known online.

  I'm assuming we're looking for a professional identity, rather than a personal page. Which means you should describe your work, again in a short, sharp and simple manner. This is not a CV. Your bio will also suggest the subject or subjects you'll be posting about.

  That's not a rigid rule. You can still talk about other matters, if you wish. But, given the bio defines your professional identity, it should outline the majority of the content a visitor will find on your page. For example, I largely talk about communication skills, but also post pretty photos from Cambridge and my travels. You might remember I'm an amateur photographer.

  Here's an example of an effective bio from an everyday user of social media. Lisa is a friend who runs a small business. She's not famous, not hugely followed, not even prolific online, but still knows how to put together a good bio (Figure 8.5).

  It's short, simple and works well, with the words and images complementing each other. But notice also Lisa's bio is not just business, business, business.

  That brings us to the quirk of the words, which adds to the trickiness. Remember, social media is supposed to be social. So we need a sense of your character as well as your work, just as Lisa offers. The Twitter/X bio of the UK television presenter and former England football captain, Gary Lineker, is another good example:

  ○ *Once kicked a ball about. Now talk about kicking a ball about.*

  Lineker manages to convey his professional identity. But his warm and humorous character is very much on display too, which is exactly his television persona.

  In summary, the words in your bio should tell a visitor what you'll mostly be posting about, and the kind of style in which you'll be doing so.

  Profile picture

  This is probably the easiest part of your bio as it's likely to be a photo of you. It's as simple as that.

← **Lisa Singleton**
7,640 posts

··· ✉ ⌕⁺ (Following)

Lisa Singleton
@lisazebra Follows you

Devon based graphic designer. Lover of beaches, travel, sunshine, fun, food and friends. Life is short....live it

⊙ Exeter, England 🗓 Joined May 2011

251 Following   **1,523** Followers

Figure 8.5 Bio of Lisa Singleton on Twitter/X

A shot taken on a phone is fine. But make sure it's good quality. An image which is half in darkness, or out of focus, can look unprofessional. A helpful rundown of the essentials of smartphone photography will follow later in this chapter.

Here it's worth mentioning how to handle social media bios if you're an organisation or business. Most tend to play it straight. That's corporate life, I suppose. But it's still perfectly fine to incorporate character, and usually much better.

The American space agency, NASA, offers a fine case study (Figure 8.6).

The words are lovely in saying what NASA does, but in a warm and playful, characterful way. The profile picture is its logo, which is standard for organisations and companies. That long banner full of the beauty and mystery of space builds on the institution's work. It's called the cover image, on the subject of which . . .

Figure 8.6 Bio of NASA on Twitter/X

- **Cover image**

  This is generally used to promote your professional identity, as we've just seen with NASA. For example, here's my profile on Twitter/X, Figure 8.7.

  The cover image is a version of the website banner for Creative Warehouse. That's the classic Cambridge skyline, full of historic colleges, in case you were wondering. The profile picture is yours truly, looking as human as can be achieved given the raw materials available.

  See how the words work to give a strong sense of the professional me, but also a slice of character. *Lover of words, thoughts and feelings* is very much at the heart of yours truly.

Simon Hall
17.5K posts

Edit profile

Simon Hall
@SimonHallNews

Course Leader, Compelling Communication Skills, University of Cambridge ~ Journalist ex BBC ~ Author ~ Communication Coach ~ Lover of words, thoughts & feelings

🖆 Education ⊚ Jesus College, Cambridge ⌀ thetvdetective.com
🖸 Joined March 2011

551 Following   **5,093** Followers

Figure 8.7 Bio of the author on Twitter/X

For businesses or organisations, the United Nations (UN) profile on Twitter/X is an excellent example of how a bio should be done.

I particularly like the cover image, a gun with a knot tied in its barrel. That's ideal for the mission of the UN. The words – *For peace, dignity & equality on a healthy planet* – sum up its purpose, and the profile picture is its logo.

Which brings us to my favourite social media profile. A ten out of ten, if ever there was one. I won't spoil the beauty of the surprise, but have a look at Barack Obama's profile on Twitter/X.

See how the words, profile picture and cover photo work together in beautiful harmony? And as for using only four words to describe himself, and in that order, just think what it says about his character and priorities in life. Genius!

- Exercise: Think about your bio. Do the words, profile picture and cover photo work well together? If not, how might you change them?

Picking Your Platforms

Given the array of platforms on offer, and the endless content being posted, you could spend your lifetime on social media. Indeed, some people appear to do just that.

But, assuming you have less time, and other ambitions for your precious days on planet Earth, you'll want a strategy to maximise your impact. Which is what we'll talk about in the next sections.

Firstly, we'll look at picking your platform from the sometimes bewildering range of choices. Happily this isn't anything like as daunting as it sounds. It just requires being clear on your goals.

Again, I'm going to assume you're using social media for business and professional purposes, not just wanting to impress your friends with your latest holiday. In which case, ask yourself this fundamental question:

- Where are the people you want to reach?

If you're not sure, then do some research. A little online searching, along with spending time on the platforms will tell you.

There's also a cunning short cut you can take here. Look up your competitors, or others in your area of work. Where are they on social media? You don't have to copy them, but knowing their strategy can be a useful indicator of the way you should be thinking.

For many people, one platform will be a simple choice. If you're in business, want to spread word of your work, see what competitors are doing, or perhaps need to recruit staff, then LinkedIn dominates the market. The vast majority of companies and professionals have LinkedIn accounts.

Figure 8.8 Bio of Chloe Ambrose on LinkedIn

I prioritise LinkedIn and get a lot of good business from doing so. There are plenty of communication professionals there, whom I like to keep an eye on for innovations and opportunities. I've also spotted great recruits for Creative Warehouse on the platform. I can see how they write and the work they're doing.

Marketing is big on LinkedIn, so a friend here in Cambridge targets the platform to publicise her work. Chloe (Figure 8.8) tells me she gets plenty of potential leads from her posts.

After LinkedIn, to a lesser extent I use Twitter/X. That's because most writers and journalists are there, which is a large part of my community. Another friend, whom I've worked with on several occasions, is a wonderful author and uses Twitter/X well. Hazel tells me it helps with her profile, book sales and invitations to events (Figure 8.9).

A friend who's a chef at a restaurant in Cambridge targets Instagram. It's a heavily visual platform, which is ideal for his culinary creations, as you can see (Figure 8.10).

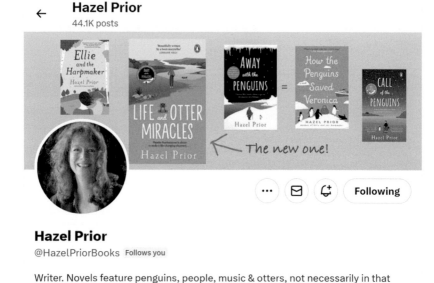

Figure 8.9 Bio of Hazel Prior on Twitter/X

Instagram is where most of the food lovers on social media appear to be. It works for Kareem, showing off his dishes and bringing in customers. Fashion, the arts, fitness, lifestyle and many other visual and touchy feely businesses love Instagram.

If video content is your thing, then you'll probably want to head to YouTube. Should you be seeking a younger audience, then TikTok is the platform of the moment. Facebook remains the most popular social media site by number of users, if you're seeking the broadest range of audience.

The moral of the story – or stories from this diverse range of professionals – is to do your research and pick the best outlet for you.

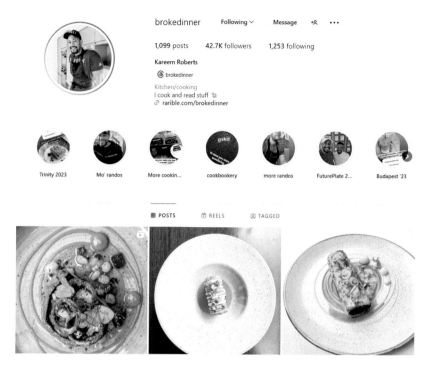

Figure 8.10 Bio of Kareem Roberts on Instagram

But, as I mentioned, life moves fast on social media. What's hot today in terms of platform can become tepid tomorrow. So if you are going to invest time in posting, occasionally review your platform, or platforms, to make sure they're the most effective for your purposes.

Despite the differences in their audiences and appeals, all the platforms work in broadly similar ways. Photos and videos are critical, along with the use of hash tags, tags and links. If you're not familiar with some of these, don't worry. We'll come to them in a minute.

It's also well worthwhile getting to know a platform and how it functions before you begin posting. A BBC colleague once sent what he thought was a private message to a friend about a guest on his programme. Unfortunately, he was new to Twitter/X and didn't appreciate the difference between a public post and a direct message.

His thoughts about the interviewee were far from complimentary, which ensured an entertaining controversy when he inadvertently shared them with the world. Take heed and take warning.

- Exercise: Do some researching and thinking. Which platform or platforms would you target for your own social media presence, or that of your business?

Creating Your Social Media Strategy

With social media, you tend to get out what you put in. Like so much of life, really. If you're part of a sizeable company, and you've got full time social media staff, you can work across a range of platforms because you have the resources.

But if not, as I imagine will generally be the case, then you have to prioritise. Which means selecting one platform, or two at most. Far better to work a small number well than spread yourself too thinly. So use your research from the previous section to choose a platform or two, then start to think about your posting strategy. These are the elements to consider:

- **Frequency of posting**
  The first point to make here is that you don't need to post every minute of each hour of every day. Although, again, some people seem to make it their life's work to do so.

  I don't particularly like blabbermouths, and if I see someone popping up too often in my feed I tend to mute them. That's a feeling many share. So don't talk too much for risk of being ignored. Remember my friend who isn't called Stuart and his ill-fated date.

  The optimum number of posts per week varies depending on the platform. For example, Twitter/X is fine with lots each day as it's so fast paced, continually reacting to events. LinkedIn and Instagram are slower, so there you're probably looking for one post per day at most.

  There are no real rules, and there's plenty of disagreement among the social media experts about the optimum number of times per week you should chirp up online. I post, on average, about three times a week, or every other day, and that seems to work well for me.

But here's the critical point, on which there's widespread agreement. Quality trumps quantity. Only post when you've got something worthwhile to say.

One of my three posts is always about the weekly blog I write. Another tends to be about some teaching, or an event I'm speaking at. The third is usually based on my pictures and observations of life, dabbling philosopher and photographer that I am. That strategy gives me a pleasant rhythm, makes me feel I'm visible and vaguely interesting, but without talking too much.

- **Interacting**

You've created a lovely post. So now you can sit back and forget all about social media for the day, right?

Nope! (And yet again, you knew I was going to say that.)

Posting is only half the battle. You also need to set aside time to interact. Don't forget, there's a clue in the name. It's *social* media. So be sociable.

Firstly, with anyone who comments on, or shares, your post. Be warm and polite. Manners matter, even online. OK, there are plenty of unpleasant people and posts out there. But being a good citizen of social gets you a lot further, in my experience.

Also, you shouldn't just be focusing on your own posts. Like and comment on those of others. Again, it's good citizenship. It's also a powerful way to help build your community, and thus the number of people you can reach.

- **Time of day**

There are optimum times of day to post to get noticed. Many studies have looked at this across the various platforms, and again there's much disagreement about when you should target. As a broad rule, it tends to come down to when the audience you want to reach is likely to be online.

My best suggestion is to experiment and see when you get the most traction for your posts. I've found that Twitter seems to like lunchtimes, perhaps because it's when people are taking a break, get out their phones and scroll away to see what's going on in the world. But, on LinkedIn, I've found posts at the start of the working day, soon after nine o'clock, perform best. That seems to allow workday time for interest in my musings to grow.

If you're going to invest time in social media, it's worth giving yourself the greatest chance of making an impact. Which makes the timing of your posts an important factor to consider.

Tags, Hash Tags and Links

You can increase engagement with your posts by including tags, hash tags and links. Their importance, and the best ways to use them, varies across the platforms. Again, it's worth some research on your chosen outlet, or outlets. But they broadly work in the same way.

- **Tags**

  To understand tags, let's zip back in time to the playground and the joyous game. When you tagged someone, you gave them a touch, usually yelling *You're it!* in the process. Similarly, tags in the social media sense are a digital touch.

  Say you've been part of an event for a charity. You might write a post, talking about what an honour it is, and tag in the charity. Usually, because of the busyness of social media, it would be hit and miss whether the charity's social media team saw it. But by tagging them they're alerted to the post, making them much more likely to share, like, or comment on it. That then expands the reach of your post.

  You can tag organisations, businesses or individuals, but as a rule only those who would be involved or particularly interested in whatever you're posting about.

- **Hash tags**

  Hash tags are a categorisation system for posts, which helps them to be found. They can be for subjects, such as the writing trade. For example, on Twitter/X, #amwriting is popular amongst authors.

  When they post about their work, they include the hash tag and other writers can find their content when searching for what fellow scribblers are doing. (Writers can find endless ways to distract themselves from the actual business of writing.)

Hash tags are also frequently used for days of the week. #Mondaymotivation is a common one, to help people through what is often the toughest day. They also appear for conferences, so delegates and visitors can find what people are saying about the event, as well as concerts, marches, rallies and endless other gatherings.

- **Links**

  You have a limited number of characters in your social media posts, restricting their length. By using links, you give a reader a chance to experience your more expansive thoughts.

  Links are commonly used with blogs. When I post about my weekly musing, I'll typically write four or five lines as a tease. I'll then insert a link, which will hopefully tempt readers to try the blog in its glorious entirety.

  You can use links to take a reader anywhere. To your website, details of an event, a form to sign, to add your name to a petition, whatever you want.

Each platform has its own etiquette and rules for how links, hash tags and tags are used. But incorporating them can help to increase the impact of your posts and thus your online presence.

Figure 8.11 gives an idea of how a finished post can look, complete with tags, hash tags and a link, courtesy of yours truly on LinkedIn.

As you can see, there's a big hook of an opening line. I then expand on my subject a little, all attractively laid out, of course.

Following that, we come to the link to my blog. There are a couple of hash tags, because public speaking and communication skills are what the blog is about. Finally, there are two tags. The University of Cambridge Online, because that's my main employer. Thomas is an academic and friend at the University, who helped to create the online course.

- Exercise: Imagine creating a post to preview an event you're attending. How would you write it, and lay it out? What hash tags, tags and link might you include?

If you want to avoid public speaking nightmares...

Worse even than being in an exam hall...
Turning over the paper...
And not being able to answer a single question...

This simple trick can help.

How? Well, it's all a matter of time. Or timekeeping.

See my new blog: https://lnkd.in/encMsSib

#publicspeaking #communication University of Cambridge Online Cambridge
Network Thomas Roulet

Figure 8.11 A post featuring tags, hash tags and a link by the author on LinkedIn

Photography

I mentioned the power of pictures in social media at the start of this chapter. Now let me show, rather than tell you. Because, as I hope you'll recall from Chapter 3, showing is always far more powerful.

I've gone viral a couple of times in my life, both when I was working at the BBC. This is the story of the second time, from just before I left the corporation to come to Cambridge.

We received a tip off that a group of boys at a school in Exeter, Devon, in the south-west of England, were going to stage an unusual protest. It was June 2017. Unusually for an English summer, the weather was hot. The boys had asked their headteacher whether they could wear shorts to school to help them keep cool.

She heard them out, but said no. It was against the school's uniform policy. But then one of the young gentlemen piped up with something like, *Yeah, but, right, then we can wear skirts, yeah? Coz you can't stop us doing that, coz it'd be sex discrimination, and you can't do that, right?*

(Excuse the writer's liberty with *da yoof speak*, but I'm trying to give a sense of the conversation.)

Of course, the headteacher replied. *Yes, of course you can wear skirts*, never thinking they would. And how delightfully naïve, and indeed fateful, that belief turned out to be.

Myself and Geoff, my cameraman that day, waited outside the school, just before lessons were due to start. We really weren't sure anything was going to happen. But then, around the corner the boys marched.

While Geoff filmed, I snapped some photos and popped them on Twitter/X. I then forgot all about social media for a while as we interviewed the boys, along with their parents, and filmed the gang of youthful protesters heading into school.

It was only when I took out my phone to call the newsroom, perhaps half an hour later, that I realised something strange had happened. My mobile had stopped working. I didn't know why, so I borrowed Geoff's to call in. I was met with the amused news that my Tweet (Figure 8.12) had, in only a few minutes, zipped around the world and was trending merrily.

Simon Hall
@SimonHallNews
...

Boys at Isca Academy in Exeter wear skirts to school in protest at not being allowed to wear shorts in hot weather.

👤 Spotlight and 3 others

8:44 AM · Jun 22, 2017

ılı View post engagements

💬 1.3K   ↻ 49K   ♡ 141K   🔖 134   ⬆

Figure 8.12 Viral post by the author on Twitter/X

That's why my phone had packed up. The poor thing was overwhelmed with notifications of likes, retweets and comments. The story featured everywhere across the BBC. We also got requests from media all around the world to use it.

And the reason my humble Tweet made such an impact? I'd love to tell you it was the beautiful, elegant and highly effective words I wrote. But I can't. Of course not.

It was the photos.

That's the power of the picture in social media. So now let's explore the essentials of smartphone photography to help your posts make an impact. For your added entertainment, I'll take you on a tour of some of my favourite Cambridge landmarks as we examine the various concepts.

Error Number One

Let's eliminate error number one first, if that doesn't sound too much like a secret agent on an important mission. I have another of my questions for you. The kind that sound daft (usually), but make sense when you think about them (hopefully).

How much of your house, flat or room do you live in? If that does indeed sound silly, let me put the question this way. I presume you don't use just

Figure 8.13 Fountain at the Cambridge Botanic Garden, wide shot. © Simon Hall

80 per cent of the kitchen, 65 per cent of the living room, 70 per cent of your bedroom, and so on?

No, I thought not.

Then why would you use only 75 per cent of the space available for your photo?

That's probably the most common error in everyday photography. Not filling the frame with the subject. Take a quick look at one of your favourite news websites. Scan through the photos of the people and events. How much space is wasted?

Here's an example of mine, from the beautiful Cambridge University Botanic Garden. Two pictures of the splendid fountain which sits at its heart, Figures 8.13 and 8.14.

Figure 8.14 Fountain at the Cambridge Botanic Garden, tighter shot. © Simon Hall

Which is the more interesting, attractive and effective of the pair? I'm very much hoping you think the latter picture, given that it's far more fountain and far less paving.

So, when you're taking a photo, remember to fill the frame with your subject. That's whether it's a person, a pet or a pretty petunia. If you have to walk a few metres to do so, then walk a few metres to do so. It's worth the effort for a much better shot.

Once again, I'll repeat the repetition and reiterate the reiteration. You're in a tough battle for attention online. The more striking your photos, the more chance you have of a post getting noticed.

Making the Picture Pretty

The word in the world of photography is composition. But that's a form of jargon, which we're well aware by now gets in the way of understanding. So making the picture pretty is what we'll tackle next.

Here, we have a kind friend to help us. Remember when we talked about soundbites and I mentioned the power of threes? The trick works with photography too. But in this case it's known as the rule of thirds.

Imagine dividing the phone's screen up into thirds, both horizontally and vertically, so you have a grid with nine rectangles. Just like Figure 8.15, showcasing another part of the Botanic Garden.

In fact, you don't even need to imagine the rectangles. Your phone will kindly create them for you.

This might work slightly differently, depending on which mobile you have, but go into the settings. Then scroll down to camera. In there, you should find a button marked grid. Turn it on. Now go to take a photo. I trust the grid which marks out the thirds in your picture has appeared?

Figure 8.15 Trees at the Cambridge Botanic Garden, picture using the rule of thirds. © Simon Hall

When you take a photo, put the key features of the picture roughly on those thirds and it should look appealing. Something like Figure 8.16, in other words, from another part of the Garden.

Whereas if you don't follow the benevolent guidance of the grid, you can get a picture which looks nothing like as pleasing, as in Figure 8.17.

That's the rule of thirds in action. Again, the visual impact of the picture helps to catch the eye and get your posts noticed.

However, one more point. Although it's called a rule, it's actually just a guideline. But I suppose *The guideline of thirds* doesn't scan anything like as well.

Photography is an art, and what works, works. If you think breaking the rule of thirds will make for a better picture, go for it and see what happens. That's part of the joy of the job.

- Exercise: Find an object in your home, garden or nearby green space and practise using the rule of thirds, as well as filling the frame with it. Then try not doing so. See the difference?

Figure 8.16 Trees at the Cambridge Botanic Garden, picture using the rule of thirds. © Simon Hall

Figure 8.17 Trees at the Cambridge Botanic Garden, picture not using the rule of thirds. © Simon Hall

Focus and Exposure

Your smartphone isn't just smart, it's brilliant. Given all it can do, it's a wonder we managed to live before the things were invented. So it might come as a surprise to know you can change the focus and exposure of a photo, just like with an old-school camera.

Sounds complicated? And why would you be interested in this, anyway? Because then you can take photos full of detail, colour and beauty. Like Figure 8.18, of the famous wisteria at Jesus College, part of the University of Cambridge.

Yes, that picture genuinely was taken on a phone. And not even one of the best on the market. Like its owner, my iPhone is getting on a bit. So, given how it can make your photos look so striking, I trust you're more interested in how to change the focus and exposure now?

Figure 8.18 Wisteria at Jesus College, Cambridge. © Simon Hall

Good, because, even better, it's easy to do. Open your camera as though you're going to take a picture. Now tap the screen where you want to focus the shot.

Again, what happens next might vary a little, depending on the make and model of your phone. But generally, you should see a small box appear, like in Figure 8.19.

Now hold your finger in that box. What happens? Something like what we see in Figure 8.20?

AE/AF lock means auto exposure, auto focus lock. In other words, you're locking the focus on the area covered by that small, yellow square. The exposure of the picture is locked too.

Now comes the really clever part. See the faint sun symbol to the right of the square? Brush your finger up or down it. The picture should become lighter or darker. That's you changing the exposure. Play with it until the amount of light is ideal for your shot and snap happily away.

Figure 8.19 Flower with yellow box showing area of focus and exposure. © Simon Hall

Figure 8.20 Flower with letters showing focus and exposure are locked and faint yellow box indicating where. © Simon Hall

Smartphone cameras are programmed to expose and focus automatically. In fairness, they usually do a good job. But, by changing the settings yourself, you open up a whole new world of taking pictures, some of which can be stunning. And, as discussed, pretty pictures tend to work very well indeed on social media.

Angles

This is a lovely trick of photography. You can make a dull picture far more interesting simply by taking it at an angle. It might require muddy knees if you're outdoors, but it's worth the effort.

For example, here's another of my now infamous compare and contrast exercises. Which of these two pictures of a family of statues at the Botanic Garden looks the more interesting? Figure 8.21 or Figure 8.22?

Figure 8.21 Giraffe statues at the Cambridge Botanic Garden from eye level. Image of statues courtesy of Break, www.break-charity.org. Photo © Simon Hall

Figure 8.22 Giraffe statues at the Cambridge Botanic Garden from low angle. Image of statues courtesy of Break, www.break-charity.org. Photo © Simon Hall

I'm hoping you said Figure 8.22. Because, for me, the picture is far more appealing with the family of giraffes looking down on you like that, compared with the flatter shot of Figure 8.21.

By the way, you don't just have to get down low to make angles work. Sometimes a high shot can be just as effective. As with this view, Figure 8.23, from the rockery, over part of the lake in the Botanic Garden.

Then there's the super creative sideways look at life. Not everything has to be squared and centred in the inventive world of photography. Here, for example, the lovely cherry tree blossoms by the side of the Cambridge University Library, Figure 8.24.

Figure 8.23 Elevated shot of the Cambridge Botanic Garden. © Simon Hall

Figure 8.24 Cherry blossom outside the Cambridge University Library. © Simon Hall

Whatever picture you're taking, stop for a second and think whether it would be improved by an angle.

Those are the main tricks for taking impressive photos, which should help you make a splash on social media. But it's also worth mentioning panoramic pictures. I often use these in my posts, as they can be striking and are easy to take.

Just find 'panoramic' when you open up your camera and the phone will guide you through what to do. It's only a case of a steady hand and a gradual panning of the shot. An example of an effective panoramic is shown in Figure 8.25, the First Court at Jesus College.

You can also experiment with filters, modes, lighting settings and any other functionality your phone has to offer. There's plenty of it, and more being added all the time. But it's wise not to get too carried away.

As I've said before, and many times, simple is not stupid. Simple is smart.

Like my viral skirts tweet, the most effective photos are those which are well composed, exposed and focused, without the need for gimmickry. As with a final example of another of my photos which attracted a lot of attention online, Figure 8.26.

Figure 8.25 First Court at Jesus College, Cambridge. © Simon Hall

Simon Hall
@SimonHallNews

Promote ...

If you want to cause controversy in Cambridge, try introducing change.

But! Just occasionally, change can bring sunshine and smiles.

Like the wildflower meadow at King's College.

Once a pristine lawn, it's now a blaze of beauty, a haven for nature...

And already much loved. 😊

King's College, Cambridge

Figure 8.26 Twitter/X post by the author

Videography

Social media loves videos. Just like photos, they can help your posts to make an impact.

Here's an example. I like to feed the birds in my garden, but, come an ordinary Thursday morning, I received an unexpected visitor. Looking out of my kitchen window, on the garden table was a sparrowhawk, busily stripping the feathers from its unfortunate lunch (Figure 8.27).

I managed to grab twenty seconds of video, before the killing machine got tired of being recorded and flew off. It took lunch along, trailing in its talons, naturally. I posted the video on social media and it received lots of attention. You can see the brief film on the companion website to this book, www .cambridge.org/compellingcommunication.

I know recording video might sound complicated, but it's actually not. For all the fuss about the array of effects which you can add, editing and that sort of thing, the best videos are simple and focus on interesting content. Just like with my sparrowhawk. Just like with pictures.

Even better, the art of recording videos is very similar to taking photographs. So, here's your quick Hall guide:

- **Filling the frame**
  Exactly the same as with photos, this is probably the most common error. Make sure your subject dominates the shot.

Figure 8.27 Sparrowhawk. © Simon Hall

- **Composition**

  Or making the image look pleasing to the eye, as we now know. Once again, the rule of thirds is your faithful friend here.

- **Focus and exposure**

  Just as with photographs, you can vary the focus and exposure. You can also zoom in your shot by pinching the screen outwards. However, it's better to be physically closer to the subject if possible, as that preserves the technical quality and detail of the recording.

- **Hosepiping**

  It's a common temptation, when taking a video, to swing your shot around from here to there, then somewhere else, and then back again. But resist. The best videos tend to be fairly static. If you need to move the shot, whether up or down, left or right, try to do so gently and smoothly to avoid the viewer feeling giddy.

  There's no set formula for how long you should stay on a single shot. But about five seconds is a good general rule. That should give the viewer time to take in the scene, but without getting bored.

  If it's fascinating, like the sparrowhawk, then the shot can sustain considerably longer. Or if the story is developing in front of you, like fireworks going off, you need only keep recording. If what you're watching retains your interest, it probably will for an audience too.

You can also compile a number of shots and then edit together your own video. Your phone will have built-in editing software and it's easier to use than it looks. If you're going to try this, make sure you record a series of clips which will edit together well. Generally, that means wider shots to establish a scene, followed by close ups to explore details.

You're looking to create a form of visual storytelling. For example, imagine you were going to a history museum and wanted to put together a video of your visit.

Your first shot might be the magnificent, imposing exterior of the building, to set the scene. Then, when inside, a wide view of the opening gallery, say the First World War. Following that, you could cut to some of the exhibits, like a glass case full of uniforms. From there, you could move even closer with your shots, picking out details like the shiny buttons, or medals.

If you have the time and inclination, try learning about editing and putting together a video. It can be fun and is often effective at generating interest online.

Blogs

Blogs are a wonderful showcase for your work. I write one a week and they've brought me more business than I can remember. So many times a potential customer has got in touch with the words, *I saw your blog about public speaking/powerful writing/storytelling etc. etc., and was wondering if you could come and talk to me/my company/my organisation . . .*

If you're not blogging already, you should certainly consider it. Even better, we've covered almost everything you need to know to write a successful blog. Here's a quick rundown of the important ingredients:

1. **Title**
   Titles are even more important than ever online, because – yet again – of the ferocious competition for attention. So take the time to make yours particularly good. You know how by now, if you'll excuse the rhyme. Remember the three letter Is.

2. **Opening line**
   Once you've hooked a scroller with your title, you need to lead them into the content. So a strong opening line is critical to make sure they don't simply click away to the next distraction.

3. **Content**
   Make sure your blog is worth reading. Information and emotion are your watchwords here. Offer value with professional insights. Many of my blogs, for example, contain tips to help readers improve their presentation skills. Remember, your aim isn't just to keep a visitor reading, but for them to want to come back next week, and the week after, and so on, to benefit from more of your wisdom.

4. Storytelling

Yes, I know I keep going on about the power of storytelling. But let me go on some more and tell you a brief tale about the impact of stories in blogs. Each Christmas, I republish my five top rated blogs of the year. And guess what?

Pretty much every year, each of those top five blogs contains a story. The moral being the power of storytelling in captivating an audience.

As I believe I may have mentioned before?!

5. Strategy

This is so basic, but so often forgotten. It also gives me the opportunity to ask another of my slightly odd questions, and I know how much you love those.

What kind of books did Agatha Christie write? The genre which she became famous for, and made her a good living?

OK, that's a no brainer. Crime is the answer. And why am I asking?

Well, imagine Agatha suddenly wrote a romance. Readers would be baffled. They'd wonder what was going on. It would probably harm her reputation and likely lose her some fans.

The point being to confine your blogs to your subject area. I write about communication skills. Within that overarching theme, there are thousands of insights I can offer, from public speaking tips, to storytelling, to writing.

A friend who's a marketer writes about marketing techniques. Within that, there are an infinite number of stories about marketing to tell. A pal who's a designer writes about design ideas. And so on it goes, depending upon your field of expertise.

Far too often, I've seen a blogger stray outside of their subject area just because there's something they want to write about. And all it tends to do is confuse and alienate their audience. To build a happy and valuable following for your blogs, stick to your subject and find stories to tell within it.

6. Character

Yet again, it's not just what you say but how you say it. Readers click on blogs for content. But the character, or voice, of how you write is important in keeping them engaged. So let it rip.

I certainly do. And OK, that generates some groans about my offbeat – to put it kindly – humour. But they're good natured and make me happy in showing that my audience is well engaged.

7. **Search engine optimisation**

You've doubtless heard of this, but just in case, it's the practice of trying to make your work prominent in search engine results. There are books and books on the subject, so read up if this is particularly important to you and you'd like a more in-depth understanding.

I tend to keep it simple. I think of my ideal customer and imagine what they would be searching for. Then I make sure to use those words repeatedly, but without looking like I'm doing so.

Search engines also pay particular attention to titles. Which is why my blogs have examples such as: *Blue Sky Thinking for Powerful Public Speaking*, or *Handling the Ultimate Public Speaking Nightmare*, or *Stand Up for Public Speaking Success*.

The words public speaking, as well as presentation skills, will also be liberally scattered throughout the content.

One further tip is geographical references. Much of my work comes from in and around Cambridge. So I imagine a potential customer typing *Public speaking training Cambridge*, and take care to mention the city as I write. From the number of enquiries I receive, I know the tactic works.

8. **Layout**

If it's not simple to navigate, you risk losing a scroller to content which is. People don't have the patience to decipher. Easiness on the eye is essential.

9. **Pictures**

Blogs love photos. So include them and show off your new found photography skills. I rarely write a blog which doesn't contain at least one picture, and often more.

10. **Show not sell**

Celebrate the difference you make, rather than trying to sell your products or services. As previously discussed, it's far more effective that way.

I don't think I've ever been offered work on the basis of a blog which has simply advertised a new course. Whereas, if I talk about someone I've coached shining at an important presentation, or triumphing at a job interview, that's far more appealing.

11. Modern writing

As we've also said before, beware of jargon, long words and even longer sentences. Remember, most blogs will be read on a phone. If in doubt, don't forget to KISS: Keep It Simple, Silly.

Once you've written a blog, post about it on social media to help draw in readers. I find having a rhythm helps, so people come to expect to hear from you. I publish my blog every Monday, which seems to work for me.

One final word on blogging, and this also goes for social media. If you're going to commit to giving either or both a try, be sure to give them time. Audiences don't tend to spring up overnight. It usually takes months of consistent and quality posting before you build up a reasonable following.

That may sound like a long slog, but it'll be worth it in the end. I've certainly found it so.

- Exercise: Think of three blogs you could write to showcase your work, but in a way that celebrates the difference you make rather than sells. What title would each have?

Artificial Intelligence

You might be tempted to use AI bots like ChatGPT to help you create blogs, social media posts and any other content. I would understand that, and – prepare yourself for a shock – I wouldn't necessarily discourage you. Despite the threat to my living!

I've used such bots and believe they have a place. They can take some of the hard labour out of creating content, but only up to a point. I'll show you why courtesy of a challenge I set ChatGPT.

- Write the introduction to a book on compelling communication in the style of Simon Hall, Cambridge University, in 150 words.

This was how it answered:

Welcome to 'Compelling Communication', a guide to mastering the art of persuasive communication. In today's fast-paced world, effective communication is a critical skill that can make all the difference in achieving your personal and professional goals.

As the renowned scholar Simon Hall of Cambridge University once said, 'Words are the most powerful tool we have for changing the world.' Whether you're giving a speech, writing a report, or simply engaging in everyday conversation, the ability to convey your ideas clearly and persuasively is essential.

In this book, we will explore the principles and techniques of compelling communication, drawing on the latest research from fields such as psychology, linguistics and rhetoric. We will examine how to structure your message for maximum impact, how to use language to influence your audience, and how to adapt your style to different situations and audiences.

Whether you're a seasoned professional or just starting out, *Compelling Communication* will help you enhance your communication skills and achieve greater success in all areas of your life. So let's get started on this exciting journey towards becoming a master communicator.

What do you think? Not bad, if we're honest? The first paragraph works fine. The second one actually quotes me, and I'm not sure I'd quote myself in an introduction. That seems odd, not to mention excessively egotistical, even by my standards. But the content itself is decent.

As for *renowned scholar,* frankly that's hilarious. I may have a thorough knowledge of communication skills from a career of practice, but academic I'm certainly not. It's classic chatbot hallucination, yet stated with remarkable confidence. Which is a warning. You should always check the 'facts' that a bot presents you with.

The final paragraph is also reasonably good. I can imagine myself writing something similar. So, overall, I'd say ChatGPT has done a reasonable job.

But here's the but. Do you sense something missing from that AI-inspired introduction to *Compelling Communication*? If it helps, think back on how the book actually began. To save you flicking there:

> Communication is nothing less than a secret superpower for success.
>
> Now, I realise that's quite a claim to start our odyssey together. But stay with me. Because I've got plenty of evidence to back it up.
>
> Firstly, an insight of my own. A confession, if you like:
>
> I fear that without the world of words I would have achieved nothing much in life.

If you're shouting out loud *it's our dear friend, the character of the writing*, I would agree. That second introduction actually sounds like, and feels like, the genuine me. I suspect, and heartily hope, that artificial intelligence will never be able to create that very essence of human communication, and indeed connection.

So, by all means use bots to harvest information and even offer suggestions. You'd be daft to ignore the technology while others around you indulge. But, for true compelling communication, the sacred goal of this humble book, write from the heart and soul in your own inimitable style. There's simply nothing like it.

- Exercise: Try using an AI bot to generate some content which might be useful to you. Now rewrite, so it feels like it's really you.

Trolls

I have two final brief but important thoughts before we exit the online world.

The first concerns the dreaded trolls. They're sadly a feature of life online. Almost everyone gets insulted or abused. That's just the way it is, unfortunately.

The Internet has brought many remarkable gifts to our world. But it's also given a voice to some people who, until now, had no voice. For which there was a good reason.

They didn't deserve one.

Trolls find bad news particularly irresistible. If you're facing a situation where you'll have to deal with difficult issues in public there are tactics for doing so. We'll explore those later, when we get to the chapter on strategic communication. They should help insulate you or your organisation from attacks.

But in general, my strategy with trolls is simple. They're best ignored.

The creatures are desperate for you to react, so don't. Just hit the block button. You'll find it a remarkably pleasing experience, letting a troll seethe away unheard in its own pool of bile.

If they persist, report them. But never react. As the saying goes, they're not worth it.

Think Before You Post!

So to my last sage words for this chapter. Which are these, once more indented to emphasise their importance:

- Always think before you post.

In fact, think, then think again, before doing so once more for good measure. And never, ever post in anger. Or, indeed, when tired, or emotional, or a little merry after what, in a triumph of euphemism, is sometimes known as *a good lunch*.

What's posted online can spread frighteningly fast. Not to mention remain forever. Genies very much don't pop back into bottles in the modern world.

No matter how tempting it might be to vent, react, wield sarcasm or simply go on the attack, don't. Take a breath, take a pause and thus take care of your precious reputation.

Finally for this chapter, my traditional nudge. The companion website to the book has a quiz and challenge for you about communicating online. On the off chance you'd forgotten, you can find it at www.cambridge.org/compellingcommunication.

9

• • • • • • •

Mixing It with the Media

At a glance: To spread your message through the media you need an effective press release, along with understanding the tricks and tactics for dealing with journalists.

News coverage is usually the most powerful form of promotion, whether for a company, organisation or individual. If you get it right, your message can travel across the entire planet, with remarkable effect. I've been involved in several stories which have made the news internationally and brought great benefits for those featured.

One concerned a research project on the application of artificial intelligence to recognising human emotions. The academics needed 1,000 people to sign up in order to have sufficient data for a robust study. But they only managed to gather around fifteen volunteers through using social media, conference talks and word of mouth.

I helped them put together a news release, which was picked up by the media here in the UK and then globally. The result was more than 5,000 people signed up for the research, creating a highly credible set of data.

A life sciences business I work with embarked on a fundraising round, seeking almost 100 million dollars. We approached a couple of journalists about the company's work, which resulted in stories in prominent business publications. The coverage aroused the interest of investors who were impressed by what they read, which helped to raise the money.

A mid-ranking manager at a company had to face the media to promote a project he was running in his spare time. He was raising money to support healthcare in poorer countries. Not only did the coverage help his charitable work, but also he was noticed by the bosses at his company, congratulated on his efforts, and secured a promotion soon after.

There are many more such examples of the benefits of media coverage. So, given that a good press would be in our compelling communication interests, let's examine how to make a splash online, in print and on air.

The News Release

The news release, or press release, is the standard way to approach the media. And here, I've got more good tidings for you.

We've already covered most of what we need to put together a press release. But there are some important extras as well. So here's the anatomy of what's commonly known in the trade as *a presser*.

- **The title/headline**
  We examined the importance of titles and headlines way back at the end of Chapter 2, along with how to create them. But if time is in short supply for just about everyone, then journalism is perhaps the most time pressured of all the professions.

  I had more days than I care to remember when I didn't have a moment to stop for a break. Hacks are also bombarded with press releases. I used to receive dozens daily.

  All of which means it's absolutely critical to interest a journalist with your headline. That will often determine whether they read the rest of the release. So take time to create an effective headline, using the principle of the three Is which we discussed before: interest, inform and intrigue.

  For example, here's the headline for the AI research release, which was picked up around the world:

  Smile, Scowl and Even Scream at Your Screen in a Mass Experiment to Investigate Artificial Intelligence Emotion Recognition

Use the headline for the subject box of the email you send out to the media. If you get it right, it should draw the journalist into reading the rest of the release.

- **The opening sentence**

  Next, you have to build on a good start by further tickling the journalist's interest. We've talked at length about the importance of opening lines. That's even more the case in the media, where editors are obsessed with how a report begins.

  Once again, you're looking to set out more of your story, establish your authority, and make the hack want to keep reading. For the AI release, this is what we wrote:

  A new project from researchers at University of Cambridge and University College London lets people try out an emotion recognition system for themselves to see how it scans their faces and interprets their emotions just by clicking on a website.

- **The facts**

  Here's a sad but true insight into the modern media. You might have heard of the word churnalism. It's a product of the cutbacks which many newsrooms have suffered, along with the drive to keep churning out content.

  In essence, rather than a reporter looking at a news release, then checking the information, reading around it, as well as talking to a variety of experts about it, they simply cut, paste and publish. This happens more often than I, and many others who believe in good journalism, care to think.

  It means that you can easily send out a news release and find it published, just like that. Which might be bad for the media, and society, but that's another debate. For our purposes, if you're seeking publicity, it can be useful.

  However, for it to happen, your release has to include all the information needed to make a story complete. So remember what Rudyard Kipling taught us back in Chapter 2, when we were exploring how to write with impact. Be sure to include the who, what, why, where, when and how, the enlightening gang that make up his Six Honest Serving Men.

  One further point is worth bearing in mind. If you can structure your release in line with the inverted pyramid principle, it will help. Journalists like the most important information first.

- **Quotes**

  Now you've got the journalist interested, and they have all the necessary information, you need to add some colour to your release. There's a principle in the media that the reporter provides the facts, the interviewees the character or emotion. That means you should add a couple of paragraphs of comment.

  This is important, because good quotes can make the difference between a story being picked up or not. It's why the print media will often feature boxes with interesting quotes highlighted on their pages. Or the broadcasters will use brief clips of interviews in their headlines.

  Which means this is no time to be modest. If something is revolutionary, say so. Likewise, if you're drawing attention to a dreadful development in the modern world, feel free to make that clear too. Hacks love strong comments.

  For example, in the AI release:

  'Many people are surprised to learn that emotion recognition technology exists and is already in use. Our project gives people a chance to experience these systems for themselves and get a better idea of how powerful they are, but also how flawed,' said Dr Alexa Hagerty, project lead and researcher at the University of Cambridge Leverhulme Centre for the Future of Intelligence.

  'Technologies as far-reaching as emotion recognition require input from everyone whose lives they touch,' added Dr Hagerty. 'We have to be sure such technology benefits society.'

- **Pictures**

  Images are critical in the modern media. You should include a photo of anyone who is quoted, but also of an event, if that's what you're talking about, or an innovation, if that's your subject.

  The AI story was based around a simple and user-friendly website, which volunteers could experiment with. So, naturally, we included a photo of it (Figure 9.1). Along with Alexa, the lead researcher, testing it to its limits!

- **Important extras**

  You should now have everything you need for the release in terms of content, but there are some extras which the media expect.

Figure 9.1 Screenshot of the AI emotion recognition game

Most important are your contact details. Although journalists will have an email address from your sending out of the release, they're impatient creatures. If they want the story, they may well want it now.

You wouldn't believe how many pressers are sent without a phone number. Be sure to include one. You could miss your chance of some lovely publicity if you don't. An opportunity right now could be gone in another five minutes when a different story comes in.

It's also a convention that you include the city and country from where the release is being issued, along with a date and time. Lastly, you should say whether the presser is for immediate use, or under embargo to a later date and time. That's a perfectly standard request, which journalists will usually honour.

The date and location, and whether the story is under embargo or not, generally come at the start of a release, the other extra information at the end.

Once you've put the presser together, it's simply a question of sending it to whichever media outlets you choose. Their email addresses are listed on their websites. All want to receive stories, and often get some of their most interesting news that way, so it's in their interests to be accessible.

- Exercise: Think about a story you might like to see in the media. Can you draft a news release which would appeal to a journalist, using the guidance above?

The Timing of a Release

Now you've created your release, don't just send it out. Stop and think for a moment about the best time to do so.

Some days are busier for news than others. If you were seeking national attention, you wouldn't want to email journalists on the day of a set piece occasion of great importance. The budget, for example. Most of the airtime and column inches would be taken up with reporting and commentary on what had been announced. It's quite possible your presser wouldn't get properly read on such days, they can be so chaotic.

Far better to be tactical. Check what's coming in the week ahead in the way of big announcements. There are plenty of websites to help with this. Then send out your release on the quieter days.

Weekends are always worth considering. They tend to be far less boisterous on the news front and so offer more opportunities for placing stories. The so-called *silly season* is another time when journalists are often scratching around for news to cover.

The fabled silly season covers the summer holiday period, when politicians, business leaders and other important figures tend to be away. Not much is getting done in terms of making decisions or announcements, which often means less important or stranger stories grace the media.

A brief aside, if you don't mind, because it's both legendary and entertaining. In the media here in the UK, a silly season report is sometimes referred to as *a skateboarding duck story*. The roots of this go back to the 1970s and a much loved BBC TV programme called Nationwide.

One edition featured a white duck called Herbie who could, apparently, skateboard. Before you think it, don't. This is not one of my jokes. It really did happen. Yet, strangely enough, not in the silly season. The report was broadcast in May.

But nonetheless, Herbie the skateboarding duck became synonymous with the silly season. I suppose, as the old media adage allegedly goes, *Never let the truth get in the way of a good story.*

Anyway, such silliness aside, back to business. There's also some evidence that the time of day when you send out a release can be important in making sure it gets read. The media relations company Prowly carried out a survey which identified the period between ten in the morning and two in the afternoon as the best time.

My experience supports that view. The first hour of the news day tends to be taken up with a flurry of deciding what should be covered. Life then feels a little quieter for a few hours, before the pressure builds again in the afternoon as the stories are written and edited, the headlines created, and the programme or publication compiled. The time you send out your release may be a small factor in securing coverage, but it's worth considering nonetheless.

Eek! (a Journalist Calls)

Sorry, I couldn't resist that title. I was getting concerned I hadn't exhibited the eccentricity of my voice lately (the duck was factual, honestly), and I didn't want you thinking I was losing my touch.

The point of the heading is that your news release has worked. You've just received a call. The editor likes your story. A reporter is on the way to interview you. Eek indeed.

So now we'd better ensure all the right messages come across when your moment before the awaiting microphone, or poised pen, comes. It's time to explore the tricks and traps of the media interview, and how to present yourself and your story well.

- **Interview structure**

  For a typical interview, when a reporter comes to visit, there's a standard interview structure. This can vary, but is worth knowing as a template for what to expect. I think of it as the three Os, and I'm assuming the journalist has read through the release you've sent out.

  The first O is to outline your story. This is the easy part. The reporter will usually want to talk it through, to make sure they understand it, and to pick up on any extra details in which they might be interested. If your interview is for broadcast, this part may not be recorded.

  O number two is your opinion. Now the interview is becoming more interesting. This, and the third O, are the parts which are likely to feature in the published or broadcast story.

  Remember, your job here is to provide colourful comments, just as in the news release. You're likely to be asked questions such as: *Why is this important? How significant a development is this? How unusual is this event?* In other words, the kind of questions which give you the opportunity to voice an opinion. Notice these are open questions, which offer a lot of freedom to construct an answer.

  The third O is the most important to prepare for. This is where the journalist will oppose what you say. Never forget that it's a reporter's job to play devil's advocate and challenge you. They might agree with every word you say, but will still find ways to test you.

  This is where the tone of your answers comes into play. It's important not to get annoyed, or appear defensive, no matter how irritating you might find the inquisition. We'll look at how to deal with difficult questions, and the art of tone, a little later.

A word of caution. The three Os structure doesn't usually apply if you find yourself in a radio or TV studio for a live interview. Here, time is at a premium. You'll have a fixed slot, which can be as little as two minutes.

That means the presenter is likely to go for the kill from the very start and pitch straight in with the most challenging questions. If you find yourself in such a studio interview situation, be ready for that. Otherwise, you can get caught out and flustered, which is far from ideal when you want to look calm and commanding.

The great advantage of knowing what to expect from a media interview is that it allows you to anticipate the questions which are likely to come up. And, of course, be ready with some strong and effective answers. Which – surprise, surprise – is exactly what we'll look at next.

Predicting Questions and Preparing Answers

Some of this work should already be done. If you've written good quotes for the news release, you can use them as the basis for your second O, the opinion question.

For example, with the artificial intelligence release, Alexa, the project lead, could expect questions such as:

- Why is this project important?
- What's the significance of your work?

Because the questions are open, she can then produce an answer similar to the one she created for the news release:

Many people are surprised to learn that emotion recognition technology exists and is already in use. Our project gives people a chance to experience these systems for themselves and get a better idea of how powerful they are, but also how flawed. Technologies as far-reaching as emotion recognition require input from everyone whose lives they touch. We have to be sure such technology benefits society.

If I was still a reporter, I would be very happy to hear a response like that. It's authoritative, thoughtful and colourful. I could see it sitting happily in my story.

Notice also how short the answer is. The modern media looks for responses which are brief and powerful. At just sixty-five words, that would be ideal. It could easily make up part of a report in a print outlet, or be used as a clip of interview in a radio or television news story.

You don't need great reams of quotes. Just a paragraph will be fine. Most interview clips on the radio or television are fifteen to twenty seconds long, as a broad rule. That equates to around fifty to sixty words. A similar number for print outlets is about right.

You also know you're on track with an answer if you can imagine part of it in a quote box on a page, or as a brief clip in the broadcast headlines. The test is whether it would grab the attention of a viewer, listener or reader. For instance, I could see this excerpt doing so:

> *Technologies as far-reaching as emotion recognition require input from everyone whose lives they touch. We have to be sure such technology benefits society.*

On, then, to the final part of predicting questions, the most important element. Anticipating the challenges which may come from the reporter. In this case, I could foresee questions such as:

- Why should anyone volunteer for this project?
- Isn't it too late for this work, given these systems are already in use?
- Don't such systems potentially offer big benefits to society?
- How can you hope to influence governments and big business to do the right thing with artificial intelligence emotion recognition systems?
- Isn't AI itself inherently dangerous for humanity?

It's usually the case that your list of potential challenges is the longest stage in your preparations for a media interview. And quite rightly so. This is where the going gets toughest, so thinking about anything that could come up is wise. Forewarned is forearmed.

Drawing up possible questions yourself is a good start. But you can also do as we discussed in the section on the Q&A, from the last chapter. Family, friends and colleagues can be helpful in suggesting the sort of questions you might face.

- Exercise: Think of a story which you might have to talk to the media about. What challenging questions can you imagine being asked?

The Message House

Next, we should look at how to prepare your answers for a news interview. Here, I have another trusted friend to introduce. It's a staple of pretty much all media training, as it's known.

The message house is an effective technique for dealing with any question which a journalist might throw at you. It's simple, which is always a win in the communication world, and it's visual, to help you remember it (Figure 9.2).

As you can see, it's not called a message house for nothing. Each segment, from the roof, to the pillars, to the foundations, should be summed up in a sentence. Remember, simple is smart, and – yet again – less is more. Discipline yourself to include only the most important points.

So here's how the components of the message house break down:

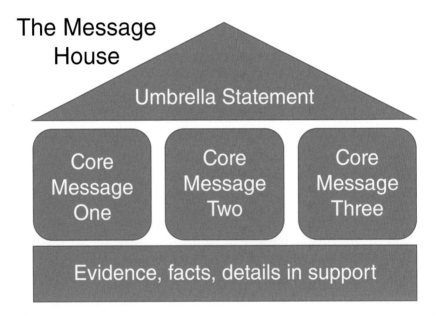

Figure 9.2 The message house

- **Umbrella statement**

  This is the most important message you would like to get across in the interview. If there's one thing you want the audience to remember, it should be the umbrella statement. It's likely this will be the first answer you give a reporter, the one you keep coming back to, and the one you repeat most often.

  For example, in the artificial intelligence emotion recognition story, the umbrella message was:

  > *Emotion recognition technology is already in use, is powerful but also flawed, and we need input from everyone to be sure such technology benefits society.*

  See how that summary of a sentence is the absolute boiled down basics of the quote which Alexa offered in the news release? That was what she felt was most critical for people to remember.

  Your message house doesn't have to be made up of fully formed answers. It should just capture the essence of what you want to say. An interview is supposed to be a conversation. So long as you know what you need to get across, you can then express it in a manner which comes naturally. That way, your appearance in the media will be most effective.

- **The core messages**

  Three is the maximum here, not a target. Sometimes you might only need two. It depends what you want to communicate. It's OK to keep coming back to an umbrella statement, along with two core messages, if they're what you want an audience to remember.

  Once more, you have to be ruthless. After the umbrella statement, what are the next most important points you want to establish? In the case of the AI story, we decided on three:

  1. We've created a program that lets people try out an emotion recognition system for themselves just by clicking on a website.
  2. Volunteers are invited to share their perspectives on the system as part of a citizen science project.
  3. Companies already use such systems to test customer reactions, from breakfast cereal to video games. But also in much higher stakes situations

like courtroom trials and job interviews – largely without public knowledge or consent.

You may have spotted that all this information comes from the original press release. That's absolutely fine. If you've put it together well, you'll find very similar messages coming across in a media interview.

- **Evidence, facts and details**

Finally, we come to the evidence you need to support your argument. This part, the foundations of your message house, has a common trap. Just as with presentations, you really want to persuade an audience of the validity of your case. So you're going to bombard them with data, right?

What do you think I'm going to say next? How well do you know me by now?

Once again, I'm suspecting you'll think a strategy based on a blizzard of facts and figures would be an error. Are the words *less is more* whispering in your mind, by any chance? If so, quite right too. An audience will only have the processing capacity to take in the key points.

There's no rule about how much supporting information you should cite. But, for a pleasing symmetry, and ease of recall, I like five facts. That way, you have **one** umbrella statement, **three** core messages and **five** facts. For the AI story, these were they:

1. The Association for Psychological Science conducted a review of the evidence and concluded that there is no scientific support for the common assumption 'that a person's emotional state can be readily inferred from his or her facial movements'.

2. Racial bias may be encoded into emotion recognition technology. A study shows these systems consistently read black faces as more angry than white faces, no matter what their expression.

3. In the EU, a coalition of more than forty civil society organisations has called for a ban on the technology.

4. Racial and gender bias in AI systems came under scrutiny after researchers at the Massachusetts Institute of Technology showed that facial recognition technology is most accurate for white men.

5. Major technology companies including Microsoft, Amazon and IBM halted sales of facial recognition technology, pending further research.

If constructed well, the message house should provide everything you need to answer any question a journalist poses. When I'm training people in how to deal with the media, there's a mantra I repeat time and again:

- Stay in the house and you'll be safe.

But that, of course, raises a question. How can the message house possibly help with anything whatsoever a journalist might ask? What if something comes up which doesn't fit easily into its structure?

That's a very good point. So next, let's explore a technique which provides a very good answer.

- Exercise: Construct a message house for a story which you might have to face the media to talk about.

Bridging

Bridging is probably the most well-known and commonly used device for dealing with difficult questions. You'll have seen and heard it in media interviews hundreds of times, but perhaps without realising. We also mentioned its value when we discussed the question and answer session, back in our tour through public speaking.

To understand the technique, ask yourself: what is a bridge for?

That's not meant to be a philosophical question, or indeed another plain daft one. Instead, it's intended as a reminder that a bridge takes you from a place where you don't want to be to one where you do. Which is exactly the purpose it serves in a media interview.

Imagine Alexa Hagerty had been asked a question she didn't expect and didn't like the look of in an interview about the AI emotion recognition system. Say it was something populist, perhaps designed to grab a headline with her answer: *Isn't this system in danger of equipping robots like the dreaded Terminators with all they need to take over the world and exterminate humanity?*

OK, I exaggerate, but you know me, and it helps to make the point. She certainly won't answer with a yes. But if Alexa responds with a no, then the journalist still has the option of a scary headline:

- Cambridge scientist plays down threat of 'Terminator' AI

That's very much the kind of screaming headline you could see in the less reputable media, however silly it might seem. Clickbait it may be, but this sort of thing happens. It wouldn't do Alexa's reputation any good, or that of the University, should it be splashed around. So it's best avoided.

This is where bridging comes into play. Instead of a denial, or acceptance of the premise of the question, Alexa could say:

Intelligent robots have long been a staple of science fiction. People may not be aware that artificial intelligence emotion recognition systems are already in use. What our project seeks to ensure is that they're used ethically and responsibly, for the good of all society, with the support of populations across the globe.

By bridging, Alexa can move from an area she doesn't want to be, speculating about the potential dangers of AI, to one where she does. Which, would you believe it, just so happens to come back to a form of her umbrella message. The answer is fifty-two words long, or about fifteen seconds. Which also just so happens to be around the ideal length.

The great advantage of bridging is that, done well, it appears as though a reporter's question has been answered. Which should avoid them persisting with it, and the interview can move on. It also means there's none of that irritating experience you may well have had when witnessing a politician being interviewed. *Just answer the question*, I often find myself yelling at the TV or radio.

Bridging makes it feel as though a question has been dealt with, by initially responding to it but then quickly moving on to safer ground. Indeed, that's the technique in summary: address the question, then rapidly shift to what you want to be talking about, rather than what the journalist has raised.

For another example, Alexa could be asked: *Do you condemn the fact that these AI emotion recognition systems are already in use, largely without public knowledge?* She might wisely not like the look of a headline which hollers:

- Cambridge researcher slams governments and big business on secret AI emotion rollout

Once again, such a headline could easily be written. But only if Alexa gave the journalist an answer which allowed them to do so. In which case, why not try some nifty bridging to avoid such an unpleasant fate? She could use the technique to reply:

- *It's true that these artificial intelligence emotion recognition systems are already in use, and largely without public knowledge. Our project intends to change that, by showing people what they are and how they work, openly and responsibly. From there, we want to gather views to ensure that the use of these systems has public awareness and support.*

Once again, bridging saves the day. It takes you smoothly from somewhere you don't want to be, outside of the message house, to back inside again. A happy place, where you're safe in the knowledge that the message you want heard is coming across from your interview. And once again, at fifty-eight words, or around twenty seconds, that answer is the right sort of length.

The best bridging comes when you make it seem effortless and thus unnoticeable. That takes practice, but it's worth the investment of time if you're facing the media. A good interview can be a great ally in your cause. A bad one can be nothing less than a disaster.

On the off chance you're not aware of the champion of awfulness in the field, just look up *Prince Andrew, BBC interview*. Then place your head in your hands.

That's not to put you off appearing in the media. I just want to emphasise that it's important to treat the moment with respect and work hard to make sure the right messages come across. If it helps, you know all you need to do so from everything we've covered in the book thus far.

Finally for this section, you may come to find certain phrases appear repeatedly when bridging. They're often a giveaway of the technique in action. I'm thinking forms of words such as:

- That's an interesting point and it needs investigating, but for now what's more important . . .
- One point of view certainly sees things that way, but I'd say what's more relevant is . . .
- I'd rather not deal with speculation, but what I can say for sure . . .
- There are concerns in that area, but a more likely explanation is that . . .
- I understand why people might think that, but another way of looking at the issue . . .

As you've probably spotted, the small yet resonant word *but* tends to feature a great deal in the world of bridging.

If you'd like to see the technique in action, look up *bridging in interviews videos*. You'll find plenty online. Spot the bridges being built and indulge in a knowing smile.

But, importantly, ask yourself whether you would have noticed the bridging if we hadn't explored – and exposed – the art. And indeed whether it works in helping the interviewee avoid any potentially dangerous comments, instead getting across the message they want.

- Exercise: Go back to the story which you might have to face the media to talk about and the challenging questions you can imagine being asked. How could you use bridging to help you answer them in a way which ensures the messages you want heard come across?

Tone

As we've discussed before, it's not just what you say but how you say it. Which makes the tone you adopt in a media interview every bit as important as the message.

So, before you face the press, think carefully about your manner. If this is a sad or difficult story, then feel it and behave accordingly. If it's upbeat and positive, then a happier tone is appropriate. But whatever you do, just think about how you look and sound.

If you're ever unfortunate enough to be involved in talking about bad news, tone becomes critical. The former Chief Executive of Rolls Royce, Warren East, notoriously smirked on camera while being interviewed about cutting thousands of jobs. Look it up. His apparent flippancy caused a storm, which added insult to injury in terms of the story. If you've got bad news to bring, you don't want to make it worse by getting the tone all wrong.

Contrast that with an example of what can happen when you sound exactly the right note. I'll declare an interest here, and a sizeable one. You're about to read a story concerning my wife, Dr Jessica Gardner. She's the Director of Library Services at the University of Cambridge, and I worked alongside her team on the media campaign I'm about to describe.

When Jess took up her role, she found that two priceless artefacts were missing from the Libraries' collection of historic treasures. They were notebooks written by the celebrated naturalist and pioneer of the theory of natural selection Charles Darwin, no less. That would be bad enough, you might think, and you would be right. But even worse, one notebook contained his iconic Tree of Life sketch, in which Darwin first formulated his thoughts about how species evolve from common ancestry (Figure 9.3).

Despite extensive searches, the two notebooks couldn't be located. So Jess decided to launch a public appeal for help in finding them. This was a huge step, to put it mildly. We knew there would be intense international media attention, given Darwin's celebrity. Importantly, getting the public onside could be the key to finding the notebooks.

Months of work went into the messaging for the appeal. But also, vitally, the tone. Search for *Darwin's missing notebooks, an appeal by Jessica Gardner*, and you'll see the result. You should be looking at a video which lasts one minute and forty-four seconds. As well as the words, pay particular attention to Jess's tone.

Figure 9.3 Darwin's Tree of Life sketch. Reproduced by kind permission of the Syndics of Cambridge University Library.

For such a difficult story to share with the world, the reaction was overwhelmingly positive. Countless kind people got in touch to try to help, sharing their thoughts about what might have happened to the notebooks. Which brings us to the ending of the story, and fortunately it's a happy one.

Around six months later, a package appeared at the Cambridge University Library. It was addressed to Jess, left outside the doors of her office, and bore the cryptic message:

- Librarian
  Happy Easter
    X

The package contained the two missing notebooks and, even better, they were in perfect condition. To this day, we have no idea who took them, why or indeed where they were kept. But most importantly, they're back where they belong, safely in the Cambridge University Library vaults, preserved for future generations.

Now for the punchline. I can't tell you that it was Jess's heartfelt tone which helped to get the notebooks back. But I interpret that X at the end of the note as a kiss. Which, in my view, suggests whoever returned them saw Jess's public appeal and experienced the emotion she was clearly feeling. It made a connection and so they brought the notebooks home.

That, in my reading of the situation at least, is a powerful example of the importance of tone.

- Exercise: Go back to the story which you might have to face the media to talk about. What would be the right tone to adopt?

Soundbites

Once more, a technique we've explored elsewhere in the book can be put to good use in another area of communication. From way back in Chapter 2, and as wielded again when we were talking about public speaking, soundbites can also be highly effective in media interviews.

You'll often be in a competition to get featured in a story. Many people want to appear in the media. But there's only so much airtime, or space on a page. Editors love strong quotes, so when you're thinking about the comments to include in your news release, consider getting creative.

As ever, there's a balance to strike. You don't want to be outlandish and undermine your credibility. But if you can find a standout way of expressing your umbrella statement, or core messages, it can help to ensure your words get used. This will also be handy in making your comments memorable for the audience, just as we've discussed before.

One of my favourite examples comes from former UK Prime Minister Tony Blair. It was April 1998, and a critical point in the negotiation of the Good Friday Agreement, which largely ended decades of bloodshed in

Northern Ireland. With the talks close to collapse, Blair addressed the waiting media pack with these words:

> A day like today is not a day for soundbites, we can leave those at home, but I feel the hand of history upon our shoulder with respect to this.

It is, of course, entirely debatable how much impact his words had on the talks. But they certainly resonated with many people. And ultimately the Good Friday Agreement was signed, heralding a new era for Northern Ireland.

One of the delights of Blair's words is the paradox. To say it wasn't a day for soundbites, but then to produce one anyway. Brilliant. Whatever the debate about the linguistic merits of the phrase, or the politics, it certainly made an impact.

Before we leave soundbites, another of my nag notes. You must be getting fed up with these. But it is an important point.

Just as with public speaking, if you're going to use a soundbite in a media interview, limit yourself to only one and one only. More and you run the risk of looking superficial.

- Exercise: Can you create a soundbite for the story which you might have to face the media to talk about?

Online Interviews

Image is important in interviews, so I'm going to spend a while discussing how to look for your moment in the media.

This is particularly relevant for TV interviews carried out online. It used to be the case that editors would rarely accept video contributions via Zoom, Teams and other such platforms. But the Covid-19 pandemic and the widespread travel restrictions changed all that. So now it's perfectly standard to be interviewed from your home.

However, you still need to take care about your appearance, however tempting it is to just climb out of bed and onto the airwaves. The principle is that nothing should distract from what you have to say. So, if the audience is talking about how you look, rather than your words, you've got a problem. For example, how many shots have you seen which look similar to Figure 9.4?

I don't really have a good side. But if I did, it wouldn't be up my nose.

You can imagine what the viewers might think if I appeared on TV looking like that. It would be all they talked about and my message would be lost. At least if I get the shot right, as in Figure 9.5, I've got a much better chance of being heard.

So, how to go about making sure your shot looks professional and not distracting? Don't worry, it doesn't require a great deal of work. Just a little thought in these key areas:

Figure 9.4 The author from a low angle

Figure 9.5 The author from eye level

- **Camera angle/distance**

  To avoid the far from flattering view of your nasal cavities, or the impression that the audience is looking down on you, the camera should be roughly level with your eyes. Prop your phone, laptop or tablet up on some books to make sure that's the case, if need be.

  The shot also tends to look best when the camera is about an arm's length from your face. That makes sure you dominate the frame, but without looming large in too scary a manner.

- **Lighting**

  The main light source, whether a window or electric lights, should be facing you. If it's behind, you'll appear as a silhouette. Adjust some lights or your position if that helps. The lurking in the shadows look is never a trustworthy one. Viewers like to see eyes and faces to help with their assessment of the interviewee.

- **Sound**

  If you're in a quiet environment, like your home, then the built-in microphone on your computer or phone will probably be fine. But, for the best sound quality, plug in your earbuds or headphones. Audiences are perfectly used to seeing these in interviews now and they're particularly important if you're in noisier surroundings like an open office.

- **Background**

  Always check what's behind you before you go on air. Then check again. Because there have been all manner of horrors in shots, from explicit books to devices which should surely be better kept in a bedroom. A plain, neutral backdrop is best, so as not to risk any distraction from your wise words.

- **Look at the camera**

  Most video conferencing systems will offer a picture of you on the screen. The temptation, of course, is to keep glancing at it. That's only natural. But looking away from the camera can appear shifty in a TV interview. After you've set up the shot it's best to turn off the image of yourself if you can, to help ensure you keep looking at the camera.

- **Framing**

  Check back on the two pictures of yours truly from the start of this section. Apart from the awful lighting, the first one has far too much headroom, which looks odd. You should aim for a picture more like the second version, with an inch or two of headroom, and a little space either side of you.

- **Make-up**

  Most of my BBC career was spent on the road, reporting from location. But occasionally I had to do some studio work. And you could almost hear the groan from the poor people tasked with applying my make-up. Suffice to say it was neither a brief nor a simple task.

  But a little make-up is worth wearing, particularly if, like me, you're challenged in the hair department. Shining on screen as you sweat nervously is distracting and can seem untrustworthy. Some translucent face powder solves that problem and is well worth the investment.

Dress to Impress

Finally for this chapter, three more brief thoughts which are important to keep in mind when mixing it with the media. You probably noticed that I missed out what to wear in the section above. That's because it deserves a mention all of its own.

I appreciate I'm in no position to lecture anyone about clothes. On a good day, I can resemble a scarecrow caught in a storm. But clothing is important in how you're perceived when being interviewed.

As with tone, the golden rule is to dress appropriately for your story. If the news is difficult, smarter clothing is wise. That shows respect for whatever it is you're talking about and the people involved. If the story is upbeat or offbeat, you have leeway to dress more casually.

Here, yet again, the mantra of keeping it simple can help. TV cameras don't like fussy or ornate. Avoid dangly earrings, showy jewellery, tight stripes, small check patterns, paisleys or anything else which is full of detail. At best, they distract. At worst, they may strobe, gauze and flux, which can look strange. Plainer clothes tend to work better.

In terms of colour, black and white are both best avoided. Black comes across as a dense block of depressing nothingness. White can glare. Gentle shades, like pastels, are usually the most effective. Again, you're looking to avoid anything which draws attention away from your words.

Before we leave the wardrobe department, I have yet another of my notes of warning. Even if you think you're being interviewed for the radio, or a newspaper, dress appropriately in terms of smartness.

The Internet means that publishers can now also be broadcasters and broadcasters publishers. It's perfectly standard to be asked to say a few words to a video camera, or be photographed, even by those reporters who used to work solely for newspapers or the radio. So be ready for that.

- Exercise: Go back to the story which you might have to face the media to talk about. What would you wear to come across appropriately to the audience?

Interview Checklist

The more you know about what you're getting into with a media interview, the better you're likely to perform. So it pays to have a checklist of questions to ask a journalist before you agree to an inquisition.

I suggest you keep this handy and refer to it when the moment comes. It may save your professional life:

- **What's the angle?**
  Remember way back in Chapter 1, when we talked about the angle which runs through every story. The journalist will probably know what it is before they interview you. Ask what angle they're taking and you can start to predict the questions you're likely to face.
- **What will I be asked?**
  It's perfectly legitimate to want to know what you're going to be asked. Most journalists will tell you, in outline form at least.

    In the BBC, we had a rule that you should always reveal your first question to a contributor. That way, you had a better chance of the interview getting off to a good start, which helped all concerned. It always pays to find out as much as possible about what the reporter is planning to raise with you.
- **Live or recorded?**
  This sounds so basic, but is often a cause of confusion and indeed alarm. It's usually nerve racking enough to be interviewed for the radio or TV, but even more so when you suddenly find out you're going live on air in ten minutes' time. Always be clear whether your contribution is to be recorded or live.
- **Any other contributors?**
  If you're appearing live, it's quite possible there will be other contributors and sometimes you'll be expected to argue with them. Knowing this in advance can help you prepare. If you look up the other interviewees, you'll get an early warning of what they're likely to be saying and can ready your responses accordingly.
- **Radio, TV, newspapers, online?**
  This goes back to the point about publishers now also being broadcasters and broadcasters publishers. It helps to know where your contribution is going to be used. In the BBC, the answer was generally everywhere.

- **Full interview, or just a clip?**

  It's very common in TV and radio interviews to record several minutes of material, but only use a twenty-second clip. If you know that in advance, you can focus on getting your most important, umbrella message into the clip by continually returning to it.

  I appreciate that may sound strange, to keep giving essentially the same answer. But it's a perfectly standard trick for dealing with the media. After all, this is your opportunity to get your message across to potentially millions of people. So why not make sure it's the message that you most want heard?

- **For publication/broadcast when?**

  Some interviews will be used in the next hour, some next week, others next month or even next year. Be clear on when the report is going to be published or broadcast.

  Journalists won't thank you for writing lots of social media posts about the story if they're not planning to release it yet. Knowing when a report is scheduled for means you can build on its impact by doing some promotion on your own channels, whether social media, website, blogs, vlogs or podcasts.

- **Social media use?**

  Most news outlets and journalists will promote their stories on social media. Keep an eye out for the posts and then join in the discussion by sharing or commenting. It all helps to enhance the impact of the story.

Dirty Tricks

Journalists often get a hard time. The profession is commonly rated down in the basement on the trustworthiness scale, along with estate agents and car sales people. (Apologies to any estate agents and car sales people reading this, but sadly it's true.)

So I'm going to say a little something in defence of my former profession. The vast majority of journalists are honest, decent and reputable in my experience. They try to get their stories right, even if they sometimes fall short. That's just being human. I made plenty of errors in my career, if never deliberately.

But, ruefully and regrettably, there are a few journalists who are far less honourable, as the opinion polls suggest. I wouldn't say truth is no object with them, but it's certainly peripheral in their field of vision. This is often the case with the tabloids, or some of the more populist websites. Those with specific agendas to peddle. You know the type.

I hope you don't encounter them, or suffer at their hands. But it's my job to prepare you for everything you might face when mixing it with the media, so we'll conclude this chapter with a look at some of the dirty tricks of the trade.

- **Off the record**

  Say hello to the oldest trick in the book. If a hack smiles at you and whispers these words in their most beguiling voice, take fright and – most importantly – take warning. There is no such thing as off the record.

  What's *off the record* in a cosy conversation in a hidden corner can quickly become the headline of a news story. Tell a journalist only what you would be happy to share with the world. Remember always in your dealings with the media: *there is no such thing as off the record*.

- **Treat all microphones as live**

  The moment you see a microphone, or camera, you should assume it's recording. Some of the biggest media embarrassments have come from unguarded comments, or even singing, when someone doesn't think they're being observed.

  Just ask the former UK Prime Minister Gordon Brown. In 2010, at the height of a General Election campaign, he was caught by a microphone describing a voter as *a bigoted woman*. The story made headlines around the world and caused significant damage to the Labour Party's standing. They subsequently lost power.

  You might be wondering why I mentioned singing. It's hard not to enjoy this as a lighter example of what being unguarded in front of the cameras can do, even if it also caused great embarrassment. Look up Mike Coupe, Sainsbury's CEO, singing while being interviewed about the company's merger with Asda.

  That should certainly help you remember to treat all microphones and cameras as though they're recording.

- **Behind you**

  Similar to checking your backdrop before a video interview from home, always look behind you when being filmed or photographed. The media can be mischievous.

  Are there billboards saying *The end is nigh!* over your shoulder when you're talking about the future of your company? Or T-shirts proclaiming *Don't panic* in a display when your message is one of reassurance?

  A quick look behind you before beginning an interview can prevent a lot of mockery.

- **Beware the trap of silence**

  Not so much a dirty trick as subtle psychological pressure, you should always beware the trap of silence in an interview.

  You might remember back at the start of Chapter 7, I told you the story about my good friend who isn't called Stuart and his lamentable date. Why did he want to fill every second with chatter? Because about the worst thing that can happen on a date – apart from spitting your soup over the other person – is an awkward silence.

  It's human nature to fill such a void. Which can mean you start chuntering away and end up saying something you regret. So it goes in media interviews. The best interrogators know when to keep quiet and just stare at you.

  The hope is you'll feel the pressure and go on to say something you didn't intend, an utterance which may become newsworthy. So beware the trap of silence. Say what you have to say and then STOP.

  It's not your job to keep the discussion going. It's the interviewer's. Knowing when to keep quiet is an invaluable art, not only in interviews but in life. Just as our friend Stuart, as he's definitely not called, would tell you.

- **Resetting interviews**

  Finally for this chapter, a cheeky gift from yours truly. Behold, a turning of the tables and a dirty trick which you yourself can put into practice when dealing with the media.

  If you start saying something which isn't planned and you fear you're going to regret, this is a way to reset the interview. Simply fake a boisterous fit of coughing and the recording or notetaking will have to stop.

Of course, you can only do this once. And it assumes you're not live on air. But if you need an emergency release from an interview, keep the coughing trick in mind. You might find it rides handily to your rescue one day.

Lastly, the companion website to the book has a quiz for you on mixing it with the media. You can find it at www.cambridge.org/compellingcommunication.

Strategic Communication

At a glance: You can use communication to achieve your aims, but to do so you need to set a goal, produce a strategic communication plan and know how to deal with difficult issues.

You should now have an absolute warehouse of communication skills at your disposal. In fact, if I were to wax lyrical – as you know I sometimes do – I imagine it as an Amazon-type depot: full of fascinating subject areas with absolutely everything you need for any occasion in there somewhere.

But enough of my flights of fancy, not to mention immodesty. The point is, for this, our final chapter together, we'll look at ways to make the best use of that repository of abilities.

First, a word about strategic communication. Most people have heard of it, but often the power of the art isn't fully appreciated. To help with that, the moment has come for another contribution from one of our renowned communicators, and this time the most quirky so far. Well, you know me.

It's time to hear from the Cambridge Dictionary, no less. And before you start to argue, yes, I would count it as a renowned communicator. Just think of all the hundreds of thousands of words which grace its pages, and how much it can teach us about language and communication.

The Cambridge Dictionary definition of strategic is shown in Figure 10.1.

Figure 10.1 The Cambridge Dictionary definition of strategic. © Cambridge University Press & Assessment

Which makes strategic communication the art of deciding on your goals, and using talks, presentations, reports, briefings, the media, even emails and social media posts to help achieve them. So come join me for our last waltz, as we take a tour through how it's done.

Setting Your Goal

This is another of those concepts which sounds so basic, yet is often forgotten. You can't achieve your goal unless you're clear on what it is.

Duh, you might be thinking. Obvious, or what? And I would agree. But I've lost count of the number of times a potential customer has come to me and said:

- We need to get media coverage. The boss says he's seen our competitors in the papers so we want to keep up. Can you put something together to help us, ASAP?

This is where I can be a rubbish businessman. But I have to say, I'm proud to be that way. Because I tend to reply:

- Yes, I can. But why do you want to be in the news?

The answer comes back that it's because the boss says so. Which may be valid as a superficial response, but not as a true reason. So I tend to advise against attempting to secure media coverage. Which can lose me work, hence my honest, if somewhat dangerous, admission to sometimes being a rotten businessman.

The reason I counsel against a splash in the news is because the request isn't strategic. There's no goal to it, apart from satisfying a random command from on high. Which, in my humble view, isn't good enough. As previously discussed, you tend to get limited opportunities to appear in the media, so they're not for the wasting.

Now reimagine the scenario. Say a potential customer gets in touch and says:

- We've got a big fundraising round coming up and we want to do everything we can to ensure it works out. What do you recommend?

This time, we're good to go. Because there's a clear goal. So now I say, *Yes, of course, I'd be delighted to help. Let's sort out the key messages you want to come across first. Then we can put together the pitch. And just before you deliver it to investors, we can trigger some media coverage so they're already half convinced before you even utter a word.*

Then, when we've got the funding, we'll do some social media, blogs and a podcast, as well as more conventional media to celebrate that. Because such publicity will help to attract collaborators and new staff, and whet the appetite of future investors too.

That's strategic communication in action.

I mention this example because it's something I've done time and again with fundraising rounds. It works, I can promise you. But strategic communication doesn't have to be confined to businesses or organisations. It can apply just as much to achieving your personal career goals.

Here's an example. An executive I work with was struggling to connect with his staff and it was important he did so. He had to make significant changes to the business and needed his teams to buy into them.

He was a warm, kind and friendly person, but wary of letting his humanity show at work. So it sometimes goes. But the result was that he was perceived as cold, distant and aloof. I encouraged him to talk more about his personal life, his children, their schooling and sporting achievements. He also began to support local sports clubs through the company, asking his staff to nominate worthy causes.

It was a slow process. These things often are. Overnight conversions followed by major announcements can just create suspicion. But the eventual result was that the executive felt his teams were looking differently at him and he was making far more of a connection. Which helped him to bring in the changes, improved morale at the company and also made it significantly more productive.

Before you think such a strategy might sound cynical, it's worth remembering the importance of authenticity. We covered it way back in Chapter 1, if you need a reminder. It was part of the foundations of communication for good reason. Authenticity is absolutely essential. If the executive hadn't been a genuine family man, and truly passionate about sport, he could never have talked convincingly about both.

That story may sound like a tiny example. But it made a real difference to the executive, his staff and his business. And it's another illustration of strategic communication in action.

Here, of course, is the lesson of this section. Both the executive and the company which was fundraising had clear goals. Which made them much more straightforward to achieve.

- Exercise: What are your goals, whether personal or for your organisation? How could strategic communication help to achieve them?

Strategic Communication Plans

So, once you've established a clear goal, where next?

The answer is to have a plan. A strategic communication plan, no less. Hence the title of this section.

If you're starting to yawn here, there's no need to worry. The plan doesn't have to be long, detailed and dull, requiring endless hours of meetings and acres of paper. A bit of brainstorming, a little strategizing, and that should be sufficient.

Allow me to introduce another good friend of the communication world. This time, one who's going to help us with our plan. Please join me in welcoming the legendary grid.

You may have heard of the grid in a political context. Parties put them together, week by week, to help promote their policies. The idea is to be clear on what they want to say, one day to the next, with no risk of mixed messages. I'd love to be able to show you one, but they tend to be kept secret as politicians don't want to give away their plans.

However, I can invent one for you as an example. I know this will be a scary thought, but imagine I was leader of the newly founded Compelling Communication Party. Our core mission is to help people communicate better with each other, so making for a happier world.

Naturally, we've been a huge success. I've got lots of Members of Parliament (MPs) under my command in Westminster, home of the UK government. Figure 10.2 is our grid for the coming week, so all my staff and MPs can be clear on the messages we'll be promoting, day by day.

Firstly, notice how simple the grid is. Yet again, simple is best. My team, and the public at large, are busy. Neither has the time or bandwidth to take in vast amounts of complex information.

Each day has a single, clear policy or message which the Compelling Communication Party wants the electorate to notice. And by focusing on that, and that alone, we maximise our chances of being heard.

The left hand column outlines first the main news, the story we'll be talking about for each of the days of the working week. Below that comes the events we're holding, or are part of. Next is a list of what's going on in

	Monday	Tuesday	Wednesday	Thursday	Friday
Main news	Email debate	Teach comms skills in schools campaign	Social media regulation	Better broadband campaign	Wonderful weekends for families and friends
Events		Simon interview on Big Politics programme		Midlands rally	
House of Commons	Start a debate on better use of email		Prime Minister's Questions: Raise social media rules		
Visits				Simon and MPs visit Birmingham for rally	All MPs home for family and down time

Figure 10.2 A political strategic communication grid

the House of Commons. That gets a row all to itself as debates and discussions there tend to dominate the political agenda. Finally come the visits that myself or other members of the party are carrying out.

So, on Monday we're going to start a debate about better use of email and perhaps even try to get people to talk to each other more, rather than just typing. Wouldn't that be wonderful?

As the grid shows, we'll do so by raising the matter in the House of Commons. All our MPs and staff know that better use of email is the subject they should be talking about that day, whether in speeches, debates, media interviews or social media posts.

On Tuesday, I'm being interviewed for the flagship Big Politics TV show. I'm going to use the opportunity to launch a campaign for communication skills to be taught in schools. Again, that's what everyone else in the party should be talking about that day.

On Wednesday, we're going to raise the regulation of social media at Prime Minister's Questions. On Thursday, we're holding a rally to campaign for better broadband across the UK, hence doing so in Birmingham, England's second city. On Friday, we're on to what I'm sure will be a great vote winner. That's our drive to free up family and friends' time on Fridays and into the weekends, so we can all communicate much better with those closest to us.

That's the grid. Each day has one clear message we want to convey. Everyone knows it and should thus be doing their best to promote it. Hence the familiar phrase *on message*.

Notice also how all that we've covered in the book works its way into a strategic communication grid. There are the essentials in terms of our core messages, style of communication, simplicity, brevity and everything else. We use our writing, public speaking and presentation skills, plus storytelling, along with our abilities with the media, both social and mainstream. The grid harnesses them all to work together in harmony and promote our cause.

Of course, there'll be times when our plans get blown off course. We may have to respond to events. If the Prime Minister suddenly resigns, for example, we'd expect to be talking about that as it would eclipse our own plans for the news agenda. But at least, by having a plan, we give ourselves the best possible chance of being in control of the agenda and getting our chosen messages across to the masses.

One of the wonders of the strategic communication grid is that you can readily translate the concept from politics to a company or organisation. In that case, you probably won't be planning day by day, as you're unlikely to be as big or important as the Compelling Communication Party. Who could be?! But in that case, when I work with a business, we'll often produce a grid for six months or a year to help raise awareness of our work.

Once again, it can easily be overtaken by events. That's life. But, more often than not, it tends to work out and help us get publicity. For example,

	January	February	April	May	June
Main news	New year, new image	Simon's birthday offer	No fools us for wonderful websites	Pitching for investment day	Partnership with Cleantech Tomorrow
Events	Free business core messages health check	Free online public speaking webinar	Day series of tips for top websites	Pitching sessions critiques	Launch party
Mainstream media	Radio Biz UK interview			Local and regional media	Local and regional media
Social media	Promote Radio Biz UK interview	Vlog and all social channels before/after	Podcast and all social channels	All channels with pitching businesses tie in	All channels with Cleantech Tomorrow

Figure 10.3 A commercial strategic communication grid

if I was drawing up a grid for Creative Warehouse, a version from the swirls of my imagination might look like Figure 10.3.

Starting with our goal, of course. That's simple and clear. It's to maintain and enhance our profile with a view to attracting new customers. We go about that by celebrating the work we do, showing the difference we make, and being proud of our contribution to the business community. But never, ever do we say, *Come buy our services*. See previous discussions on the importance of show not tell, show not sell.

In terms of what we're planning to do to raise our profile, this is where the brainstorming element comes in. The team got together, played with some ideas, and the grid shows what we came up with. It's then written on a whiteboard for all to see and understand.

With discipline, the whole process, from ideas stage to completed grid, takes no more than an hour. So it really doesn't have to be a chore. And, in terms of raising our profile, I expect the return on that investment to be well worthwhile.

Regarding the details of our plans, six months felt about right for the grid. We're always taking on new projects, as well as coming up with new ideas, so we didn't think it worthwhile to look further ahead. Remembering that people don't like blabbermouths, and tend to tune out if a company talks too much, five significant pulses of publicity also felt appropriate. Again, we can always amend the grid if something happens and we need to respond, or a new project comes in which we just have to talk about.

In between our planned announcements, we won't just go quiet. We'll still talk about events we may be part of, blogs we write, stories that make the news, or congratulate our partners and community on their successes. We'll just do so in a low-level way, rather than the greater significance we give to the initiatives detailed on the grid.

Once again, it's important to speak only when you have something to say, rather than just talking for talking's sake. For Creative Warehouse, January sees a classic move, to mark another successful circuit of the sun by our dear Planet Earth. *New year, new image* is a free analysis of a business's core messages, to see if they're working.

As you can see, the mythical Radio Biz UK are interested and so interviewing me about the subject. For maximum impact, we'll promote that interview on social media, both before and after me gracing the airwaves.

To celebrate my birthday, in February (cards and gifts to Cambridge University Press, please), I'm holding a free online webinar about public speaking. We'll promote it using a vlog, social media and our website.

There's no mainstream media planned for the webinar, as it isn't a big enough event. Perhaps more importantly, we've got other initiatives planned which might make the news and it's unwise to come across to journalists as an attention seeker. Again, as previously discussed.

In March, we decided to keep quiet. We didn't have much to say for that month, so we said nothing. That's because the words of a couple more of our renowned communicators have always stayed with us. This quotation is often attributed to Abraham Lincoln, or Mark Twain, but, as with so many great sayings, it's disputed. However, whomever may be the author, the wisdom is beyond doubt:

- Better to remain silent and be thought a fool than to speak and to remove all doubt.

Next, on the subject of fools, to mark April Fool's Day, a stroke of marketing genius (ahem!). We're going to start the week with a podcast on the subject of making sure there's nothing foolish about your website. We'll follow that up with more brief tips on social media to ensure a site is the best it can be.

In May, we're inviting young businesses to come and pitch their wares to us. We'll then give them a critique of their performance, to try to help them on their way. As you can see, that's attracted the attention of the local and regional media.

Cambridge is a hotspot for entrepreneurship, so journalists are always interested in business initiatives. We can amplify the mainstream media coverage with social media posts, mentioning all the companies we're working with.

Finally for the grid, in June we're going to trumpet the launch of our partnership with Cleantech Tomorrow. It's a major new organisation which will promote a greener future through innovative technologies, and we're proud to be a part of its work. Because cleantech is such an important issue, our partnership has also attracted media attention, as you can see. Once again, we can amplify that by cross promoting on social media with everyone involved.

Finally for strategic communications plans, a thought which might come as a surprise. You can just as well draw up a grid for yourself as for a business or political party.

I didn't formally set out a grid when I was a News Correspondent for the BBC. But, looking back, I certainly had something similar in mind. Imagine, for example, my annual appraisal was in three months' time. It's an important moment, not least because it tends to determine any bonus awards.

News editors are frenetically busy and don't usually remember anything much beyond the previous month. So, being cunning and strategic, perhaps I drew up an imaginary grid like the one in Figure 10.4 to prepare the ground for a glowing appraisal.

Once again the goal is clear and simple, to make me look like a shining star of a member of staff. Notice that's mostly – but not solely – rooted in the fundamentals of my job: breaking important stories. I'm also making clear I'm a valuable member of the team, with my offer to chair the staff working group. Furthermore, I'm doing my bit for the BBC's contribution to the community, with the suggestion for an outreach programme for schools.

Again, before you raise a hint of suspicion, this is not cynical. I genuinely investigated and broke stories like those mentioned in the grid in my BBC

	Week 1	Week 2	Week 3	Week 4
Event	Release exclusive story on long delays in criminal cases coming to court	Propose outreach to schools programme	Reveal story about planned new development on green belt land Offer to chair staff working group for coming year	Release exclusive story on rivers and sea pollution levels

Figure 10.4 A personal strategic communication grid

days. I did set up an outreach programme and gave talks in schools, and I did also, in my earlier days, look after some staff-management relations.

OK, the timing of what I'm proposing in terms of stories and initiatives might be helpful for my goal of a glowing appraisal. But everything in the grid is still very me. It's worth saying again that communication campaigns will struggle if not underpinned by authenticity.

Once more, when you put together a strategic communication plan for yourself, all that we've discussed so far in the book will help. You'll be clear on your message and know how to get it across. That's whether in a report or a presentation, by using storytelling, or any and all of the other techniques we've explored.

- Exercise: Imagine a grid for you personally leading up to an important moment in your working life, perhaps an annual appraisal or job interview. What can you include to help achieve your aim?

The Elements of a Strategic Communication Plan

To ensure you maximise the chances of success, it's worth working through a checklist of the key elements of a strategic communication plan:

- **Who you're talking to, your target audience**
  This can vary widely, from millions of people, to just a handful, or even one key individual.
  For example, my BBC appraisal plan had only my editor in mind as the target audience. When we released the artificial intelligence emotion recognition story, without being immodest, we were aiming at the whole world. We wanted to sign up as many people as possible, of as many ages as could be, from as many places as we might reach. That way we would get the best possible data set.
  Sometimes you can seek out a select audience, as when I worked on a fundraising round for a biotechnology company. We were asking for £80

million, and there were only about thirty individuals who were interested in the particular field and had the resources to invest such a sum.

Whether it's your boss, your colleagues, a section of society or the whole wide world, being clear on the target audience is critical for a successful strategic communication plan.

- **How you're communicating with the target audience, the channels you use**

Once you've identified the target audience, the question is how best to reach them. That can be as simple as talking to your boss, or your fellow workers in the office. It might be speaking to a networking group.

For example, I needed to get to know some marketers in my early days in Cambridge to partner with on projects. So I got myself an invitation to talk to a monthly meeting of marketing professionals. They benefited from my insights into the media and I made several good contacts who I have worked with many times since.

For the biotech company's fundraising round, we did some research and found that our thirty target investors all tended to read the business section of a certain UK newspaper. So we built a relationship with a journalist there and placed a story. Because the investors had already heard of the company, and seen a report on the power of its technology, they were much more interested in the pitch. Which helped to secure the money we needed.

That, incidentally, is another example of the power of getting yourself media coverage, when strategically required.

Choosing the right channels often requires a little research. But it doesn't usually take long to find out where your target audience gathers, either online or in the real world, or how they consume information.

You can use social or mainstream media, your database of contacts and customers, talks at a conference or professional organisation, or any way which works. So long as the people you need to speak to are in the room. Even if that's metaphorically so.

- **What you're saying, your message**

Clarity of message is critical in impressing and influencing any audience, as discussed so many times now.

My message for my appraisal was simple. I was a top performing journalist and highly valuable all-round member of the team. With our biotech fundraising, it was the power of the new technology and hence the potential profitability of investing.

For Creative Warehouse, we wanted it known we're an outstanding communication agency which can make a real difference to the businesses we work with. In the case of me and the marketers, it was that I needed partners for some interesting and lucrative projects.

Keep the message clear and simple and keep coming back to it in order to maximise your chances of cutting through and being heard.

- **When you're talking to your target audience, your strategic timing**
  So much of life is about timing. I don't just mean that as a profound and philosophical point such as changing career, even if I've found it to be happily true. Timing is critical in your strategic communication plan, too.

  With the fundraising, we triggered the media coverage just as we launched the round. That helped to get us space in the diary of the busy people we were targeting, so we could pitch our proposal. With Creative Warehouse, we often target bursts of publicity when we launch a new service.

  The timing of my sudden bout of BBC civic dutifulness and strong stories, just ahead of my appraisal, may have been a little obvious. But hey, sometimes obvious is the only way.

- Exercise: Once again, imagine a grid for you personally, leading up to an important moment in your professional life. Now work through the key elements of your strategic communication plan.

Bad News

Despite my past as a journalist, official purveyor of doom, I don't like bringing bad news. But, as we all know, and all too well, life isn't all happiness. Which means I'd be failing in my duty if we didn't look at how to handle difficult tidings.

And here's the strange thing about news management. However dark and dirty this area of strategic communication may be, people still find it fascinating. It can undoubtedly also be useful. So next, let's have a look around the shadowy crypt where the tricks of the trade for dealing with bad news are kept.

Getting Your Retaliation in First

This is a critical principle in handling difficult news. It's far better to be in control of the agenda, if you can.

Why? Well, think about these two different scenarios.

Imagine your organisation has been hit by a cyber-attack. There's been a significant data breach. You're trying to keep it quiet, but the story leaks to the media. It's splashed first on one website, then lots more as they pick up the news. That happens. Journalists love to pile onto tasty tidings. It's a pack thing.

Next, a social media furore starts raging. Then broadcasters begin running the story. You're deluged with requests for information and comment. But it takes you time to get the senior people together and a response formulated.

In the absence of any authoritative information, rumours start to spread. They're far worse than the true picture. Now your customers and partners are getting in touch, alarmed and angry, demanding to know what's going on. Why have they been kept in the dark? Don't you care about them?

In short you suffer a dreadful day, which might even threaten the very existence of your organisation.

Now think about a different scenario. You uncover all the information you need about the data breach. You put measures in place to deal with it and ensure it can't happen again. You tell your staff, partners, customers and all your stakeholders, calmly and efficiently, then put out the news to the media and the public.

OK, you still take a battering. But! At least you're in control and can make sure that comes across. The boss has recorded a reassuring video to put on your website and social media. You have all the answers when journalists come calling. Senior staff are there to be interviewed, to soothe the worries of the outside world. Your social media team is able to dampen the online outcry.

That's the importance of getting your retaliation in first, as the old saying goes. Or just setting the agenda, as it's more calmly known.

Kitchen Sinking

Now we move to specific strategies for dealing with difficulties, and I imagine you're wondering what that heading means. Well, if you think it's strange, wait until we get to the next section. I told you this would be curiously fascinating!

But first, before I digress further, another of my golden rules. In this case, it's to remember when dealing with strategic communication. You've probably seen it in action repeatedly in politics and business, but once again it works wherever, whenever and whatever:

- Good news in stages, bad news all in one go.

The principle behind this is the corrosive effect of drip, drip, drip bad news. People can take one dollop, maybe even two or three, but if it becomes relentless they tend to snap. Which means, in politics, vowing never to vote for a certain party again. Or shop with a certain company, if we're talking business. Or, perhaps, on an individual level, not renew a contract for a member of staff if they become tarred with failure.

That gives rise to the concept of kitchen sinking. It's not, as the name suggests, the room where you do the cooking suffering subsidence. Sorry, excuse the Hall humour. But it is about getting all your bad news out and done with in one go. It's an associate of the phrase *Throwing the kitchen sink at it*, meaning chucking everything you've got in one foul fling.

A good example comes courtesy of the UK's biggest supermarket chain, Tesco. In 2015, the company announced its worst ever financial results.

It lost more than 6 billion pounds. Quite a sum, I think you'll agree, and bad enough on the reputational front.

But here's the cunning strategic communication move. At the same time, Tesco also revealed it had a huge pension scheme deficit. And, as if that wasn't enough, that its stock was worth half a billion pounds less than previously estimated, too.

Ouch. To put it mildly.

So, why did Tesco adopt such a painful self-flagellation strategy?

Because by getting all the bad news out in one go, the company avoided the corrosive effect of several horribly negative stories appearing over a series of weeks. Which would have been far more damaging for Tesco's reputation than one single burst of ugly publicity.

The kitchen sink strategy relies on the relatively brief news cycle. With twenty-four-hour news channels always rolling, and the Internet never slowing, never pausing, there's a voracious demand for fresh stories. Bad headlines tend to fade away after a day or so, as the media and the world turn their focus to something new.

(Sometimes, just occasionally, the brief attention spans of modern life, which we've referred to so often, can be useful.)

Now contrast the kitchen sinking approach with a series of good news stories you might have to bring the world. You would never, but never, put all those out in one go. Far better to bask in the repeated glory of happy headline after happy headline, rather than just one batch of glowing coverage.

You can even find slightly different ways of announcing the same good news, then repeatedly 'unveiling' it. Politicians do this all the time.

The ignoble art of kitchen sinking might well be useful to you in the business context one day. But it can also work on a personal level.

If you've got lots of good news to bring the boss, you can do so day by day, week by week, and earn a reputation as a model employee. But if you have bad tidings to deliver, far better to do so all in one go, however tempting it might be to try to paint a rosier picture.

That way you can focus on it, let it dominate discussions for a while, but also deal with it. Which hopefully means you can then move on, giving you a far better chance to recover your reputation.

The Dead Cat Drop

I did warn you the title of this section would be even stranger than its predecessor. Yes, I know this sounds disgusting, as well as bizarre. But it really is a real concept in strategic communication, really.

The dead cat drop is pretty much the exact opposite of kitchen sinking. It relies on the cunning art of misdirection. If you don't know it, that's the trick which magicians use in order to help make their shows so impressive. Spoiler alert here if you're a romantic and just want to enjoy a magic act without thinking about how it's all done.

The theatrics of the show aren't just there to build up the drama and create a spectacle. They serve a more practical purpose. You know all those bangs and flashes, smoke and lights which catch your eye? They're drawing attention away from where the magic trick is going on, whether it's switching a card from a deck, apparently producing a coin from thin air, or whatever. That's misdirection.

In terms of the dead cat drop, the name comes from this scenario. Imagine you were at a dinner party and the host really didn't like the topic of conversation which had just come up. Now try to visualise that host pulling out a dead cat and dropping it on the table.

What would happen? Apart from a fair few screams and you vowing never to go to a party at that house again, I mean.

Yes, of course. Everyone's attention would be on the poor deceased feline, however horrified and disgusted. The previous topic would be forgotten, just as the host wanted. That's the dead cat drop. It's an extreme technique, to say the least, but it can be effective in an emergency.

I make no partisan points here. But you do tend to see the trick used a lot in politics.

Donald Trump, the former US President, was a master of dead catting. In 2016, for example, he attacked the cast of the hit musical *Hamilton*. It was surely just a coincidence that the move distracted media attention away from a legal settlement which was creating bad headlines for him.

It's also a standard ruse of the Conservative Party in a UK General Election. If they're facing a difficult story, a senior figure will often start talking about the future of the BBC and whether it should lose public funding. The media love that story and tend to flock to it, eclipsing whatever news was proving awkward for the Tories.

Burying Bad News

This is another sneaky trick for reducing, or sometimes simply eliminating, the impact of bad news. It works in exactly the way that the title suggests. The troublesome issue is conveniently buried under other stories.

Imagine, for example, a business had some difficult news to reveal. Perhaps a story about hundreds of job cuts in a restructuring. If said company chose to reveal that on a normal news day, it would create hours of uncomplimentary airtime, and upon yard of troubling newsprint and internet pages. That's before you even get to the inevitable social media pile on.

Now revisit the scenario. But this time, say the company revealed the news just an hour after the Chancellor had been speaking in the House of Commons, detailing the UK's annual budget. That's a huge set piece event in the news and business year. Pretty much all media and public attention is fixed upon it, as we digest the latest tax rises, spending cuts and prophecies of doom.

There's only so much newsprint, internet interest and airtime to go round. The vast majority of which would be dedicated to the budget. The job cuts story would probably get a brief mention in a few news outlets, here and there. And maybe there would be a ripple or two online. But the impact would be nothing like as bad as if the story had emerged on a much quieter news day.

That's the art of burying bad news.

Again, it's cynical. Yes, I accept that. But ours can be a cynical world. And this is a very real and very commonly used technique, which is worth knowing.

Like many of the dark arts of strategic communication, burying bad news has become a well-known tactic. These days journalists are not only watching for it; they have a habit of pointing it out to audiences as well. Which can be a nuisance if you're the one doing the burying.

But be that as it may, the trick still works. Cynically speaking again, a brief mention in a few news stories is far preferable to big headlines, half-page features, extended radio and TV coverage, and a social media furore. All of which put a big and painful boot into you, your company or your organisation.

- Exercise: Reflect on the techniques we've just discussed for dealing with difficult news. Could any (theoretically, of course!) be of use to you personally, or your employer?

Crisis Communication

This is a fascinating field of strategic communication. So we'll spend a little time on it, as one day – one sad day – the techniques involved could come in handy. And if they do, on an individual level they can save your professional life.

In the wider context, they might just preserve the very existence of your organisation. Yes, the stakes really are often that high. As we'll see.

There's a big curiosity about crisis communication. Every time I teach it, or write about it, I'm in the strange position of saying to the audience that I sincerely hope this is a waste of your time. By which I mean that you never have to use what we're about to discuss.

But you know how life can be. So, on the off chance they might be required, here's a quick rundown of the principles of crisis communication. We'll do this with another of my now famous/infamous/delightful/painful (delete as appropriate) compare and contrast exercises, as it's so revealing.

Case Study A – How It's Not Done

We'll start with what's often considered the gold standard for how not to do crisis communication. Here's a challenge of memory for you. When I mention the oil giant BP, and a serious problem the company had on the pollution, human suffering and reputational front, does anything come to mind?

I'm wondering if you quickly recall the dreadful Gulf of Mexico oil spill. Does it sound familiar? Are the horrible pictures of the pollution, and the heart rending stories of those who suffered, surfacing painfully?

As a quick recap, it goes back to April 2010. An explosion ripped through a rig called the Deepwater Horizon. Eleven workers were killed. More than 5 million barrels of oil leaked into the Gulf, according to the United States Environmental Protection Agency. A beautiful and precious environment suffered appalling harm.

It was America's worst oil pollution disaster and made news around the world for months, causing untold damage to BP's reputation. That, in itself, was plenty bad enough. But the company's reaction caused even more harm. It's unfortunate to say, but it was a catalogue of defensiveness and denial.

Following the explosion, BP's Chief Executive, Tony Hayward, initially tried to shift the blame. He said it wasn't a BP rig, but owned by one of their contractors. Following that, he subsequently tried to downplay the size of the disaster, saying the Gulf of Mexico was a very big ocean, which meant 'the amount of oil we are putting into it is tiny'.

Cue, unsurprisingly, much anger raging in BP's direction. And so the controversy grew. But it got yet worse. Hayward also then said the containment of oil on the surface was very effective. He somehow neglected to mention the vast plumes sullying the waters beneath the waves. That was left to independent scientists to point out.

With BP now under fierce attack from all sides, you might think the company would get their act together. But no. Their handling of the disaster grew still more inept.

BP initially estimated the leak rate at 5,000 barrels of oil per day, a figure they slowly increased to between 12,000 and 19,000 barrels. Now why might that be, you could wonder. Perhaps because fines for such oil spills are based on the volume of pollution? It hardly helped that the revision of the rate oil was being spilled was partly based on new video footage of the leak, which BP only released following serious pressure from the US Congress.

And by the way, see previous thoughts on good news in stages, bad news all in one go. This was the very reverse of that principle.

The oil leak eventually took almost three months to cap, raising questions about whether BP had ever taken the pollution seriously. And finally, Tony Hayward added insult to the grievous injury of BP's disaster by declaring in an interview, 'There's no one who wants this over more than I do. I'd like my life back.'

The reaction of the families of the dead workers was, unsurprisingly, outrage. Public and politicians felt likewise.

In summary, what was the result of the way BP handled – or horribly mishandled, to be more accurate – the Gulf of Mexico oil spill?

It was an utter disaster for the company. The scandal remains in the public mind, even all these years on, and is often referenced in news stories about BP.

Case Study B – How It Is Done

Now let's look at a very different model of how crisis communication can be done. Here we turn again to Tesco, whom you'll recall from their exemplary use of kitchen sinking.

As will become apparent, the company take their strategic communication very seriously. They obviously employ highly competent professionals to help them get it right. Because Tesco provide us with the template for how to handle a crisis and the use of strategic communication to help calm it.

So to another of my questions. When I mentioned Tesco, did you think of any reputational disasters which have befallen the business? I'm not talking profits or pensions, as we mentioned before. Instead, I'm hinting at something to do with the food they sell and a scandal stemming from what it contained.

I suspect you're struggling to think of anything. Which, I hope, helps to make the point.

I'll stop teasing now. Instead, let me take you back to 2013. If I nudge your memory, I wonder if you can remember when horsemeat was found in some Tesco products?

It was a shocking story. DNA tests found 100 per cent horsemeat in some meals which were supposed to be made up of beef. Yes, you did read right. That's 100 per cent. Not just traces. The whole meal.

The discovery prompted an absolute scandal. The story made the front pages of many newspapers, was all over the radio and TV, and ran around the world. It was dreadful for Tesco's reputation on so many levels. There was horror amongst animal lovers, amongst shoppers, amongst pretty much all and everyone. In summary, the horsemeat scandal was one of the worst crises an otherwise generally slick and highly successful company had faced.

And so comes the question. How did Tesco deal with it? Did they do a BP, for want of a better expression, and resort to defensiveness and denial?

No. Not a bit of it. Quite the opposite. Instead, Tesco reacted immediately and effectively with strategic communication at the heart of their work:

- Firstly, and critically, Tesco immediately focused on and took ownership of the issue. They made very clear that this was their problem and they would deal with it, whatever that might require.
- They also recalled a range of products, and did so without a hint of hesitation, argument or delay.
- Tesco apologised to the public and the world. It was a move which seemed sincere, as the company placed large and expensive adverts in a series of national newspapers to do so.
- Loyalty card customers received emails headed *We are changing*, with information about how Tesco would make sure such a failure never happened again.
- Tesco also committed themselves to sourcing more food from the UK and Ireland to help reassure customers about the quality standards of their products.

And so we come to the key point, the moral of the story. The result of all the effort and expense which was expended to deal with the issue. Why did I ask you that question earlier, about what you think of when you hear the name Tesco?

Not the horsemeat scandal, I suspect.

Today, the issue is only vaguely remembered, despite it being huge news at the time. It's also very seldom referenced by the media, politicians or the general public. In other words, the horsemeat scandal is largely forgiven and forgotten. Which is quite a contrast to the fate of BP and the Gulf of Mexico oil spill.

So, courtesy of Tesco, that's an example of how to handle a crisis from a strategic communication standpoint. And, courtesy of BP, an example of how very much not to do so.

In summary, here's a checklist for what to do if you're ever faced with a crisis:

- **Own it**

  Blame shifting, ducking and diving, along with wheedling is banned. Remember how it helped BP (not).

- **Openness and honesty**

  You're going to think me hypocritical here, after taking you through the dark arts of dead cat drops and the like. But, as the old and wise saying has it, honesty is the best policy. It's always better to be straight and open about your issue.

  Since I've mentioned sayings, there's another old and wise one which dictates: *It's not the crisis that kills you, it's the cover up.*

  That's been proven true many a time with scandal after scandal. Watergate is perhaps the best known example. It wasn't the break in to the Democratic National Committee headquarters in the Watergate Building, Washington DC, which ultimately led to the resignation of American President Richard Nixon. It was the attempted cover up.

  Honesty is even more critical in the online age. The modern world is leaky, which means it's very hard to keep problems quiet. They've a habit of spilling out, what with everyone now having ready access to social media, or being easily able to contact news outlets, politicians or regulators through their websites.

  Far better to come out and be straight with the world than be forced to. As BP found out to their cost.

- **Focus on it**

  I know everyone is busy and diaries are full. And yes, I appreciate the boss has got lots of important meetings to get through. But it's a common error not to appreciate the scale of a problem, and a crisis takes precedence over all else.

  Remember, this could be a make or break, life or death moment for your organisation. If it's that bad, then everyone needs to be focused on it, and at the very highest levels

- **Apologise**

  I know this can be difficult, and the lawyers don't like it because an apology can be taken as an admission of guilt. But sometimes, you just have to say sorry. It's what a situation, and the world, can need and expect. Tesco did so with the horsemeat scandal, and it helped them.

If the lawyers dispute making an apology you can point this out, as I've sometimes had to.

It's no good having a legally arguable defence if you don't have a company or organisation any more to wield it. And all because your handling of a crisis has been so dreadful that everyone, from customers, to partners, to funders and friends, has deserted you.

- **Deal with the problem**
  Take tangible and effective action. And not just that. Also, communicate, communicate, communicate that you're doing so, to everyone in your organisation, your partners, stakeholders, the media and the wider world.

  It's wise to remember that you can't communicate enough in a crisis. If a vacuum of information develops then rumour and speculation will quickly fill it, and that's never helpful. So use all we've learned in the book to get out there, get on the media, and get communicating.

- **Resource the issue**
  Dealing with a crisis can be expensive. Accept that, face down the finance team and do what's necessary. It'll be worth it in the long run. Again, remember this could be a life or death moment.

- **Change**
  Learn your lessons and don't let it happen again, whatever the problem may have been. And don't forget to show the world how you're not going to let it happen again either. Or, at least, do your darndest to make sure it doesn't.

I have one final matter to mention while we're talking crisis communication. It may feel that the principles we've worked through apply only to organisations and businesses. But not so. As with strategic communication grids, they can have personal uses too.

Just about everything we've discussed works every bit as well if you've made a big, bad mistake at work. Bosses hate being kept in the dark and blindsided; they hate staff not taking responsibility; they hate them not focusing, working hard and dealing with an issue; and they hate lessons not being learned.

Now, I appreciate that's a lot of hate, which isn't my style. But you get the point. Should you ever be faced with a real stinker of your own making, the principles of crisis communication might just help you live to fight another day.

Recovery Plans

Finally for this chapter, if you, your company or your organisation has been through a crisis, you'll want to recover your reputation afterwards. The good news is that's perfectly possible, as Tesco have shown us.

Even better, you now know exactly how to do so. Back we come again to the strategic communication grid.

If you go through a painful time, gathering the team together to brainstorm ideas for positive publicity for the days, weeks and months ahead can help restore morale and motivation. If it's a personal issue, do the same but with family, friends and trusted colleagues.

Pick out the best of those thoughts and translate them to your grid. Then start working your way through it and rebuilding your reputation.

- Exercise: Imagine, if you can bear it, a crisis hitting you, your organisation or your company. Can you brainstorm enough ideas to fill a strategic communication grid and recover your reputation?

Finally, it'll come as no surprise by now to know that the companion website to the book has a quiz for you on strategic communication. So, here's one last reminder! You can find it at www.cambridge.org/compellingcommunication.

A Compelling Conclusion (Hopefully)

It's time to relax. Celebrate. Shed a tear of sadness, or perhaps relief.

Whatever you wish. We've reached the end of our journey together.

You now know everything you need to be a compelling communicator, whatever the subject or situation. Well done on all your hard work, and I really do mean that. I appreciate we've covered a lot of ground.

But! Our great journey is not quite at an end. I have a couple of final thoughts for you, the morals at the end of the story. I suspect you sensed they were coming, given your knowledge of me and my love of storytelling. Although they can wait a moment.

First, a super quick recap. Which I'll begin with a question.

Did any of what we explored surprise you? I'm thinking particularly in the first chapter, when we established the foundations of effective communication.

I ask because there's a curiosity of teaching communication skills that always appeals to me. A lot of the essentials of the art go against so much of what we were taught at school and college, or learned in the world of work and our passage through life.

To recall, should we try to squeeze as many ideas into our content as possible? Use big words, even bigger sentences, and lots and lots of them?

Take up hours with our presentations? Repress our character and talk, talk, talk to impress?

Or, in one more tribute to our beloved less is more, should we instead always cherish:

- Clarity
- Simplicity
- Brevity
- Authenticity
- Humility/listening

A confession here. I've been looking for a smart way to summarise those fundamentals so that they stay with you. A neat acronym, perhaps, like KISS, for keeping it simple, silly. But all I managed to come up with was SCHAB, which sounded unpleasant. I also thought of BACHS, which alluded to beauty and elegance, as with the great composer's music. But it still didn't quite work.

So instead, I've shamelessly borrowed from Rudyard Kipling and adapted his Six Honest Serving Men, whom we met way back in Chapter 2.

> I keep five communication rules,
>   (They taught me what to do);
> Their names are Authenticity, Brevity, Clarity, Simplicity,
>   And never forgetting to Listen, too.

OK, it's not great, I admit. And I very much doubt it'll still be quoted in a century's time, unlike Kipling's elegant and excellent words. But I hope my bumbling rhyme will help to remind you of the foundations of effective communication. Just about everything else we've discussed follows from there. Imprint those five principles upon your mind and you shouldn't go wrong.

Secondly, I'd like to say thank you. A big thank you, in fact. And several of them.

To start with, to Jess, my long-suffering wife. (That prefix always seems to be applied when anyone mentions her in the context of me, although why

I don't know – ahem!) Also to Niamh, my almost as long-suffering daughter.

Both were indulgent enough to not mind when I disappeared into myself to write and was either monosyllabic or entirely oblivious to their questions; whether I'd like a cup of tea/a beer/a sandwich, or a jug of water poured over my head if I didn't pay them some attention soon.

But, just as importantly, it's a very big thanks to you, my kind and patient reader. For giving the book – and, even more generously, me – the precious investment of your time, focus and thought. I trust it's been worthwhile.

If you'd like to keep in touch, I would love to do so. And before you raise an eyebrow, no, I'm not just being polite and saying that. I really do mean it. Writing *Compelling Communication* has been a love thing for me, as I'll explain in a moment. If what we've worked through helps you, I'd be delighted to hear about it.

Probably the easiest way is to connect with me on LinkedIn. You can find me at Simon-Hall-Communications, or just search online for Simon Hall. I often post tips for effective communication on LinkedIn, along with links to my latest blogs, which might be useful. I'll look forward to hearing from you. Always assuming you haven't had plenty enough of me by now.

And so to those last thoughts. I hope this book will help you to become a good communicator, perhaps even a great one. But I wonder if you still harbour doubts. Perhaps you think it's easy for me to talk about all these skills and putting them into action, but I'm lucky to be blessed with a natural talent with words.

Prepare yourself for a shock. I think you may be right, although only up to a point. I suspect I do have a certain way with words. But there's another factor in play, which I want to mention. Because it's far more important. And I'm going to reveal it in the form of a final story.

Well, of course I am.

When I first came to Cambridge, as I cast around for work, I was asked by one of the colleges to talk to their undergraduates about careers in the media. I was excited by the opportunity. I thought it could also be a breakthrough moment, a gateway to more work with the University.

So I carefully prepared and rehearsed the session. I polished and perfected. It was a fine mix of insights and interactions, informative but also entertaining. I was nervous as I walked to the college. I knew this could be a very important moment in my Cambridge life. I was all psyched up, ready to perform at my best.

Guess what happened?

Three students turned up. Just three. And OK, they were lovely, and it was all worthwhile, but . . .

I was still deflated, to put it mildly. Floored, to be frank. Where were the hordes of an adoring audience who should have flocked to rejoice in my wisdom?

Ego duly battered and bruised, I did some forlorn reflecting. The trouble with Cambridge is that the city has lots of brilliant people offering all sorts of talks, experiences and insights. I might wish it, but the sad reality starkly said I wasn't in any way special here. I realised I would have to up my game and enhance my repertoire of teaching if I was going to have any chance of making a success of my new life.

So I worked at it. I challenged myself to learn more about public speaking and forced myself to give lots of presentations. In order that I could truly understand the art, teach it, and teach it well.

Likewise with writing skills. I studied the minutiae of the craft and practised and practised, in order that I could truly understand it, teach it, and teach it well. Likewise with storytelling.

I worked and worked at it, and, over time, my knowledge and abilities grew. I travelled and taught, learning all the while. Different age groups, different professions, different backgrounds, so many different challenges about how best to explain and enthuse. I reflected, refined and refined again.

Until now, here I am, a course leader at this magnificent institution, as well as writing a book for its prestigious publishing arm.

And here comes the punchline.

A few months ago, I was invited back to that same college to teach public speaking. And, as chance would have it, they gave me that same room. Just as the first time, those years earlier. When only three students came along.

But this time, the room was packed. Full to the far corners with more than sixty people. Undergraduates, postgraduates, even members of staff. There was also a waiting list to join the workshop.

What a feeling it was as I left the college that evening.

So yes, maybe I do have a certain gift with words. But I doubt it's anything much greater than you possess. Which, I trust, means I need say no more on that score.

Go, then, and practice your new skillset. Because only that way will you become good. Then very good. Then, perhaps, a great communicator.

Finally, you may have asked yourself at some point during our journey why I wrote this book. Given my sense of humour, you may well have asked the question through gritted teeth, but forgive me that. After all, as we know very well by now, character is critical in communication, however curious.

Anyway, the motivation for writing the book goes way back to Chapter 5, when we discussed the gold standard of storytelling. Remember the teachers' tale I told?

Of all my adventures in life, this time now, when you find me writing *Compelling Communication*, is the absolute pinnacle. The reason stems from the story about Nigel and Jerry, and the benevolent ambush they staged which transformed my world. The influence of those two wonderful teachers has never stopped echoing through my life. Even now, all these many years on.

I read sciences at university because I wanted to teach. I wonder if, even subconsciously, I'd already come to appreciate the remarkable power which a great teacher can have. OK, I was beguiled by the media for a while. But even in those days, I taught younger journalists at the BBC and gave talks in schools to encourage the students to aspire to uplifting futures.

Teaching has always called me back. It's part of the reason I moved here, to ancient and learned Cambridge.

Every time I see a spark of understanding in a student's eyes, each message I get thanking me for my help, every success story I've been a small part of, each and every one fills me with the warmest and fuzziest of warm and fuzzy glows.

I have found my place. It may have taken a while, but I've found it. And I feel incredibly proud, fortunate and fulfilled to have done so.

Which brings us to this. Nigel and Jerry gifted me a beautiful legacy, allowing me to follow a richly rewarding path and to realise my potential. I've carried their spirit with me through all of my days.

Compelling Communication is part of handing on that precious legacy. I ask only that you honour the ideals of Nigel and Jerry, the reason for me writing this book, and continue that noble tradition. Use the skills we've explored to make a better world for yourself, for those around you, and for those of the future. Thank you.

Simon

Index

Printed in the United States
by Baker & Taylor Publisher Services